PART 1

The Strategy

———

Chapter 1

PASSING THE RELAY BATON

> *"And the things you have heard me say in the presence of many witnesses entrust to reliable men who will also be qualified to teach others."*
> —2 *Timothy 2:2*

*I*ntense determination filled his blue eyes and opened a picture window deep in his searching heart. The misled 15-year-old boy had just come to the startling realization that his father had duped him into thinking that love was no farther away than a condom dispenser and that true intimacy was reserved for fairy tales.

I saw him as I stepped away from the microphone after delivering a sex-and-dating talk at one of our sports camps. Through the crowd of 300 socializing kids, he was wending his way toward me. Across his face, the word *HURT* was scrawled in capital letters, yet determination marked his step. When our eyes met, he reached out to shake my hand, fumbling for words.

"Uh, may I have the picture for my room?" he asked, pointing to a piece of butcher paper on the easel behind me, where I had painted a heart-shaped mix of tempera paints to illustrate the undefiled marriage bed.

"What's your name?" I replied.

"Eric, sir . . . and, umm . . . would you mind signing it for me?"

"Of course not, but what do you want with that crazy picture, Eric?" I asked as I peeled it off the makeshift easel, scribbled my signature, and rolled it up for easy packing. I'll never forget the look of sober appreciation in his eyes as he quickly summarized his deepest desire.

"I . . . I want it for a reminder," he answered with tears beginning to swell. "You see, sir, my dad gave me a condom on my fifteenth birthday and told me to always carry it with me in case I felt the need. He said to use one as often as I wanted. He said it would keep me out of trouble. What you said tonight really got to me. I knew there had to be more to love than what my dad was telling me. I just didn't know what it was. But now I know. I want to love my wife like you love yours. That's why I was wondering if I could take the picture home. I want to hang it in my room to remind me what real love is." He hesitated for a moment, then added, "And . . . and I guess having it would be sorta like you coming home with me to be my dad, since mine isn't telling me the truth."

Now, I'm not usually at a loss for words. But I tell you, as I stood there in the middle of that spirited youth rally, where the singing raises the roof and the level of fun is just shy of a Mardi Gras festival, I suddenly felt very _alone_ with Eric, very connected to him, and very, very tongue-tied. So I just shook his hand and held it reassuringly to let my hand-to-hand embrace speak its own message. Then he walked away with the picture tucked under his arm and disappeared quickly into the sea of teenage friends.

There has to be more, I said to myself, recalling Eric's words. And since that night, those five monosyllables have lingered somewhere near the edge of all my thinking. In my 20 or so years of kid-work, I've found that a no-nonsense, straight-to-the-point talk about sex has always been appreciated by teenagers. But today their culture is so misled by Hollywood, Madison Avenue, school sex clinics, and even many parents that teens like Eric are fairly begging for the truth. At the very core of their being, a tiny voice cries out, "There has to be more!"

Well, I'm here to say there _is_ more. Life has much, much more to offer our teens if we would only learn to point them toward it. However, more pain is on the horizon if today's parents don't rise up to face the challenges of this decade.

If America was roaring in the twenties and warring in the forties, then

I'm not too far afield when I declare this country has gone value-starved in the eighties and nineties. Certainly history will record this period as the time when our family values were torched with a barrage of antifamily education, legislation, entertainment, and leadership. As always, the fire is the hottest and most lethal when it reaches the hearts of our kids, whose generation will close out this century with more promiscuity, suicides, abortions, drug addictions, and countless other examples of moral bankruptcy than any other generation of kids in any nation during any period of time since "In the beginning."

As you grab your breath, however, let me step up on a handy soapbox and raise my eyebrows, cup my hands around my mouth so my voice will carry from the Atlantic to the Pacific, and say, "There are fire trenches being dug in these flaming nineties!" I see them in the homes of rich, poor, and middle class. I see them in the suburbs and in the city. I see them in farmhouses and high-rises. I see them in two-parent homes and single-parent homes. Those of us whose homes are in this category may not be the majority, but our numbers are growing dramatically each year.

We are the moms and dads who, in the midst of an era of cultural arson, are stubbornly trying to preserve and pass on our ways to our kids so they can pass them on to theirs, and so forth. We can be encouraged, for others have gone before us on the same path. The apostle Paul, for instance, undertook the difficult task of spiritual parenting with his favorite son in the faith, Timothy—and in a culture no less twisted than our own. With his eyes fixed on the gospel of Christ Jesus, Paul imparted his values to his young pastor friend in the same way a relay runner hands the baton to a team member. Listen to what my Olympic track star friend Madeline Manning Mims has to say about this vital aspect of a relay:

> I've had batons slip, drop, slide, and even bounce off the track back into my hand on the way to victory. But of all the crucial moments in an Olympic relay race, there is none so crucial as the pass. *It is the approach, the timing, the grip, the exchange, the power, the pressure. It is the all-important transfer. It is where the race is won or lost. Period.*

Moms and dads, Madeline knows relays. She has won more gold and silver from Olympic and other international competitions than Fort Knox has room to hold. But what makes her glitter is the absolute dazzle in her eyes from her enthusiastic love for God, family, and kids. So when Madeline talks about the all-important transfer of faith, I listen. I'm impressed with her exhortation to make a good pass or lose the race. But as a dad, I'm far more impressed with the high calling of Christian parents to be faith trainers—to make a good pass to their children, who will carry the baton of faith into the next generation.

Effective Faith Trainers Are Good Baton Passers.

The baton is a message.

It's a message of faith.

I believe that God has kids, not grandkids. Just because Joe White is a Christian doesn't guarantee his children will be, too. Faith does not get passed along genetically like brown eyes or freckles. It must be handed from runner to runner, generation to generation. Every child of God must receive it, grasp it tightly, and run the race that cannot be run by anyone else.

Based on his experience, the president of one of America's largest youth ministries (working with more than 250,000 kids in 600 cities) told me he estimates that 80 percent of the young people who accept Christ in high school turn their backs on the faith during their college days. Paul had similar sobering thoughts. After traveling with Timothy for years, he poured himself out in writing so that his friend might develop a firm grip on the baton of faith and be firmly committed to passing it on as well. Read now the depth of Paul's fatherly exhortation, penned in the presence of the Spirit of God for our successful journey as parents:

> *"Fan into flame the gift of God, which is in you"* (2 Tim. 1:6).

> *"What you have heard from me, keep as the pattern of sound teaching"* (2 Tim. 1:13).

> *"Guard the good deposit that was entrusted to you—guard it with the help of the Holy Spirit who lives in us"* (2 Tim. 1:14).

> *"Be strong in the grace that is in Christ Jesus"* (2 Tim. 2:1).

"Remember Jesus Christ, raised from the dead" (2 Tim. 2:8).

Paul, knowing his time was short, lived and died to place the truths of the faith deep in Timothy's heart so that Timothy could carry the baton to the next generation.

I'm weary of hearing about Christian parents who drop the baton. Too often, the consequences of their blunders end up sleeping in a bunk bed at one of our camps. Little Tommy in cabin nine wonders why his daddy keeps all those bad magazines under his bed at home. Annie in cabin four hopes her mommy will say her prayers with her at night just as her counselor does, but she knows she's only dreaming. I could give you account after account of former campers who—just like Eric at the beginning of this chapter—are crying out, "There has to be something more!"

Every so often, however, I hear of a parent who takes the baton pass seriously, and I'm encouraged. One such mom lives in Wichita, Kansas.

Doris Howard knew the significance of being a Christian mother. She knew that as God blessed her with a daughter in the delivery room, He wasn't just saying, "Congratulations. You're about to become a parent!" He was saying, "Push, Doris, push! And with a few more pushes, you're about to become the coach of one of my dear little runners. Train her to run well, Doris. For her success depends on your training."

Doris trained her daughter, all right. She passed on the baton of faith and the courage to go along with it! By the time her daughter was a sophomore in high school, she was leading a Bible study in a classroom each Friday morning before school (Equal Access Law; Supreme-Court tested). Two years later, she inspired 13 kids from other campuses to do the same. Two years after that, those 13 had grown to become 3,000 wide-eyed Wichita Christian teens determined to tell every junior-high and high-school student in the area about their priceless faith in the Savior.

Those 3,000 young evangelists personally invited 30,000 area students to a youth rally. Of the 30,000 invitees, 10,000 showed up, and 6,000 made written commitments to follow Christ. And it was all because of one committed faith trainer and a jillion baton passes practiced over and over and over. Nice job, Doris.

There is no set pattern for the perfect faith trainer. The baton can be passed by any Christian with a willing heart and a relentless spirit. The single father in Houston can get the job done, as can the abandoned mother in New York City, the poverty-stricken couple in Chicago, the millionaire in Miami, and countless others I know from every conceivable socioeconomic circumstance on the planet. I'll say it again: All it takes is a willing heart, a relentless spirit, and the desire to see your children run the race of life for God's glory.

Do you want your children to run well in life rather than stumble through it? Would you like to see them among that increasing number of teens who are making pledges of virginity, praying around school flagpoles, presiding with integrity over student bodies, sharing Christ on the sidelines of football games, closing love letters with verses from Scripture, creating Christian music groups, starting antidrug and alcohol accountability pacts, and participating in Bible study teams, missionary trips, and other creative initiatives too numerous to count? I'll tell you, it's happening! And it's happening because moms and dads all across the country are exchanging their Just-a-Parent membership cards for invisible coaching jackets with two bright words stitched across the shoulders: FAITH TRAINER.

Will you become one? Will you wear the jacket? Will you pass the baton? If your answer is a resounding *yes*—or even a weak-kneed, hesitant one—this book will help you meet the task.

Effective Faith Trainers Are Relentless Learners.

When our oldest child was crossing the threshold into junior high, my foresighted wife bought a used set of *Encyclopaedia Britannica* for upcoming theme papers. The purchase has proved to be invaluable. Year after year, theme after theme, we've gone to that shelf for quotations, ideas, and references. The books will be tired and dog-eared by the time our fourth child makes it through school, and no doubt some of the information will have become outdated. But do you think we'll throw them away? No way! We'll tape them up and give them to the grandchildren.

Moms and dads, in the same way, you'll want to refer to this book again and again in the coming years. I urge you to find an easily accessible place for it in your home and then use it daily to write a godly life theme on the hearts of your children. Don't shelve it in the library until your youngest goes to college! Some of this book will help you give your little ones a rock-solid foundation under their precious size-three feet. A great deal more of it will help you produce strong, happy, virgin, pure-in-heart teenagers who will carry the baton of faith with courage.

All in all, I have enjoyed (celebrated) the privilege of distilling thousands of pages of information to make this growing-up syllabus an efficient and effective use of your time with your kids. I pray it will become a one-a-day spiritual and intellectual vitamin for your family, with the result that some day you will send your kids off to college secure enough in Christ to stand up against any atheistic, humanistic professor who dares to try to tear their faith apart. What a challenge to build godly children in these last days! What a thrill to get the job done well!

In the dead of January, I was pondering this book. *What does it really take to be a faith trainer?* I asked myself. *How can I teach on paper the art of baton passing when it's hard enough to do it in real life?* Across the living room, the last NFL playoff game had just been settled. In the victorious locker room, champagne spewed wildly, and I heard John Madden proclaiming, "There's nothing greater than going to the Super Bowl!" That caught my attention. I laid my pencil down on the yellow pad and began to recall the three bowl teams I'd been part of as a college player and coach.

Maybe John Madden had never been there to see a woman return home from the hospital with a chubby little package that would soon call one man daddy and win his heart with her mother's charm. Possibly he'd never sat at the dinner table listening to his high-school daughter describe how she led her locker mate to Christ. Perhaps he had never watched a proud father give away his godly daughter in marriage to the Christ-centered man for whom he'd been praying diligently since the girl was born. Come to think of it, John, there are a lot of things greater than going to the Super Bowl! And the greatest of them all is raising kids who walk hand in hand with God.

My experience working with kids tells me that Paul was a master at passing the baton of faith to a young person. That is exactly what he was doing when he wrote 2 Timothy. So that book of the Bible will be our guide as we consider how to train our children. Then, following the 15 chapters on how to do it, you'll find a bunch of resources to help you actually roll up your sleeves and get to work as a faith trainer. You'll see resources to help teach your kids the truth about Jesus, the Bible, human origins, other religions, and so on, as well as three family Bible studies that will take you through the books of Mark, John, and James.

This book is for all the children in the world who wait expectantly in the baton-passing zone, who instinctively know there's more to life than Super Bowls and condom skydiving yet lack the training to find it. Is there an Eric in your household? Is he floundering around life's racetrack, dying for you to show him how to quit smacking into all those hurdles? Is she standing there with her hand out, waiting for you to give her the baton? If so, commit today to becoming a faith trainer, because before you know it, you'll be watching your sons and daughters walk out of your daily life, just as Paul watched Timothy go . . . and just as I watched Eric go.

I pray your children will be clutching the baton of faith the way a three-year-old grasps her first cotton candy at the county fair!

Chapter 2

JOIN THE RACE

"To Timothy, my dear son."   —2 Timothy 1:2

Ask any relay runners about "the zone" and they'll tell you it's the one place on the track where everything must come together. If the baton pass is not completed within that allotted space, the team is disqualified and the race is lost.

You and I have a zone to contend with, too. It's about one inch wide and 18 years long. From the moment our children are born to the time they go out on their own, we have the awesome responsibility of training them to run on life's narrowest path—the one that leads to godliness. All other paths are broad and treacherous, with a herd of reckless runners careening headlong to their destruction. It's simple to train children to run on those wide tracks. You merely put them out to pasture with the rest of the herd, then sit on the fence to watch what happens.

The results are always ugly.

But if you and I take seriously the fact that there's a zone of time within which we must pass the baton of faith to our young runners, we won't sit on the fence. Instead, we'll bend all our energies toward faith training so that when our children finally leave us, we can say as Paul said, "I have finished the race" (2 Tim. 4:7). With that in mind, here's another significant guideline for us: The effective faith trainer gets involved.

The Effective Faith Trainer Gets Involved.

In other words, *he or she joins the race.* How long can we parents remain idle before we realize our idleness is making clumsy, stumbling, handicapped runners out of our children?

Before you answer that, let me tell you how this former fence-sitter of a father almost waited too long before getting involved with his own family. The only thing that's not average about our family is the size of the baggage I brought into the relationship. Believe me, I brought a trunk load.

My first wife left me for my best friend after only 14 months of marriage. I've never really blamed her. The divorce was devastating, but it put me squarely on my knees, groping for the touch of a heart-healing Savior. He continues to touch up that scar to this day.

My oldest boy learned to ride his bike with his baby-sitter. My oldest daughter used to put notes on my desk asking for an appointment. (I weep inside as I write.) My workaholic temperament left my second wife and four eager young ones begging for attention. But before I could give it, God had to get mine. What the divorce didn't do to wake me up, my kids did when Jamie was 11, Courtney was eight, Brady was seven, and Cooper was two.

That summer, Courtney attended one of our camps for 13 days. Like all parents of campers, I agreed not to visit until the closing ceremonies. (I was too busy to worry about it anyway.)

After a few days, Courtney became homesick because of some insecurities I had graciously provided. Her counselor dried her tears and assured her she was doing great, was growing, and would soon get to be with her dad again.

"I never get to see my dad," protested Courtney beneath a curly, blonde mop of hair.

The counselor didn't know what to say. When the camp director heard the story, he made a beeline to my office.

"Sit down!" he commanded.

"What's the problem?" I asked.

"This may not be easy for you, Joe, and it may not make any sense, either," said the director. "But we're going to sit here and talk until it does."

As he told me the story, I dug my chin deeper into my hands and wished I could melt into the chair. My personal stock market had crashed, and I was ready to jump. Still my friend didn't let up.

"We're not leaving this room until you make some serious commitments," he asserted. "Joe, your life is going to change—and I'm going to hold you accountable to it."

You know, you can buy a lot of cheap stock after Wall Street collapses. After that providential talk, I scraped up every last penny of self-worth to my name and invested it all. By God's grace within me, I became a husband and a dad. Did you catch the key word in that last sentence? It's the tiny, monosyllabic miracle big enough to make Pauls out of Sauls and effective faith trainers out of absent fathers. We call it *grace*.

By grace, I got on the right track. Since then, I haven't become a world-record holder or even All Backyard at this thing called faith training, but my heart beats passionately to get better at it every day. Delegation in the workplace has become the fun side of life for me. Saying no to wonderful opportunities so I can say yes to a bedtime story or seventh-grade band concert is becoming easier every day. Many nights I pray, "Lord, make me a more effective dad." For all my efforts, I have no trophies to show. But I have four growing children and a better-than-I-deserve wife whom I now consider my best friend, which makes it all worthwhile. My kids aren't major success stories (except to me), but they love their mom and they love their God. Home has become our favorite place to be. It's nearly wallpapered with pictures of happy moments and various stages of growing up together.

By grace, Joe White can tell this story. If it weren't for that, I greatly fear I'd be waving good-bye to my children some day without really knowing where they were headed—or even what track they were on. But by grace, I got involved. And oh, how fun the involvement has been! Want a little sample of it? Try the following on for size.

When Jamie turned 16, I began to realize that within that zone I described above, there are several minizones that are equally crucial and equally as demanding on the baton pass. But the zone I dreaded most was the one called *dating*. What a horribly misleading title! Poll the bulk of fathers in America, and they will tell you a date is really a coup, and the "boy" who comes calling is nothing less than a greedy usurper out to steal their daughter's loyalty. At least that's how I felt that Thursday evening not so long ago when the phone rang for my little Peanut.

"Hello, is Jamie there?" said the shaky adolescent voice on the other end.

Chills ran up my spine. The hand that held the receiver quickly became limp and clammy. I worked in vain to mask my nervousness. "Maybe," I said. "Who's speaking?"

"Uh . . . this is Josh, sir."

I had met Josh once. One of the local high-school kids had told me he was thinking about asking Jamie to the prom. Josh was 6'4" tall, the center on our high-school basketball team. *Why couldn't Jamie attract the attention of someone more my size?* I thought. *How in the world, at age 44, can I look a giant in the eyes and get his attention properly if he mistreats my princess?*

"What do you need, Josh?" The awkward conversation continued.

"Well, sir, I was, like, sorta wondering if maybe I might, like, ask Jamie to the prom or something."

It had happened. The teddy bears had faded and lost their furry toy-store texture. The fast-forward button had been on for 15 years, and as hard as I tried, I couldn't find the pause button. She was 5'6" tall and as lovely and solid as the woman I'd loved for 18 of the best years of my life. Now David had Goliath on the phone, and I was grabbing for stones to load in my tiny slingshot.

"Well, Josh, how 'bout slipping by the house one of these days, and let's you and I have a little visit about this date."

"Do I have to?" he asked, his voice cracking.

"Sure, I think that would be appropriate. I'd like to meet you first and talk over some details of the evening together."

"Uh, I don't want to go out *that* bad," he blundered, as I'm sure I would have had I been in his shoes.

"Josh, you're 6'4" tall. You weigh 220 pounds. You're the starting center on the basketball team. Surely you're big enough to come over and speak to a shriveled up, 44-year-old man, aren't you?"

"Uh, okay, sir. I'll be over tomorrow at 5:00."

I *did* want to talk about the date, but more than that, I wanted to have some fun. This was an opportunity I wouldn't let pass into the ordinary for anything.

About 30 minutes before Josh was to arrive, Jamie and I set up the video camera in some trees, pointing it toward our front door. When Josh came to the door, he would be met by two of my good friends and fellow workers at our sports camp.

Stephan Moore is a handsome African-American basketball player from Arkansas. At 6'9" tall, he looks like a world-class CIA agent when dressed in a black suit with dark sunglasses.

John Dickerson is a soldier par excellence, the commander of the Corps of Cadets from Texas A & M University. Dressed in field artillery gear, armed with a deer rifle, and his face made up with camouflage paint, J. D. looked fit for guerrilla warfare.

With my two hit men staunchly in place "guarding" my front door, we were ready for the arrival of the high-school senior coming to negotiate a date for the prom.

Roll camera.

As expected, Josh walked confidently down the pathway to my house. Stephan and John stepped forward to meet him.

"Josh!" Stephan's big, deep, booming voice stopped the teenager in his tracks. "I hear you want to go to the prom with Jamie."

"Uh," Josh managed to say, gulping air. "Yes, sir. I was hoping to ask her dad about that, sir."

"Well, you've got to get by us first, because Jamie's like my little sister."

"Wow, I didn't know that . . . sir."

"Are you going to touch her?" Stephan shouted.

"Uh, no . . . no, sir," Josh stammered.

"How you goin' to escort her then?"

"Uh, I never thought about that, sir."

The interrogation went on for about five minutes as Jamie and I watched from the bushes, holding our sides and covering our mouths to refrain from bursting out with laughter.

Just before Josh's knees buckled, I stepped out and rescued the lad. We walked inside and joked about the hidden camera. Josh assured me he'd bring Jamie home by 8:30! I gave him my consent. (I felt sorry for him!)

What sticks out in my mind the most about the serious side of my conversation with Josh is that he chose Jamie as his date because he respected her. Funny thing—that's exactly why I chose her mom some 18 years before.

Seventeen magazine (read by 7 million teenage girls) recently dedicated a spring issue to the prom—what to wear, how to act, where to go, what to say. The colorful pages hardly missed a thing. The issue was entitled "Sex and the Prom." (Note: As a teen magazine publisher myself for a time, I learned that *Seventeen* is targeted to 13-year-olds!)

Here is *Seventeen*'s prom-night counsel:

The date. The dress. The dinner. The dancing. The expectations and uncertainties. The pressure's on—just how will the evening end?

To shave or not to shave: That was the question. This, after all, was my senior prom, the culmination of my high school social career. . . .

Oh, sure, I had already bought the frilly new underwear and bra, but I could always convince myself that they were just for "good luck." . . . But the closely shaved legs? There was only one reason to shave them before I went out the door that night—because someone might feel them.

Nobody ever told me that saying yes to a prom date was like signing a Let's Get Intimate contract. So why was it something I sort of assumed? Because it's, well, prom. The ultimate date, the night of giddy romance when anything seems possible. It's fun, it's romantic, it's *sexy* . . . a whole evening of events subtly pulling at you in a way few other nights do. . . .

[T]here's a kind of silent seduction at work on prom night—something you begin to feel in the pit of your stomach hours before he even shows up. As much as it's about anything else, the prom is about romance. . . .

For one thing, the prom can feel like a mini wedding. . . .

"I had a serious boyfriend for about a year before the prom, and there were many occasions when we could have had sex," says Sally, nineteen, now a college sophomore. "But I always felt it would have been hurried and furtive and kind of, I don't know, *dirty*. So on prom night I decided, 'This is it.' We rented a room. I wanted it to be a beautiful thing, and I was waiting for a beautiful occasion."[1]

That, moms and dads, is the world our kids learn to date in! My crazy interview with Jamie's date was definitely memorable, but a dad at the door with a shotgun or an eight-foot-high electric fence won't keep a 16-year-old girl from buying into *Seventeen*'s decadent advice. Jamie's decision to have a no-kiss prom night began when she was two and three and four as we opened the Word together day after day at breakfast and night after night at bedtime. A young person's commitment to wedding-night virginity grows little by little as God's love—shown in a parent's involvement—sprouts in a child's heart and fills the need for premarital affection.

Surveys tell us that more than half of my teenage friends are going to bed on their dates. The first teenage book I wrote was entitled *Looking for Love in All the Wrong Places*. The title says it all. When your teenagers go out on their first dates, how can you be sure their hearts are so full of love that they'll never have to look for it in the wrong places?

Paul, though firm, crusading, goal oriented, and zealous, knew that affection and tenderness were relationship gold! He called Timothy "my beloved son." Paul gave us a glimpse of that loving, involved fathering style (even though he was writing Timothy from a distance) when he said, "I constantly remember you in my prayers. Recalling your tears, I long to see you, so that I may be filled with joy" (2 Tim. 1:3-4).

Notice how rich in affirmation that brief passage is. Paul told Timothy: "I think of you and pray for you constantly. Night and day, you're on my mind. I long to see you again. I remember how you wept the last time we parted. Being with you fills me with joy." Here was a "father" who obviously knew his "child" well from spending time with him, loved him deeply, and didn't hesitate to express that affection. In addition, twice near the end of 2 Timothy, Paul urged his son in the faith to come see him as soon as possible (see 2 Tim. 4:9, 21).

Practically, specifically, in today's late-twentieth-century language, how can a parent enable a teen to feel like a beloved son or daughter, with security that stands under dating pressures and the plethora of other influences that fall on a teenager's shoulders? With the help of several hundred college students who identified themselves as "beloved sons and daughters," I've compiled a list of 365 tried and true ways to say "I love you" that put love into the flesh and the strength to say no into a teenager's heart. The complete list is found in Resource A, but 30 of the ways follow. Sprinkle a few of them into your recipe for homemade "relationship pie" each week, and watch the parent-child friendship grow.

1. Have milk and homemade chocolate chip cookies together after school today.

2. When your child is participating in an athletic event or musical performance, be there watching.
3. Help your son or daughter learn a new skill: riding a bike, making a
cake, fixing a flat tire.
4. Walk with your child some morning all the way to the school bus stop.
5. Leave an I-love-you note in your child's lunch box.
6. Tonight, read a chapter together in your child's favorite book.
7. Memorize a Bible verse together.
8. Share a devotional time with your child tomorrow morning before
school.
9. When the school bus brings your child home, be there at the curb with
a welcome-home smile.
10. Talk together about your favorite memories growing up.
11. Find a new way to trust your child by granting a new area of responsibility that he or she would enjoy and benefit from.
12. Have a family picnic next Sunday afternoon.
13. Sit in church together.
14. When your child is being punished, undergo the punishment with him
or her (occasionally).
15. After your son or daughter comes in from a date, have popcorn
together by the fireplace.
16. This weekend, wait up until your son or daughter comes home (no
matter how late).
17. For a time of reflection together, ask your child, "When you pray, how
do you think of God?"
18. Listen to your child—with all your attention.
19. If your child goes on an overnight trip, leave an I-love-you note in his
or her bag.
20. Have a water-pistol fight (let your kids drench you).
21. Skip rocks together on a lake or pond or river.
22. Reminisce about your child's toddler days, and say what a wonderful
baby he or she was.
23. On the first cold day of autumn, make and drink hot chocolate
together.
24. Say, "I'm proud of you."
25. Twice this week, prepare your child's favorite dinner menu.
26. Let your son or daughter select where you eat out (even if it's
McDonald's again).

27. Allow (but don't force) your child to share in the cost of some the whole family wants. Let him or her also be a part of the decision-making process, helping select the color, brand, features, and so on.
28. Ask your child, "What is your favorite passage in the Bible, and why is it your favorite?"
29. Make up and tell stories with your child as the hero.
30. Bring home your child's favorite candy bar.

Resource A can expand your list of relationship-building ideas to the point of giggles. But I'll stop here to repeat the words of a friend that changed my parenting focus forever: The relationship is everything. (During times of fatigue and stress, I've repeated it over and over to myself a thousand times.)

The relationship is everything.

The relationship is everything.

My wife, Debbie-Jo, loves to be a mom. She also loves the Bible study she leads with several dozen spiritually maturing women in the community. She loves to help her husband in his summer camping business, too. (I couldn't do it without her. She probably could make it float more easily without me!) Most of all, however, I admire the time and dedication she employs to build a friendship with her kids! Nothing is too much trouble.

Our last boy, Cooper, is a fine student. He just couldn't read or write until fifth grade (oops!) and showed little interest in learning either. Debbie-Jo doesn't nag her kids. She's a thinker. One day, she decided to read to Cooper every night for about 30 minutes. For one solid year (except during the summer), you could always find those two, from 9:15 to 9:45 P.M., curled up on the couch, reading together. Book after book became her gift to her educationally apathetic son.

I've never seen anything like it. Because Cooper admired his mom so much, and because everyone is born with a God-given desire to learn, that boy developed an appetite to read. Today, he makes A's in reading. (Folks, hear me. I was afraid that boy would never get out of remedial reading. If the object didn't bounce or pass or shoot through a hoop, he wasn't interested in looking at it twice!)

The relationship is everything!

Relationship building between a parent and child travels in three vehicles of communication: words spoken, experiences shared, and touches appropriately given.

The Effective Faith Trainer Touches Appropriately.

I still cringe at the memory of the pressure-cooked day when Jamie, at age five, was imitating my moodiness. She spouted off with a smart-aleck remark, and I quickly swatted her bottom with my hand. I'll never forget her look of hurt and disappointment for my inappropriate touch. Oh yes, we've administered appropriate spankings with love and firmness to each of our children, but this one was evident to the giver and receiver as a touch of anger, not a touch of disciplinary care. That night, as I knelt by her bed to pray with her, I made a monumental commitment to her and to God that an inappropriate touch would never come from this daddy's hands again.

Hands are instruments of grace. Hands are messengers of trust. Hands are extensions of care.

Hands can hurt. Hands can heal.

Hands can abuse. Hands can tenderly hold.

From age three to about five, Courtney had trouble going to sleep at night, but she relaxed easily when I lay down beside her and gently laced my fingers between hers. She'd then place my hand under her tiny cheek as a security pillow and quickly let go of her worries and fears. She and Jamie still appreciate a hug, a hand to hold, a lap to jump into, or a daddy's arm around the shoulder.

Even though Brady is taller than I am, he and I still hug daily. Psychologists assure us that hugs at any age extend security and warmth and even lengthen life.

Paul accompanied Timothy's all-important moment of grace with touch. I can imagine that though Paul's hands were callused and seasoned with many rugged years, Timothy often felt them as hands of affirming touch. "For this reason I remind you to kindle afresh the gift of God which is in you through the laying on of my hands," Paul said (2 Tim. 1:6, NASB).

Let me emphasize again the point I made at the beginning of this chapter: Through time, effort, affirmation, and tender touch, *the effective faith trainer gets involved.*

Chapter 3

IT'S NEVER TOO LATE

---

*"Grace, mercy and peace from God the Father and Christ Jesus
our Lord."*   —2 Timothy 1:2

*T*he great letter of 2 Timothy begins with grace. Interestingly, it ends
the same way: "Grace be with you" (2 Tim. 4:22).

God created the world with grace, and the last chapter of His Word says
it, too, will end with grace. Appropriately, faith training follows suit to the
letter. Grace is what allows you and me to participate in the awe-inspiring
race of family life.

Put simply, God's grace is the reason we can run and train others to run.

A more vengeful god might have squashed us on the track a long time
ago. He certainly might have left me in pieces after my disastrous first
marriage or caused my dear Courtney's heart to harden so solidly that no
amount of change on my part could have softened her. Thank God, He
didn't. Instead, He lifted up this fallen runner, handed me the baton, and
put me back on a proper course. You see, that's His business; that's what
He does best. He searches out the broken, the downtrodden, the stragglers

in the bunch, and by His grace He makes them useful again. As we train others, therefore, we should do likewise.

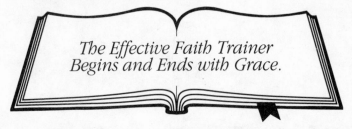

*The Effective Faith Trainer
Begins and Ends with Grace.*

Do you know what the word *grace* means? When applied to our Christian salvation, it means "an unmerited, divine assistance given to men and women for their regeneration or sanctification." In Ozark talk, that translates, "somethin' for nothin'." Get the picture?

Joe White never did a thing to earn God's favor. But for some precious, unfathomable reason, God chose to send His Son to be hanged like a criminal on a Roman cross for me. And then He lavished me with life, the love of a beautiful woman, and four invaluable children. I simply don't deserve it. And neither do all you other faith trainers who are working hard to teach your children how to run. I'm sure you'll agree with me, however, when I say that because of grace, it's never too late for a parent to become a faith trainer.

FROM HEATHEN TO HERO

Dennis is an alcoholic, plain and simple. Jimmy the Greek would've offered overwhelming odds that Dennis's one beautiful daughter, Shannon, wouldn't stand a chance against the backdrop of a modern world of allurement and debauchery. But God has always loved the dark horse. And my, what a winner He made out of that one-time heathen!

Though his sincere beginning with Christ came late in his life, my friend Dennis determined to be the best dad he could possibly be in the days that remained for himself and his budding princess. He used the "miserable wretch" of his past to ensure that God's "amazing grace" would be more amazing in his home each day.

In 1992-93, Shannon wore the Miss U.S.A. crown with dignity. The night she won, Dennis sat humbly in the audience wearing his weathered cowboy boots and chewing on a toothpick while diamonds, furs, and cameras flashed all around him. Onstage, Shannon told the panel of judges that her hero in heaven was Jesus Christ and her earthly hero was simply "my dad."

They couldn't resist her sincerity and commitment.

For the year of her reign as Miss U.S.A., she signed autographs with Scripture. Today she's willing to turn down multimillion-dollar television and movie contracts if the content of the projects is objectionable.

Dennis knew a secret about God and fatherhood: It's never too late to begin.

Grace makes heroes out of heathens, and grace gives us second chances. Grace also allowed a man named Saul of Tarsus—blind destroyer of Christians—to have an eye-opening experience with the Father of fathers. See if you relate to him the way I do. Imagine this:

Saul hated Jesus and His followers. With all his energy, he hunted the early Christians and even presided over the stoning of some, like Stephen. He was vengeful, arrogant, and unmoved by the cries of those he perse-cuted. If ever there was an unlikely candidate for "Faith Trainer of the Year," it was Saul of Tarsus. Yet at this very moment, you are holding in your hands a testimony to the truth that it's never too late for Christ to make a Paul out of a Saul. I can only imagine how many times Timothy thanked God for such a fatherly figure. (For the complete story of Paul's conversion, see Acts 9:1-28.)

Because of grace, Paul also knew that it was never too late for his son in the faith to begin again to develop his spiritual gifts. "I remind you to kindle afresh the gift of God which is in you through the laying on of my hands," Paul told his protégé (2 Tim. 1:6, NASB). As someone has wisely observed, our God is the God of the second chance (and the third and the fourth . . .).

Fellow faith trainers, when I tell you it's never too late, I'm not just talk-ing to those parents who have failed to get involved with their children. Some of you reading this have been the dictionary definition of involve-ment, yet you're wondering, *So why is my kid going down the drain?* Listen to the testimony of a relentless faith trainer named Martha who refused to let her son's alcoholism keep her from passing the baton.

Cameron is an alcoholic, though he's only 17. When he was quite young, he was abused by a baby-sitter, and for ten years he kept the secret to himself. At 12, he began his drinking. He rejected anything that had to do with Christ or the church. If I asked him to attend worship service with me, he'd angrily refuse. If I prayed at dinner, he'd mock me. Even when I did something as simple as hang an inspirational picture on the wall at home, he'd say, "Mom, you know I don't like that!" and he'd demand that I take it down. Keep in mind I knew nothing of the abuse and was therefore both baffled and hurt by his behavior. But through it all, I never ceased to pray.

Reluctantly, Cameron went to church with me one January. It was the first day of the month. I remember the date because the new year was beginning, and deep within I hoped Cameron was beginning something new as well. A miracle happened that day inside my son. The changes were neither immediate nor visible. Nevertheless, I had a sense that Cameron had at least trusted God enough to say, "If there's a Father up there for me, then here's my open hand. I will let You hold it."

Three months later, on March 18, my Cameron let his whole self be embraced by God. He stepped out of the dark world of shame and secrecy and into the light of the Lord's forgiveness and acceptance. Of course, you can imagine how I felt when he finally told me about the abuse. Since I was a single parent and working outside the home at the time of the incident with the baby-sitter, my heart was filled with guilt—not to mention the horrible pain for Cameron. However, as if to help me with this new burden, God reminded me of a prayer I had prayed not long before Cameron's conversion. It was a cry of desperation as I watched my alcoholic son and his alcohol consume one another. The prayer went like this:

"O Lord, I would gladly give my son to another mother on earth if You would someday give him back to me as a Christian brother in heaven. Amen."

It was a short and painful prayer—the hardest one a mother can pray. But I wanted so badly for Cameron to quit destroying his life that I was willing to give another woman a shot at raising him. The amazing thing is this: The more God reminded me of that prayer, the more I could see Cameron's abuse was not my fault. I had done the best a mother could do with the circumstances available to her. Eventually, I could see that all of Cameron's life had been a series of times of giving him up to God—from day one in the hospital, when I almost lost him in delivery, to all those excruciating nights when booze was his primary caretaker and I wondered if he was ever coming home.

Today, I thank God that Cameron is on the right track. Already he has introduced two of his friends to Christ, and just the other day he told me, "Mom, when I go to parties, the people there can see the change in my life." Hearing that makes all those years on my knees worthwhile. I am forever grateful God heard my prayers and gave Cameron a second chance.

Faith trainers, remember this: Whether the problem's with the baton passer or the baton receiver, it is never too late to join the race. Martha and Cameron are living, running proof of that.

The gracious cross of Calvary stood in triumph on that "hill far away" as if to say, "Yesterday is mine, moms and dads. Tomorrow is ours. Let's take it together." I learned something about God's grace a few springs ago that still brings mist to my eyes and a sense of tender passion in my heart. I think about it often. (God teaches His greatest lessons to parents through their children, doesn't He?)

My two boys and I were skiing in Winter Park, Colorado, with my best friend, Mike Trout, and his daughter Meredith. The snow was deep and powdery. The days were picture perfect, and the nights were filled with heavy spring snow.

At about 10:00 A.M. one day, Brady (age 13), Cooper (age 10), and Meredith (age 11) decided to make new trails through the forest. When you're four feet tall, new trails are lots of fun. But the combination of six feet, mid-forties, and clumsy as an ox doesn't exactly fit the Daniel Boone formula for flying through the pine trees at 30 miles an hour. Being the hyperdad that I am, however, I followed the three pups into the dark woods of deep powder. Mike gladly said "See you at the bottom" and took the groomed slopes with the 20,000 other sane adults who enjoyed Winter Park that brisk March morning.

After about 15 minutes of skiing through the forest, Brady, Meredith, and I popped out into the open slopes. For some curious reason, Cooper didn't come out. I waited at the bottom of the woods for 20 or 30 minutes, looking intently at the edge of the trees to find those bright yellow pants atop tiny skis and the familiar, blond-haired, brown-eyed, four-and-a-half-foot frame.

He didn't come out.

I called the ski patrol. They assured me he'd be out before long. My heart quickened to a semipanic that only a parent with a lost child can understand.

In haste, I grabbed a lift and, as best as I could remember it, reskied the long path we had blazed through the trees.

Still no Cooper.

The ski patrol arrived at about noon, and they, too, skied through the trees.

No Cooper.

Twice more I made the run, and each time I grew more desperate. Tears stung my eyes when I considered the gravity of the problem.

By 2:00 P.M., I was deeply worried and frantic. I knew he'd come down for lunch. My youngest can be irresponsible as all get out and miss everything, but you can bet your bottom dollar he doesn't miss food! Surely if he was okay, he'd show up for lunch. But he didn't.

At 4:30, the mountains cleared, the lifts closed, and the dark clouds and heavy snow moved across the vast Winter Park slopes. Thousands of skiers entered the warming house at the base of the mountain, happily celebrating the day's festivities.

This dad wasn't celebrating.

I waited impatiently at the base of the ski area, sorting through the skiers with my tear-filled eyes. Yellow pants, yellow pants. "Dear God," I prayed, "help him find his way out."

As the last skiers cleared the mountain, I saw a tiny, lone figure sheepishly slip down the mountain. My tears became an uncontrollable sob. I skied across the base to meet him, and we melted into each other's arms. I hugged him for five minutes, unable to speak.

A ski patrol fellow skied by. "I'll bet you're mad at him for getting lost," he said.

He obviously never was a dad with a lost son. Anger was the least of my emotions.

Cooper and I didn't talk much on the bus trip to the lodge. I just held his clammy little hand and wept softly. As I recouped emotionally, God got my attention with divine authority.

At midnight the night before, I had hurried through my personal quiet time, reading the familiar passage in Matthew 26 where Jesus, in the garden at the base of Mount Olivet, grappled with the realization that within a few hours, He would be captured, tried, and crucified. And as He accepted the sins of His children upon His sacrificial shoulders, He and His Dad would be separated for the first time since before the beginning of the beginning.

He said (paraphrased in my words), "Father, we've been closest father-son friends forever. Tomorrow in Your holiness, as I become a curse, I'll be lost from You. I don't want to be away from You, Dad. Please think of another way to get the job done. But as always, we'll do it Your way. You know best."

I missed His intense pain as my quiet time scurried by that night. You can be sure I won't miss it again. I felt it in the marrow of my bones as I considered the agony of losing Cooper.

The next day as we flew home, Cooper and I sat pensively and content-edly in the 727, shoulder to shoulder, side by side. After about an hour, I said, "Coop, buddy, what were you thinking about as you tried to find me all day yesterday?"

"I was praying that God would tell you I was okay."

I must have missed it! Perhaps God was trying to tell me something far more important.

Then Cooper looked up to me with his big, trusting eyes and said, "Dad, if I would have died yesterday, would it have been harder for you than if I would have died as a baby?"

A spear shot into my heart. I hesitated for a few minutes and pondered the awful thought. Finally I spoke up: "Yes, little buddy, it would have been worse if you'd have left me yesterday, because when you were a baby, you were my son. But now you're my son . . . but you're also my best friend."

Perhaps you think I'm belaboring the point when I tell you again: The effective faith trainer must begin and end with grace and the conviction that it's never too late. But it's too important not to drive it home one last time. You see, it's not accident . . . or your good looks . . . or anything you've ever done in all your days on planet earth that affords you the opportunity to groom your little "runner" for the race of life. It is by God's grace that you've been given the position of faith trainer in your home. And just as God has treated you graciously, so should you treat your children.

It is the rare teen who doesn't ski off on at least one minor rabbit trail during his adolescence. (You and I have been on a few of those ourselves, haven't we?) Our job as faith trainers often involves a lot of seeking, searching, and gently welcoming that teen back onto the narrow path, much as I did for Cooper. And all along the way, we must remind them that although there are sometimes hard consequences for going astray, it is ultimately not our ability to stay on the path that makes us worthy, but God's grace— God's *grace*.

If you will grasp that one aspect of the Christian faith and then pass it on to your son or daughter, you'll be amazed how much smoother life's rocky track becomes for all of you. Your teens will be eager to receive the baton of faith from you, not resistant. They will welcome your involvement, because your involvement is salted with graciousness. Oh, what friendship we find with our children when we finally understand our own heavenly Father gave us "somethin' for nothin'"! Of course, my theologian friends will argue with me on this point. They will remind me that our salvation cost God everything and should not be taken lightly. I will smile and nod my head in agreement, because they're right.

But then I'll ask them to consider: If the cross of Calvary completely bankrupted the God of the universe, if He really did pay every last penny of our sin debt for us, then what's left for us to pay? Accounts receivable have all been settled. We have a zero balance. By the grace of God, we are free to run with lightness in our step and a happy heart—and it's never too late to start. And that, my parent friends, is Baton Passing 101.

Chapter 4

SINGLE MOMS, SINGLE DADS, GRANDMAS & GRANDPAS

"I have been reminded of your sincere faith, which first lived in your grandmother Lois and in your mother Eunice and, I am persuaded, now lives in you also." —2 Timothy 1:5

*T*his chapter is meant as an extra-large helping of encouragement for those of you who are single parents, either in fact or it just seems that way because your spouse isn't very involved. So get out your Kleenex and share a heartwarming story with me, if you please! Picture a little, brown-eyed girl whose dad was too consumed in his work to go for walks out in the woods, holding hands the way they do it in storybooks. When the little girl got lonely, she would walk up the hill to Grandma's house. Her grandma was especially adept with a little girl who needed a hug, because she, too, was raised without a dad. Her mom was a single parent who poured out her heart to bring a daughter "trained up in the Lord" through the tough scramble called poverty that followed the Great Depression.

That brown-eyed girl is 19 today and a college freshman. Appropriately, her first English theme was a tribute to her grandma. It was written during a homesick day when college seemed bigger than life itself. I hope you enjoy it as much as I did the first time I read it. (By the way, the little girl is my daughter Jamie, her grandma is my mom, and her grandma's mom is now 100 years old and still calls the daughter she raised so well "my little chick.")

GRAN'MAW AND THE LITTLE GIRL THAT USED TO BE

The sun is peeking through the branches of the oaks and elms as they sway to and fro in the breeze. The water is carelessly skipping over the rocks and dancing through the moss without knowing of the falls to come. The birds are singing happily, and the squirrels are chasing each other through the trees. One can sense the Great Designer all around: the pureness of the air and the dampness of the mossy banks. The grass, leaves, and weeds are many shades of green, with the wildflowers splashing the forest with color.

Down by the waterfall, beside an old stump sit two lizards watching all that is going on. A grandmother and a little girl are talking softly about lichen and gnomes. The young girl has a flower in her hair, and she is looking curiously and imaginatively at a fungus-covered rock. She gleefully points to something in front of her, and her grandmother looks, too, with all the interest of another child. There in the woods, in their own world, they spend their afternoon. They carefully walk hand in hand through the woods and watch the birds and other animals enjoy their environment.

They follow the water and talk of deer and chipmunks and squirrels. Hand in hand the whole time, so compatible with each other and with the nature surrounding them. As they walk side by side, they talk and laugh together, occasionally stopping to pick a flower or to watch a butterfly. Here in the woods, they become friends of the Divine Creator, and all of the animals bravely watch the two enjoy their walk. The breeze ruffles their jackets, and the sun shines on their hair.

It is such a peaceful scene. They are so alone and separated from the real world in which they live. They pretend to be looking for gnomes, and the grandmother makes up stories of gnome homes while the child's imagination runs wild. Every once in a while, their trusty canine checks on them and licks the girl's face with excitement and love and then is off exploring once more. They just walk and talk and collect leaves, acorns, lichen, and unique rocks.

In my mind, this scene is replayed constantly. This event that was a consistent part of my past. My gran'maw and me, the little girl that used to be, walking hand in hand through the woods. She shared with me such a love and appreciation of nature, and I looked forward to our walks. Sitting here, I can hear the water and feel the breeze. My imagination overtakes me now as it did then, and a smile crosses my face as I remember the good times Gran'maw and I had when I was a child, and I know that she, too, walks in her mind with the little girl that used to be.

The Timothy that Paul "adopted" had a father and grandfather we know little about, but Timothy also had a mom and a grandmom who anchored him in the faith with all the strength of the Rock of Gibraltar. Those two women did their homework! Look again at 2 Timothy 1:5: "I have been reminded of your sincere faith, which first lived in your grandmother Lois and in your mother Eunice and, I am persuaded, now lives in you also."

Obviously, those women were people of strong faith themselves. And the fact that Timothy was a promising young pastor loved by the apostle Paul shows that they had been diligent faith trainers as well. They had not taken Timothy's salvation for granted. Rather, by their example and instruction in an atmosphere of grace, they had instilled in him a knowledge of and love for the Lord. They did not allow lack of support from (possibly) unbelieving husbands to keep them from passing the baton of faith firmly to Timothy. They understood their responsibility, they accepted it, and they fulfilled it.

America didn't invent distant dads, wayward moms, divorce, or untimely deaths of spouses. They were a part of Timothy's era as well. But America is definitely producing some Lois-and-Eunice-like heroes, parents who are single and going it alone with Medal-of-Honor courage.

The wound in my heart from my surprise divorce has healed greatly, but the scar that remains definitely makes me sensitive to all the folks who walk the mama-daddy road alone. My friend Rosalind Bell's one-of-a-kind husband, Paul, suddenly died. She was left to parent her teens, preteens, and little ones all alone. Through tearful eyes she told me, "Joe, we're going to make it, but there is a labor shortage around here right now."

Single parent, you are not alone! You're out there in the marketplace working hard and then going home to fix the meals, throw the house back together, somehow balance the books, and cry yourself to sleep. But you are not alone. There are a million others just like Rosalind Bell who sympathize with what you're going through.

Keith Chancey is a 30-something bundle of energy who directs one of our camps with "pogo sticks" on his legs. I've never known a man with as much sparkle in his smile and confidence in his daily walk with God. He moves industrial-sized gray clouds away from people's lives with sincere affirmation, warmth, and a touch that resembles that of a Savior with a boat full of fishermen on a stormy night on the Sea of Galilee.

Keith's dad was an alcoholic and had no contact with his family during Keith's vital growing-up years. But oh, Keith has a mom! He told me that the greatest night of his illustrious high-school football career was Dads' Night (of all things) during his senior year. All the fathers were lined up on the sidelines with their sons' numbers fastened to their shirts. Keith felt like the only guy in the huddle who wouldn't have a dad on the sidelines. Loneliness and depression crept over him as the game got under way.

Then suddenly he noticed someone standing in the line wearing his number. His heart skipped a beat: *Has Dad come home?* Looking closer, a tear entered his eye. There stood his mom, stately as any dad in the line, her hair tucked under her work hat, jeans pressed neatly, and number 24 displayed proudly on the back of her shirt.

I met a girl at Southern Methodist University (SMU) in a physical education class who awed that posh and preppy student body with charm, grace, cheerleading talent, and, most of all, a solid, day-after-day Christian lifestyle that I still can't get over! Debbie-Jo was the only financially poor girl at SMU. She was there on military aid as a result of her father's untimely death as a Navy test pilot. She was four at the time of the tragedy that sent her and her two brothers reeling in dismay. But Debbie-Jo had a mom—what a mom!

During the course of the year, I found out that Debbie-Jo loved kids, loved God, and lived her playful sorority life without a drop of alcohol (amazing!) or even a hint of promiscuity. Her cheerleading talent brought crowds to their feet on Saturday afternoons.

I sought to hire her as a summer camp counselor. Little did I know that someday I'd marry her.

I thank her mom in my mind every day for the unbelievable gift she gave me when she held that little family together and relentlessly loved her daughter through the tragic loss of husband and father. Debbie-Jo's mom, like so many others, is a modern hero to me.

Thirty percent of the suburban kids who come to our camps are raised by a single parent. Eighty-plus percent of our inner-city kids are in the same situation.

Some of those children are the nicest kids we know. Many are struggling for identity, no doubt, but not the ones who have a courageous mom or dad who continues to fight for tender moments of faith baton-passing. The common denominator all those parents possess is a magical word my wise father taught me years ago. During a time of heightened family crisis, I asked him to sum up parenting in one word. He squinted his firm yet tender eyes and said without a smile, "Relentlessness. Relentlessness, son. You never give up."

Do you understand what I am saying here? Relentlessness forms the basis of the next great milestone in the process of faith training.

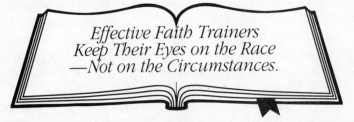

*Effective Faith Trainers
Keep Their Eyes on the Race
—Not on the Circumstances.*

I looked to God in prayer as I thought about each of you who are having a labor shortage in your home right now, and He reminded me that He has walked that road, too. He knows loneliness. He knows rejection. He abandoned His heavenly life to visit us and embrace the emptiness and desperation you feel today. He is the relentless One who went before you, an idea I tried to capture in the following poem.

The One Who Went Before You

He began the day with a father—
He ended the day as an orphan.
He began the day as a hero—
He ended the day as a penniless criminal.
He began the day with a following—
He ended the day alone.

The scent of rejection and ridicule filled the air as the Father of the father-less climbed life's tallest mountain to gain the perspective that only an aban-doned child can understand. It was the only hill under the sun where He could see the hand life has dealt you. He paid the price to come to grips with the loneliness a mother of three feels when her 41-year-old husband walks out the door—a price that cannot be measured in the dollars and cents of this world.

The God of the universe watched His Dad walk out the door as His mom looked on with helpless agony.

"John, take care of Mom."

"Mom, behold your son."

"Eloi, Eloi, lama sabachthani. [Daddy, I need you]" (John 19:26-27; Mark 15:34, my interpretation).

Even in His most desperate moment, Jesus paused to embrace every struggling single mom, single dad, orphan, widow, grandma, and grandpa on earth and say, "I know how it feels. I've been there, too. My Daddy will be there for you. He was there to meet Me, and since I cleared the way for you, He'll never turn His back on you."

"It is finished," He cried. Not "*I* am finished" but "*It* is finished"—your desperation, your loneliness, your quest for a friend and helpmate. Yes, He's there. Your colaborer is God Himself. Your kids do have a dad. They do have two parents to guide them. Each page of this book that we turn together will seek to show you how to integrate Him more and more into your family circle.

Chapter 5

I'd Like to Eat Where You Eat

"You, however, know all about my teaching, my way of life, my
purpose, faith, patience, love, endurance."
                                                    —2 Timothy 3:10

My 80-year-old daddy—who has taught me more of the simplest (and most-treasured) lessons about living life in its fullest and happiest abundance than I've learned in all the self-help books in an average-sized bookstore—is at his best when someone in need is around. He doesn't even have to think twice about meeting someone's need. He's a servant robot with a sold-out heart. Bring an abandoned child, a single mom with three kids, a minority man in a majority society, or a handicapped person of any kind, and he is there . . . quietly but effectively.

He probably hasn't even studied the subject of servanthood. He just does it. I can't begin to walk in his shoes. But one thing he has modeled so often that I just can't shake it is to "look out for the little fellow," "love the loser," "team up with the underdog."

I never really put a value on that kind of thinking until one day when my accountant told me that my 17-year-old daughter's teen clothing company (which she founded, guided briefly, and now shrugs off humbly) had just made a $213,000 net profit for the year. (As always, she donated the money entirely to an inner-city youth camp and a Cambodian children's hospital.)

I wasn't too great in math, but even a C student can tell "that ain't too bad for a kid." We're quick to give credit for the company's success to a sharp-as-a-tack woman from Little Rock named Suzette Brawner for great sales; to a very effective company leader, Bob Abel, for excellent negotiating (like Suzette, he's a first-timer in the garment industry); and to Dillard's department stores for believing in us.

The way all this ties into my daddy's admonition is how the company came into being. Had Jamie and I not had a kind, old, poor taxi driver one day who knew where the local folk ate, the Cinderella story never would have happened. Jamie and I were going on a missions trip to an impoverished city in Trinidad when Jamie was a budding 13-year-old eighth-grader. The day before we landed in Trinidad (just off the coast of Venezuela), we had a three-hour layover on a tranquil Caribbean island named Antigua. As soon as we hustled off the plane, we hopped into the nearest taxi and briskly instructed the driver, "Let's take a quick look at this beautiful home of yours."

Rozelle was a picture postcard. He had driven his antique taxi for several decades. Though poor, he was content and trusting. He had made peace with himself in this life.

We saw the scenic tourist spots, the big hotels, and the breathtaking white-sand beaches that endlessly border crystal-clear, 80-degree salt water. After an hour and a half of slam-dunk sightseeing, Rozelle leaned over in the seat and smiled as his stomach growled. "Where you two want to eat today?" he asked.

My daddy's training leaped out of my mouth: "Hey, man, we'd like to eat where you eat."

Rozelle smiled and said, "You want some local food, eh?"

"You bet," I exclaimed as Jamie gave me a puzzled glance. "We're with you."

Twenty local folks' heads turned as we walked into the café shack on the edge of a nontourist oceanfront area. The food was inexpensive and good. (I'd never heard of some of their island dishes before!)

After lunch, Jamie browsed through a small outdoor market next to the thatched-roof café. A dear Antiguan lady who made a modest living had hand sewn a few meager garments and hung them on a cotton clothesline outside her one-sewing-machine work tent.

One pair of shorts made from a throwaway cotton flour bag caught Jamie's eye. The bag had a faded silk-screen label that said CREAM OF THE ISLANDS . . . PURE 100% FLOUR in pale red and green.

The shorts were one in a million! *The $5 price tag is the biggest bargain in the western hemisphere,* I thought as Jamie (who never wants to buy clothes) asked if she could buy them.

"Sure!" I exclaimed. "What a great souvenir!"

As we said good-bye to Rozelle and began the last leg of our trip to Trinidad, Jamie and I admired the unique simplicity of her shorts and the reliclike quality of the flour-bag design. Almost in unison, we jumped on the idea. "Jamie, I think these things would sell in America!" I said.

"No doubt," she quickly responded. "Let's start our own company and call it White Sands. If it makes any money, we can give it to the inner-city camp."

Sitting in a busy Miami airport as I write this, with many happy White Sands memories behind me, I see the same kind of scenario happening all around me. As my mom and dad, my wife, and our four kids return to Antigua for a twentieth-anniversary family vacation, I see my daddy tending to a feeble old woman as she stumbles through a crowded ice-cream parlor. Just outside in the corridor, Jamie and a Cuban two-year-old girl are playing with a stuffed animal Jamie "inadvertently" purchased for the "stranger" in the airport gift shop.

The little old woman beamed from Daddy's kindness. The Cuban toddler relished her surprise gift from the unknown American teenager.

Given that we're supposedly raising a me-first generation of kids in the closing moments of this twentieth century, I just sit here and marvel as I write. Empathy, warmth, and kindness are as transferable as an iron-on appliqué. They just take more planning, more perseverance, and a lot of practice. They're caught—not taught.

Two hundred thirteen thousand dollars is a lot of money, but that's just a shadow of the value of the smile on that Cuban kid's face right now.

Thanks, Dad. I didn't know those valuable little lessons would be so priceless!

Thanks, Rozelle. Best two-dollar bowl of ham hocks and beans I ever ate.

Thanks, Jamie. Your kids will rise up and call you blessed.

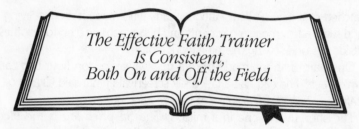

The Effective Faith Trainer Is Consistent, Both On and Off the Field.

This kind of stuff, folks, brings us to the make-it-or-break-it phase of baton passing—example, modeling, practicing what you preach. Here's where I start to squirm as a dad, but here's where it all succeeds or fails. My own failures have been too numerous to count. I can laugh at some of them.

One Easter morning, my wife was on the sixth day of a much-needed one-week vacation with my mom. I had a ball that week being Mr. Mom, but boy, did I appreciate my wife more during those hectic days! One task in particular was spelled out for me by my well-organized wife before she left town: "Be sure to take a picture before church of the kids in their Easter outfits that Grandma made them."

I never knew moms worked so hard on Sunday!

I got an early start that beautiful spring day cooking breakfast, piling all three toddlers into the bathtub, grabbing the burnt toast out of the toaster oven, drying hair, and, alas, putting the fresh Easter dresses on the girls. Everything was okay until I got to the white nylon tights for my two chubby-legged daughters. (I'd never put tights on a girl before!) I thought you did it like sacking potatoes or putting a pillowcase on a pillow—raise up the body, and shake it until it gets to the bottom!

As you can imagine, their toes never did reach the end of the nylon stockings. The harder I shook their little bodies ("What in the world are you doing to me, Dad?"), the more the nylon stretched. Finally, in frustration, I folded the excess nylon under the feet and crammed it into the shoes. By this time, the food was cold and we were late for church.

I hustled the young threesome to the table, and each took his or her place at their Sesame Street placemats. (We always reserve Oscar for the grouch of the day.) We joined hands for the breakfast prayer, and I hurriedly grumbled, "Dear God, thank You for this food and the joy of Easter. Amen."

As we dropped hands, I inadvertently knocked the Oscar placemat to the floor. When I picked it up, the sheepish little voice of my oldest daughter eked out the message, "Dad, you'd better sit by the Oscar placemat today."

"What did you say?"

"Oh, I just thought you might want to eat by Oscar today."

"Why do you say that?" (I thought I deserved a Superdad trophy.)

"Well, you prayed about the joy of Easter, but really you're sort of a grouch."

We got the picture my wife wanted, but I got a message I'll never forget. It was the What-you're-doing-speaks-so-loudly-I-can't-hear-what-you're-saying message.

Christianity, like kindness, is more caught than taught.

If my wife and I gladly submit to each other, our kids learn to be submissive.

If I have a passion for God and His Word, they'll eventually get the disease.

If they watch me on my knees a lot, they'll be good pray-ers. If I ask for forgiveness when I fail, they'll be more humble.

On the other hand, if I'm a harsh leader, our kids will be harsh. If my wife is domineering, they will be difficult to train. If I drive 75 miles per hour, they'll be lax on the laws of the land. If I buy girlie magazines, they'll sneak pornography into their lives.

This old poem has become dear to my heart as I try to remind myself continually how significant my example is to my fathering objectives:

There are little eyes upon you,
And they're watching night and day;
There are little ears that quickly
Take in every word you say;
There are little hands all eager
To do anything you do,
And a little fellow who is dreaming
Of the day he'll be like you.
You are the little fellow's idol,
You are the wisest of the wise,
In his mind about you,
No suspicions ever rise.
He believes in you devoutly,
Holds that all you say and do,
He will say and do in his own way

When he's a grown-up like you.
There's a wide-eyed little fellow,
Who believes you are always right,
And his ears are always open,
And he watches you day and night.
You are setting an example
Every day in all you do,
For the little fellow who's watching
To grow up and be like you.

The little eyes would see it all if I drove 75 with my Fuzz Buster clearing the way.

They would see it all if I sat lazily in front of the TV while my wife did the dishes alone.

They would see it all if I barked out the orders of the day.

They would see it all if I grumbled at the IRS for stealing my profits.

They would see it all if I flicked on the adult movie when they crawled into bed.

They would see it all if I repetitiously wandered through my pilgrimage with God, complaining about the time it takes out of my daily routine.

They would see it all if I criticized, complained, found fault, and nagged.

It's amazing to me how kids are born with great big baloney detectors installed like radar in their eyes and ears. Pick up any newspaper or watch the evening news and you'll see that the headline story for the day is the issue of integrity or character. We can hardly open a paper without reading about a politician or visible figure's private life and how it doesn't line up with his public image.

Paul, on the other hand, was bold enough to claim a clear conscience and was plainly aware that his forefathers could as well: "I thank God, whom I serve, as my forefathers did, with a clear conscience, as night and day I constantly remember you in my prayers" (2 Tim. 1:3).

Faith training hinges on this point: An athlete takes his cue from his coach. If he knows his coach demands one thing on the field but does something entirely different when no one is watching, it's highly probable the athlete will do the same. Similarly, sons and daughters take their cues from their fathers and mothers. If their parents live with clear consciences, they will live with clear consciences, too. Faith training requires a parent to run with integrity.

Incredible is our word for the gold-medal relay team when they cross the finish line. But when the crowd leaves, the coach goes home to bed, and that same team is still down on the track, setting their sights four summers ahead, we call them *men of integrity*.

Integrity—or a clear conscience—was the key to Paul's success with Timothy, because Timothy knew that his trainer lived the same both on and off the field. In Paul's first letter to the Corinthian church—written about ten years before his second letter to Timothy and so perhaps familiar to the young man—Paul had dared to say, "Follow my example, as I follow the example of Christ" (1 Cor. 11:1). In deed and in word, Paul set a standard that Timothy could aspire to without reservation.

At age 45, I can't remember one word my daddy said about how to love a woman. But I will never forget the countless instances I've seen of him hugging and speaking kindly to Mom throughout their 58 years together.

I can't remember him ever telling me how to pray, but time won't erase the sight of him night after night, on his knees by his bed, talking privately to his Lord and God.

Daddy never said anything to me about serving, but how well I remember him meeting the garbage collectors at our back door every Monday and Friday morning with a cup of hot coffee and a warm breakfast roll.

I'm sure Daddy didn't do it perfectly, but to this youngest child in the family, watching him was like watching the embodiment of Mother Teresa's slogan:

"Witness always.
Speak when necessary."

Chapter 6

PRIORITIES

———————

"Do your best to get here before winter."   —2 Timothy 4:21

O ur home is not a normal stopping-off place for famous people—
not in the least. Ten miles north of the Arkansas border in the hills
of southwest Missouri is not exactly Madison Avenue at Times Square. But
occasionally I get to meet some interesting people in my work.

In the fall of 1993, I got to have lunch on two different occasions with
two well-known Americans, Dick Cheney (secretary of defense under
President Bush) and Oliver North. Both men were a real treat. I couldn't
wait to hear their unique stories and find out what made each man tick.

Secretary Cheney, a mutual friend, and I were invited to fly fish for rainbow trout in a nearby Ozark stream. As I approached Cheney, he landed
a three-pound beauty with the colors of the rainbow glimmering down its
side. A smile of victory beamed from his face as he lifted his trophy from
the cool spring water.

We enjoyed trout fillets as the former secretary of defense talked about
the Persian Gulf War that he helped orchestrate with miraculous success.

Instead of the feared 20,000 to 40,000 casualties the media braced us for, we lost only 141 soldiers.

After lunch, I asked Cheney who he thought was the most impressive person in the world—and he had met them all, from continent to continent. He quickly replied, "Margaret Thatcher."

I probed further.

"I like Maggy Thatcher," he went on, "because of her great convictions and the courage she has to follow up her convictions."

Three weeks later, over fried catfish, I asked Oliver North the same question. Immediately he said, "The greatest person in the world I've ever met is, without a doubt, my wife."

Hmm.

The courage and convictions admired by Cheney . . .

The priorities of Oliver North . . .

That's not a bad formula for any parent who deeply desires to build godly kids in a Christ-centered home.

Our government spent a lot of time and money to prosecute Oliver North, and the media closely scrutinized him for many months. If that wasn't enough, one crazed leader from Libya had a band of hit men trying to assassinate him at the same time. I asked him how he held up under such intense pressure. North said his strength came from one simple act: *prayer*.

The question I put to Cheney and North is a great way to learn the true heart of a person. North had welcomed almost every great military and political leader in the world in his days with President Reagan, but his wife remained the Mona Lisa of his life in every way.

Priorities win wars. Priorities make CEOs successful. Priorities make good spouses. Priorities raise good kids.

How are yours today?

Mine are constantly struggling for survival. My telephone has 12 lines, and my hair started graying at age 35. But I love to fight (there are nuclear battles some days) for priorities.

Today at lunch, I pulled out of a couple of brush-fire meetings to have a bowl of soup with my bride. I needed to apologize for something shallow I said last night. She deserved better.

Last night, I got to see my boy put the ball in the basket a few times in a David-and-Goliath basketball game where, without a 15-year faith in God, he'd have gotten stepped on like an ant.

My year is a lot like yours—crazy. But a calendar and a watch have done wonders for me (no, they've saved me!) in the last few kid-loving years.

We keep a calendar on our refrigerator, and every September, my sweetie writes in all family times (sports and school events, vacations, etc.). Each year, there are more than in the last. (Thanks, God!) When a wonderful ministry opportunity comes up for me, I've learned—the hard way—to check the calendar first and let folks know that if a family event is planned, that day won't work because it's already spoken for.

This sentimental dad needs at least a day and three nights a week to do only family things. We need two or three weeks a year (sometimes in two- or three-day spurts or five-to-seven-day spurts) to do things with only Mom, Pop, and the kids. I need to be alone with each of my kids regularly. The calendar is the magic. I'll play golf and get a lot more social when my last boy goes to college. Until then, the calendar rules.

The other priority provider is the wristwatch. Nine-thirty to 10:30 P.M. is my time to lie by the kids and visit one on one. The Dallas Cowboys might be playing San Francisco, but they'll have to play without me during that precious bedtime hour. I often have to excuse myself from guests in the living room to tuck a child into bed. They understand. The Cowboys can win and the conversation can go on without me.

The apostle Paul wasn't able to be with Timothy every day; when 2 Timothy was written, Paul was in a Roman dungeon, and Timothy was pastor of the church in Ephesus. But do you think Timothy and his welfare were on Paul's mind? Were they a priority concern? Let me take you back to Paul's letter: "Night and day I constantly remember you in my prayers. . . . I long to see you, so that I may be filled with joy. . . . Do your best to come to me quickly" (2 Tim. 1:3-4; 4:9). There could have been no doubt in Timothy's mind about how important he was to his spiritual father.

If you want to do something really dangerous (and too sweet for words), get a pen and paper and write *every* in big letters at the top. (Watch out; this exercise will change your scrapbook and retirement memories drastically.)

E V E R Y

Under the word, make some nonnegotiable, priority commitments that the San Andreas Fault can't separate you from. For example . . .

Every night, I'll lie by my kids and memorize a Bible verse.

Every Sunday will be Daddy-kid or Mommy-kid day.

Every Monday and Thursday nights will be family nights.

Every month, I'll get each kid one on one for an evening.

Custom-make your commitments to move you as far from the Joneses as you can stand. Their kids are the statistics in tomorrow's *USA Today*. Your kids will rise up and call you blessed!

Chapter 7

USEFUL TO THE MASTER

"If a man cleanses himself from the latter, he will be an instrument for noble purposes, made holy, useful to the Master and prepared to do any good work."　　　　　—2 Timothy 2:21

S itting on the bench, you want to play so bad your stomach is tied in knots. If only the coach would notice you! Such feelings bring pain to a young athlete's soul. Maybe you're not as strong or fast as the other players out there, but if desire could be measured in pounds of strength and seconds of speed, you'd be starting for sure. Then in an instant, a team member at your position blows a play. The coach is infuriated. He begins to pace the sidelines, looking for a replacement. Your chest swells. You stand slightly on your tiptoes to stretch your stature. He looks right at you as if he's thinking, *Can he make it out there? Will he let me down if I put him in?* Then he drops his eyes and moves away to select someone else. Everything inside you dies.

I still relive some of those benchwarming looks of rejection. Twenty-five years later, my coach's laser eyes continue to burn holes in my heart.

But that pain, though great, pales compared to what I feel when I watch the same thing happen to my son and daughter. I die each time it takes place. No matter what the sport—basketball, volleyball, football, cheerleading—they're all the same. Coaches choose the most fit and leave the rest to watch the game.

As Coach Bud Wilkinson once said, "Modern-day football is 22 players on the field desperately needing rest and 22,000 spectators in the stands desperately needing exercise."

I can survive benchwarming for me and my kids in sports and school activities, however—but even oxygen isn't more important to me than our being players for God on the eternal field of life, where people's very souls are won and lost every day. To have God use your 17-year-old to lead a lost peer to the Cross is a mountain of satisfaction no Heisman Trophy winner has ever climbed on a football field. To watch a high-school sophomore choose to spend a summer in missions; a 12-year-old choose to give his allowance to feed the hungry; a daughter walk the aisle in a white bridal veil of purity; or a grandchild look up to his dad (your son) and admire his Christlike family leadership—these are nothing less than the greatest call from the Head Coach to the arena of highest value.

How does a parent prepare his child for such a call? Paul told Timothy clearly, "Take a bath. Take an inside-the-heart shower, and keep it squeaky clean" (2 Tim. 2:20-22, my loose paraphrase).

Wow! What a challenge in these turn-of-the-century years where pornography and humanism loom around every corner! A challenge? Yes. Impossible? Definitely not. God never gives a command that He doesn't supply the wherewithal for a willing follower to fulfill it.

To be "useful to the Master" (2 Tim. 2:21), kids need four parent-given attributes. Put them in place consistently, and chances are their Head Coach will call their names.

First, help your kids fathom their potential. Physiologists tell us that a child's brain has 1 trillion nerve cells and 1,000 times that many neuron connectors that enable it to absorb 100 million messages every second.[1] Every sound, every sight, every touch, every taste is packaged and stored for use (good or bad) immediately or at a later time. That magnificent mind could only be filled if a child learned something new every second for the next 3 million years. According to Leslie Hart in *How the Brain Works,* "A computer of the latest generation with anything like the capacity of an average brain, would fill several large buildings and would require electric power sufficient to run a small city."[2]

So who or what is programming your children's computer today? What kind of environmental bath do they enjoy each 24 hours?

Second, consider the potential for absolute disaster if your kids are left to the unchecked influence of modern information technology. When my oldest child landed awkwardly in the Let's-go-to-the-movies stage of early adolescence, I carefully reviewed a well-documented book called *The Parent's Guide to Current Movies*[3] over a three-year period. I was flabbergasted to learn that the average PG movie has a dozen four-letter words, ten profanities, and six sexual innuendoes, often explicit.

That number is doubled for PG-13 movies, and their packaging is exaggerated for "tasty" savoring by teens with emerging hormonal activity.

Consider a mid-1990s PG movie sold at box offices coast to coast and then marketed by McDonald's hamburger stores (of all places) to go along with a Happy Meal for an extra $5.95. Forgive me if I make you blush, but here are the facts: The movie pokes fun at masturbation, alludes to satisfying oral sex, and is laced with God-jeering profanity.[4] What's good for McDonald's (or anyone else up the street) isn't fit for a home that really desires to raise a godly daughter or son.

Studies I've read about indicate that children watch about 43 hours of violent cartoons each week—48 acts of violence per hour. Over the 10-year period between ages 5 and 15, children will witness an estimated 13,000 human deaths on television.

Top-40 radio and pop/rock music is worse still. Read the lyrics on the CD jacket in your teen's or her friend's room. "Rape me." "I want your sex." "If you're nine, you're ready." "Let's spend the night together." "Kill the cops." You name it and it's being played in Christian homes from every church denomination in our country, and the rhythm of music makes it stick the way a hawk's talons sink securely into its prey.

Donald Duck and Richie Rich have been replaced on almost every comic-book rack by drugs, sex, rock & roll, and graphic superhero violence, all packaged for young children. Nintendo, Sega, and other multibillion-dollar electronic game makers boast of their most popular games for eight-year-olds that feature demons, witches, and Satanic-style violence. *Seventeen* magazine (for the 13-to-15-year-old market) battles *Sassy* to be the most chic, sexy stimulant of the day. *USA Today* has its own 900 phone number for horoscopes, and *Sports Illustrated* is the new leader in soft-core pornography sales with its swimsuit issue. (What happened to baseball, hot dogs, and apple pie?)

I recently counseled a confused and angered 16-year-old boy who said he was receiving his new mental-violence/four-letter-word programming from an underground computer network. This is the latest of the new evil-world thought producers. Apparently there are on-line services all over the country, available to every home, where teenagers connect with other computer sharks and play Dungeon-and-Dragon-type games that are about as evil as anything on the market.

On TV sporting events, bikini-clad females are used to sell beer, and a nude man and woman kissing in the shower MTV-style are used to sell a wet-dry electric shaver. Ask a 19-year-old boy and girl who walk shamefully away from an abortion clinic if they bought the shaver or bought the sex.

I was so outraged at one point that I offered my kids a fat (for our lifestyle) monthly allowance if they'd watch TV just one time a week. All four gladly agreed. The crazy thing about the plan is that it *worked* with four fun-loving kids, a matinee-movie-loving mom, and a sports-loving dad for over a year. Better still is the way the allowance taught the kids to manage, save, and give away their money! It hasn't been flawless, but we're playing games again in the living room. We're actually discussing the day's activities quietly after dinner. We're enjoying great movies like *Old Yeller* and *It's a Wonderful Life* on the VCR.

Third, remember that parents are still the boss in the home. (No thanks, Phil Donahue.) We're not in the tyrant business, but we are firmly planted in the leadership and skillful-decision-making business. I get all the input I can from my spouse (who is so wise) and my kids (who teach me every day), but the final yes or no is mine to give, and the responsibility of that yes or no is mine to endure. Only a fool would pridefully lord that authority over a family, but a greater fool would not exercise it wisely.

*The Effective Faith Trainer
Gives Clear Instructions.*

I am amazed at the tendency of today's parents to be nondirective with their children when they wouldn't dream of doing so with their employees, the appliance repairman, or their tax-return preparer. Somewhere along the line—and I'll mention no names (but his initials are Carl Rogers)—the public was tricked into thinking that children arrive in this world with all the information they'll ever need to become productive members of society, and therefore our job is to just stay out of their way and watch the beautiful process unfold. Under that plan, our society should be flourishing by now.

Question: So why is our Congress spending so much time talking about crime and unemployment?

Answer: Because all those kids in the '70s and '80s who were supposed to metamorphose into productive citizens without our assistance did a very bad thing—they let us down.

If we look at Paul's fathering of Timothy, we see an abundance of directiveness. Note the following command words found in the text of 2 Timothy:

> *Retain the standard of sound words* (1:13).
> *Remember Jesus Christ* (2:8).
> *Keep reminding them of these things* (2:14).
> *Flee the evil desires of youth* (2:22).
> *Pursue righteousness* (2:22).
> *Don't have anything to do with foolish and stupid arguments* (2:23).
> *Mark this* (3:1).
> *Preach the Word* (4:2).
> *Be ready in season and out of season* (4:2).
> *Correct* (4:2).
> *Rebuke* (4:2).

Paul didn't say, "Does Timothy want to turn off the TV set? Does Timothy want to choose a G-rated movie instead of that PG-13? Does Timothy want to listen to Christian music instead of heavy metal?" No. And no effective faith trainer will, either.

Trainers must give clear instructions—or the baton will be dropped along the way.

Finally, children who play for God have a three-pound computer of gray matter seated securely on their shoulders that is programmed daily with wisdom. The subsequent pages of this book will, by God's grace, be a prayerfully derived encyclopedia of age-appropriate computer bytes to enable you to fill that mind with God's wonderful truths.

Chapter 8

A Man Called Trevor

"All Scripture is God-breathed and is useful for teaching, rebuking, correcting and training in righteousness, so that the man of God may be thoroughly equipped for every good work."
—2 Timothy 3:16-17

*H*e had the hands of Michelangelo, the smile of Jimmy Stewart, the compassion of Mother Teresa, the heart for God of David, and the surgical skills of none before or after him. When Trevor Mabery died in a tragic plane crash in the summer of 1987, part of me died. Trevor was my second dad, mentor, and friend.

As a young resident at the world-renowned Mayo Clinic, Trevor got even Dr. Mayo's toughest surgeries because of the divinely given skill of his hands. Behind his modest smile was a Fort Knox storehouse of medical wonder.

Funny thing about Trevor was, every patient, young and old, admired him as I did. Everyone who knew him felt that he or she must be the most important thing in Trevor's life. Trevor reminded me of these poetic lines I've seen etched on a tombstone:

He has achieved success who has the respect of thinking men,
the love of little children, has filled his niche,
and has left the world better than he found it.

Trevor built a huge medical complex in Dallas, Texas. He worked countless pharyngeal, audial, and nasal miracles, but his favorite cases were kids
from foreign soil who were born with severe facial abnormalities. His eyes
would sparkle when he'd show me the "before and after" pictures of these
little niños and niñas from South America who were once ridiculed because
they had no nose, no ears, or grotesque mouths. The "after" photos always
showed them smiling with a countenance that would grace the portfolio of
any children's modeling agency.

I will never forget the day Trevor and I met in my Ozark mountain home
and he described perhaps his favorite surgery a few days after its super-
naturally guided completion. The patient was a young boy from Brazil who
was born without ears. For his first ten years, he had never heard a sound.
He had learned to communicate, however, and often expressed his desire
to hear the birds sing.

Trevor heard of his story and helped the young Brazilian to come to
Dallas, where Trevor and his team of four charitable physicians went to work.
Trevor bored ear-canal openings in precisely the right location, inserted the
missing auditory ossicles (hammer, anvil, and stirrup bones obtained from a
bone bank), and connected them to the existing nervous system. The assist-
ing plastic surgeon built the outer ear structure from scratch.

The next morning, Trevor entered the boy's room to check on his
condition.

The boy was in his bed, crying.

Trevor asked about the tears.

The boy smiled "from ear to ear" as he gratefully spoke of hearing a bird
sing outside the hospital window. He said to his doctor friend, "I've never
heard a bird sing until today. I woke up this morning to the sounds I've
longed for since the day I was born."

Ears.

"Dear God, I pray, help us give our kids ears. May I be so motivated
as a dad, so contagious in my approach, so prioritized in my schedule
that my kids will long to hear the Word of God in their lives the way
that boy ached to hear a bird sing."

I can't give them anything greater.

Folks, without a doubt, the single most important command (yes, command) in Scripture from God's heart to a parent's Day-Timer is found in Deuteronomy 6:5-9. It spells out our duty for all of us who think "There's just not time in the day" or "I'll delegate that one to my wife or the Sunday-school teacher":

> *And you shall love the Lord your God with all your heart and with all your soul and with all your might. And these words, which I am commanding you today, shall be on your heart; and you shall teach them diligently to your sons and shall talk of them when you sit in your house and when you walk by the way and when you lie down and when you rise up. And you shall bind them as a sign on your hand and they shall be as frontals on your forehead. And you shall write them on the doorposts of your house and on your gates. (nasb)*

At this point in the book, I'm putting up the public-address system. I hope you can picture me climbing a ladder and placing the 5,000 megawatt speakers on their giant platforms: *The effective faith trainer is committed to imparting God's Word.* Throw the rest of this book away if you want, but put this chapter in your fireproof safe for annual review.

In 2 Timothy 3:14, Paul urged Timothy, "Continue in the things you have learned and become convinced of" (NASB). And what had he learned that was worth continuing in? "From infancy you have known the holy Scriptures, which are able to make you wise for salvation through faith in Christ Jesus. All Scripture is God-breathed and is useful for teaching, rebuking, correcting and training in righteousness, so that the man of God may be thoroughly equipped for every good work" (2 Tim. 3:15-17).

Clearly, Paul wanted his spiritual son to know and continue to learn God's Word, but not for mere head knowledge. He understood that the Word in Timothy's heart would produce godliness in the young man's life. Timothy's grandmother and mom had been wise enough to build Scripture into his life from his infancy; it would continue to bear fruit for as long as he lived.

The Effective Faith Trainer Is Committed to Imparting God's Word.

The process that would forever change my family's life began when my oldest child was six and my next two were four and one. I hadn't memorized anything since my sixth-grade speech class, and I was sure that part of my brain was missing and I could not retain a line or two longer than 30 minutes.

I went to a Scripture memory seminar, however, and I was blown away by all that man had memorized with his nine-year-old. I think they were in the twenty-third chapter of Luke and still cruising at breakneck speed. But that guy had twice my IQ, and I was sure his nine-year-old would pass it soon.

Then God led my wife and me to another seminar, and all I can remember the guy saying is, "You can do it," "Scripture memory is essential to life," "There is no tomorrow; do it today," and "The gold vein is discovered as you undertake it chapter by chapter."

That night, I memorized Romans 12:1. I wasn't going to quit until Romans 12 was mine. Wow, it was hard work in those early days! I wrestled and struggled and carried the book everywhere I went! Thirty days later, I was hooked. As scripturally brain dead as I was, memorizing the Bible became like oxygen to me! As my appetite grew, I read an article in _Moody Monthly_ magazine that simply and firmly let me know that as a dad, I needed to memorize Scripture daily with my kids.

I set a goal (one of those "in concrete" kind). Every night (e-v-e-r-y), I would lie down by my kids before they went to sleep and memorize the next verse with them. That was 13 years ago! We're still at it!

I told them that if they would memorize a medium-sized book, God would give them the blessing and I'd give them a chunk of money to spend any way they chose. (Both my oldest kids gave half of theirs to their favorite charity, spent about 10 percent, and saved the rest.) I told them that if they'd memorize two medium-sized books (Titus and Philemon—_not!_) and live by them, I'd give them a car—not a BMW, but a reasonable car that we could afford. (For many of you reading this, even a decent used car is beyond your means. You know what you can and can't afford. But my point is to offer a reward that's sufficiently motivating and commensurate with your child's accomplishment.)

The process has been the single most exciting adventure I've ever been on! I'm now on chapter one of book two with my youngest. None of them quit when they finished the goal. Kid number two has memorized three books to date and has the younger two memorizing Scripture in her car as she taxis them to school each day! The passion continues to spark their own initiative. We've argued, cried, failed, been through junior-high temptations and high-school broken dreams like every other family, but my how the Word of God has been there to guide us! Folks, *it works!*

I stand in awe of how my kids fight the battles in their public-school lives. One tough junior-high day, kid number two came home from seventh grade in tears. Twenty-three invitations had been issued to her group of 24 loosely held friends. It was a spin-the-bottle party. One invitation was purposefully withheld. One of 24 was omitted. She cried stinging tears of rejection, but she also took comfort in sobbing in my arms and knowing she was rejected for a great reason.

"Courtney," I said, "in the last seven years, we have spent a lot of time together memorizing and discussing God's Word."

"Yes, sir," she eked out quietly.

"Princess, has it been worthwhile for you now that things are getting crazy around you?"

She looked up and said, "Yes, Daddy, it definitely has been worth it."

"Why?"

"Well, in junior high, you have to make lots of hard choices, and with God's Word in your heart, you don't have to go home and look it up."

On another memorable occasion, I was in a café in Nashville, calling home to southern Missouri after two weeks of lonesome business travel. Debbie-Jo told me she had just come from her prized evening time of tucking the children into bed with prayers. As she had said good night to our two boys in their Superman pajamas, "Super Cooper" had said he wanted to memorize a new Bible verse so he could tell it to his daddy when he came home. "Get out my Bible," he said in his four-year-old dialect, "and wead me one, okay?"

"Cooper," she replied, "the lights are out. Can I just tell you one?"

"Okay."

She pulled out the old standby. "A good verse for every child to know is 'Children, obey your parents in the Lord, for this is right' " (Eph. 6:1).

There was a long pause. Finally Cooper spoke. "That's not in there, Mommy."

"Yes it is, sweetheart."

"No," he protested, "I think you just made that one up."

I roared with laughter as Debbie-Jo gave the account over the telephone. After I hung up and walked back to my table, the truth struck my heart like a sword. That's exactly what I tell God when I keep a safe distance from a Bible verse that demands not only my attention, but also my action—especially when He asks me to change something I don't want to change. "That's not in there; You just made that up." (Why does God keep teaching me lessons like that?)

Ready for some real family fun? Here's how it works. You can't give away what you don't have. Mom or Dad needs to get personally involved in the memory process. All you have to do is stay one verse ahead of your kids.

Enthusiasm covers a multitude of ho-hums. Make it like Hershey's Kisses. Get out the pom-poms and get excited about it. Ten years from now, be more excited than you are today.

Now, remember that word *every*. *Every*. Write it, ponder it, meditate on it, think about it. Now set a personal goal to memorize a new verse or review yesterday's verse or last week's verses every night. (Do it together.)

The best time is bedtime. As you lie down by each child in a fun, relational way, ask questions like "How was your day?" "What was the most fun thing you did today?" "What did you learn today?" Then take the verse one bite at a time, and remember that a spoonful of sugar helps the medicine go down. Plan a reward system that fits your taste and budget.

Do it together. (I think I'm repeating myself.)

Start with a few key verses that are easy for a preschooler to understand. Next, do some short psalms so each child can succeed at completing a chapter. Then pick a medium-sized book and get carried away!

Do it together. (Oops, I already said that!)

I have a black Labrador retriever named Brave. Training him to perform complex hunting and obedience skills has been a great experience. He's an amazing pet! His successes come from many *short*, enthusiastic lessons. We always "work happy"—I smile, cheer, and applaud wildly. He always wants more when we stop the day's lesson. If he's having a bad day or getting lazy, we end the training and play together.

Scripture memory work with a child is very similar. Do it *often*; do it *joyfully*; do it in many *short* spurts.

Below is the plan that has worked well in our home. Stay with a verse until your child can repeat it with a smile, and review it until it's stuck in his or her heart forever, poised like a well-armed soldier for a 15-year-old at a Saturday-night party when a date wants to go to the bedroom.

Age 3
Psalm 23
John 1:12

Age 4
Psalm 1   Matthew 5:16
John 3:16   John 10:10
1 John 1:9   Revelation 3:20
Matthew 6:9-13 (the Lord's Prayer)

Age 5
Romans 3:23   1 Corinthians 13
Galatians 5:22-23   Philippians 2:3-5
Colossians 3:23   1 Peter 2:2

Age 6
Psalm 100   Matthew 5:1-16
Romans 5:8   Ephesians 6:1-3
2 Corinthians 12:9

Age 7
Luke 2:1-20   John 14:1-4
Romans 6:23   Romans 8:1
Romans 12:1-32   Timothy 3:16-17
Philippians 1

Age 8
Psalm 103   John 14:5-11
Acts 1:8   Philippians 2

Age 9
John 1:1-14   Philippians 3
John 14:12-21   1 Thessalonians 5:16-18

Age 10
Philippians 4

Age 11
2 Timothy 1-2

Age 12
2 Timothy 3-4

Age 13
Review Philippians and 2 Timothy

Age 14
James 1-2

Age 15
James 3-4

Age 16
James 5 and review

If your child is already over three years old, jump into the plan wherever you feel is best. A five-year-old could start at the three-, four-, or five-year-old level. A 12-year-old might start with the book of Philippians.

Applying the verses to your daily lives is so rewarding! Scripture memory is to the child what the lamp was to Aladdin.

It's the diamond to the bride.

It's the bone to the dog.

It's the flag to the nation.

It's the snow to the skier.

It's the key to the lock.

Scripture memory is the single-most-effective life-shaping tool in a parent's toolbox!

A great memory expert once said, "You can't remember words, but you can't forget pictures!" In my early days of Scripture memory, I pictured every word of every verse. The more ridiculous the mental pictures were, the more impossible they were to forget! When we'd memorize Scripture with the kids in their first few years, they loved the pictures! Sometimes we'd get on the floor and act out verses like skits.

One night when Cooper was about five, we were memorizing Revelation 3:20, which says Jesus knocks at the door of your heart. Cooper kept forgetting the part where it says "and opens the door," so Debbie-Jo pictured Jesus running into the door and bumping His head. She came upstairs exhausted from the fun. About ten minutes later, Cooper came up to our bedroom.

"Okay, Mom, I've got it," he said. "Can I try it by myself now?"

He began the verse slowly, concentrating on every word, picturing it carefully in his mind. "Behold, I stand at the door and knock; if anyone hears My voice, I will come in to him . . ."

He paused as if he'd forgotten his shoes or something.

"Oops, I made Him run into the door again."

"You did what?" I asked.

"I made Him run into the door. I forgot to open it up again, and Jesus ran into the door."

Here's the way we picture Psalm 23 for year-three memory. Have fun. Make up your own memory pictures as you go along. You can even make flash cards of a verse and see which kid can get it first.

After a year or two, your memory skills grow. Then you can do what I call *transitional word memory,* where you picture the last word of one verse and connect it to a picture of the first word of the next verse. (This is where it's easy to get hung up.) For example, 2 Timothy 1:5 says, "For I am mindful of the sincere faith within you, which first dwelt in your grandmother Lois, and your mother Eunice, and I am sure is in you as well" (NASB). Verse 6 starts off, "And for this reason . . ." So I picture in my mind a well and a water bucket bringing up a big, plump raisin: ". . . in you as well. And for this reason [raisin] . . ."

People always ask me, "Where do you begin?" They're looking for a new technique to make memorization easier.

I just answer, "Verse 1."

"Verse one of what?" they reply.

"Verse one of your favorite chapter."

"Then what do you do?"

"Verse two."

Yes, the pictures help! (You can draw them, cut pictures from magazines, etc.) But mainly, it's just doing it each day and getting excited every step of the way.

One morning years ago, we were at the breakfast table. Two of our kids were scuffling over a toy (pure selfishness). The night before, we had memorized Philippians 2:5.

I stopped the argument and said, "Son, what was that verse we memorized last night?"

His sheepish reply was, "Have this attitude in yourselves which was also in Christ Jesus" (NASB).

"That's right," I affirmed. "Super job! And what kind of attitude do you and your brother have right now?"

"Selfish."

"What kind of attitude did Jesus have?"

"Unselfish."

"What do you need to do with that toy?"

"Share it."

With four teenagers in the house, the application of Scripture is even more intense as we talk about what verse applies to why not to go too far sexually before marriage, why not to drink when everyone else is, why not to watch TV much or go to PG-13 movies, and why not to give in to a thousand other daily battles. The key understanding is that we don't do or not do something "because Daddy says." I'm just a man. Instead, we decide based on what God says.

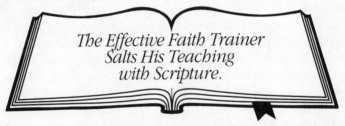

The Effective Faith Trainer Salts His Teaching with Scripture.

You know what? I am now free to fail. I can apologize when I blow it in front of my kids. I can expose my weaknesses. I don't have to be the knight in flawless armor, because ultimately they don't answer to me. They answer to God. He doesn't make mistakes. His Word is sound every time. His advice spans the generation gaps. When it's in the heart, it stays for a lifetime.

Did you ever pour fresh concrete for a sidewalk or front porch for your house and let your children put their tiny footprints and names in the setting surface? Recently a big, tender lump formed in my throat as I noticed, for the first time in many years, the dainty footprints my oldest daughter, Jamie, placed in a freshly poured concrete dog run behind our house 13 years before.

Those feet never belonged to a beauty pageant winner, valedictorian, or All-State athlete. But I thank God joyfully that as those feet grew each year, that little girl learned His Word in our Bible memory times at night. The fruit that I prayed would grow from that effort never looked riper and more delicious than on the day I discovered that Jamie had started a Bible study for eight teenage girls on a high-school campus near her college dorm. As they met together each Thursday morning for donuts and the Word, Paul's exhortation to Timothy became a 1990s reality: "And the things you have heard me say in the presence of many witnesses entrust to reliable men who will also be qualified to teach others" (2 Tim. 2:2).

Several years ago, I sat near the sidelines on a basketball court in Oxford, Mississippi, admiring my two camp-director cohorts and their basketball skills that had outlived their colorful college careers. While they played, I was (believe it or not) pecking away at my Scripture memory work. A giant African-American man sat down beside me, and we began a casual conversation as the game raged on a few feet away. Johnny played football for Ole Miss. He was a bone crusher—one of the best-looking athletes this old college coach ever laid eyes on. In a few minutes, our conversation landed squarely on Johnny's relationship with the Lord. After many difficult teenage years, Johnny was now ready for a major overhaul in his life. At 10:00 that night, Johnny Boatman became a new man in Christ.

In the months that followed, he kept growing in spite of the adverse peer pressure constantly surrounding him on the Ole Miss campus. A year after he gave his heart to Christ, I asked him what force inside him gave him the energy to say no to the drinking and sex that flowed so freely around him.

Johnny smiled a smile that would have melted a tyrannical dictator's heart. "It was my grandmom," he began, reflecting happily on his childhood. "When I was a young kid, she would memorize Scripture with me for hours. Those verses never left me!"

The next year, when our recruiting team returned to Ole Miss, Johnny was waiting for me outside his dormitory. Grinning broadly, he was as proud as a new papa as he introduced me to one of his friends, the team's NFL-bound defensive back whom Johnny had taken under his wing.

"Joe, I want you to meet Derek," Johnny said. "Tonight I want you to do for him what you did for me."

Derek prayed to receive Christ at 10:30 that night, and Johnny's first birthday present as a Christian was the soul of a friend at the throne of God.

How surprised and overcome with joy Johnny's grandmom will be when she gets to the great family reunion in the Eternal City and meets all the Dereks in Johnny's lifetime who sprouted from the fruit tree of humble beginnings in that Mississippi riverside shack where Johnny's spiritual fire began!

God's Word never fails to accomplish His purpose—that's a promise (see Isa. 55:11).

Chapter 9

FAITH THAT GOES TO COLLEGE

"For this reason I remind you to fan into flame the gift of God, which is in you." —2 Timothy 1:6

S teve, at age 30, was celebrating the joys of fathering Billy, four and a half years old and full of vitality. I met Steve after speaking at a business luncheon in Dallas, Texas. His eyes danced with the radiance that's reserved for an active parent as a prized child breaks into every amazing stage of development in those accentuated early days of discovery.

"You won't believe what Billy said to his mom a few nights ago!" Steve reported. His face grew a smile that covered half of Texas. "Billy had just celebrated his fourth birthday, and he asked Jesus into his heart. He really was sincere about it, too!

"A few days later, when his mom asked him where Jesus lived, Billy smiled and said, 'Jesus lives in heaven.' His mom agreed and said, 'Where else does Jesus live?' Billy replied after a little pondering, 'Jesus is everywhere. He lives everywhere.' Again his mom agreed, but she softly continued to probe more deeply. 'Billy, where else does Jesus live?' Billy smiled peacefully and placed his hand over his heart. 'He lives in here. He lives in my heart.' Then, to his mom's surprise, Billy blurted out, 'Why did I wait so long to do that? I've wasted so much time.' "

Aren't kids amazing? No wonder Jesus said, "You've got to become like a little child to see the kingdom of heaven" (Mark 10:15, paraphrased).

In each of my kids' rooms is a picture frame shaped like a school bus. Within the brass frame are 12 little compartments poised expectantly for each year's school picture. Baby-teeth smiles transform into no-teeth smiles, which fade to awkward smiles of junior high and finally bloom fully into smiles of twelfth-grade confidence and readiness for college harvest.

"Yesterday," Jamie's school-bus frame was peaceful, indeed, with two tiny pictures and ten empty holes waiting to be filled. I felt that eons of time would pass before they would get their respective grade pictures inside. "Today," my saddened heart noticed that all 12 holes were full. It was harvest time, and the little girl who once sucked her thumb and wore diapers had been transformed into a young lady who left me in the dust of amazement and emotional awe.

Steve, I remember so well the night Jamie, at age three, asked Jesus to live in her heart. As she prayed, she sat in my lap wearing red and yellow pajamas with little white footies attached to keep her size-½ feet warm at night.

But do you know what's even more wonderful than childlike faith in your three-year-old? It's childlike faith in your 17-year-old!

Sincere faith leaves home and goes to college.

As I mentioned earlier, 80 percent of all high-school Christian kids in America abandon their faith sometime during their college days. More college kids die from alcohol abuse (300,000 annually) than go to graduate school.[1] Seven out of ten kids are sexually active by the age of 20.[2]

No Disney movie or Broadway screenplay holds a candle to the excitement I felt the spring after Jamie's freshman year in college when that same little girl whose diapers have turned into blue jeans and whose "goo-goos" are now college English themes dove onto our king-sized bed and recounted with fulfillment the highlight of her week. God's grace had allowed her to lead her best friend back to a daily walk with Jesus Christ after a four-year detour! If that wasn't enough, I about fell over dead when I heard her on the phone counseling some notoriously wild football player toward his own pilgrimage with the Savior.

You bet we struggled through junior high.

We cried a million tears.

We shared the sting of corrective discipline.

We embraced the emptiness of chronic rejection.

But by God's grace, faith went to college the fall before. Faith left home and moved 600 miles to Texas.

It was the worst day of my life.

I've cried before, but I've never lost it the way I did on I-35 between Waco, Texas, and my hillbilly home in southwest Missouri. We had taken everything she owned, it seemed, up three flights of stairs into the freshman dorm (I'm a pack mule by trade), put up the matching curtains and unpacked the bedspreads (I was the hammer-and-nail guy), and then it was time to leave.

"Sure you don't need one more nail up there?" I asked. "Uh, by the way, when are you comin' home?"

"Thanksgiving. Guess I'll see you Thanksgiving, Dad."

"Thanksgiving? Wow, that seems like eternity." (I couldn't breathe.) As I turned to walk away, I told her, "Jamie, the trouble with you is you're so hard to say good-bye to."

I couldn't drive after that. I tried. The four-lane highway just wasn't wide enough. I literally couldn't see. Someday I've got to grow up and quit acting like that. I don't know when that will be, but I'm pretty sure it will be sometime after kid number four goes to college. (Now my older friends are telling me, "You think college is bad, just wait until your daughter gets married.")

Spiritually, the apostle Paul had also prepared Timothy to live a mature faith that could stand up under the pressures of a hostile culture. In his letter to the young man, Paul told him, "For God did not give us a spirit of timidity, but a spirit of power, of love and of self-discipline" (2 Tim. 1:7). In his first letter, he had encouraged him, "Don't let anyone look down on you because you are young, but set an example for the believers in speech, in life, in love, in faith and in purity" (1 Tim. 4:12).

Timothy's maturity can be seen in the fact that he was the pastor of the church in Ephesus. Paul had a deep interest in that church, because he had invested more than two years of his life there. Timothy also accompanied Paul on several of his missionary journeys. And when Paul was feeling lonely, deserted, and in need of a "soul mate," he called for Timothy (see 2 Tim. 4:9-12, 21). He said of the young man in another place, "I have no one else like him" (Phil. 2:20).

*The Effective Faith Trainer
Follows Through.*

After two decades of having fun with America's kids, counseling until the wee hours of the morning, and answering a telephone that has melted wires from incoming calls from caring parents with troubled kids, I have built a funny-looking ladder for you to enjoy. It's a thumbnail sketch of faith growth that works with kids as they skyrocket from diapers to diploma. The steps on the left side of the ladder are the training wheels . . . the guidelines . . . the disciplinary phases necessary to foster healthy growth. The steps on the right side of the ladder are age-appropriate, parentally guided growth steps that will make your child's going to college a successful experience.

The ladder isn't meant to be used like a recipe for baking a cake. It's simply a guideline for the steady, progressive training of children over a period of time. If your child is already above the age of one and you've maybe missed a few of the steps, don't fret! Just start at the point where you see the greatest need for your child, and gradually work your way up from there as you're able.

Like any other ladder, both sides have to be well balanced or it tips over! Also, don't try to jump steps or you might slip. Just take it one step at a time and enjoy the trip to the top with your child.

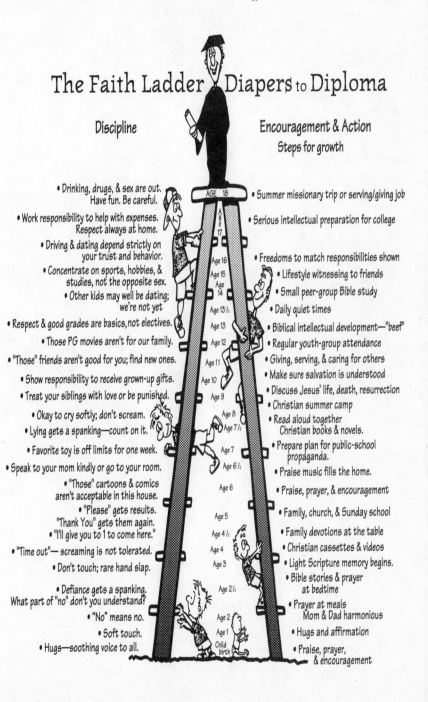

The Faith Ladder ♦ Diapers to Diploma

Discipline

Encouragement & Action
Steps for growth

• Drinking, drugs, & sex are out.
  Have fun. Be careful.

AGE 18

• Summer missionary trip or serving/giving job

• Work responsibility to help with expenses.
  Respect always at home.

Age 17

• Serious intellectual preparation for college

• Driving & dating depend strictly on
  your trust and behavior.

Age 16

• Concentrate on sports, hobbies, &
  studies, not the opposite sex.

Age 15

• Freedoms to match responsibilities shown

Age 14

• Lifestyle witnessing to friends

• Other kids may well be dating;
  we're not yet

• Small peer-group Bible study

Age 13½

• Daily quiet times

• Respect & good grades are basics, not electives.

Age 13

• Biblical intellectual development—"beef"

• Those PG movies aren't for our family.

Age 12

• Regular youth-group attendance

• "Those" friends aren't good for you; find new ones.

Age 11

• Giving, serving, & caring for others

• Show responsibility to receive grown-up gifts.

Age 10

• Make sure salvation is understood

• Treat your siblings with love or be punished.

Age 9

• Discuss Jesus' life, death, resurrection

• Okay to cry softly; don't scream.

Age 8

• Christian summer camp

• Lying gets a spanking—count on it.

Age 7½

• Read aloud together
  Christian books & novels.

• Favorite toy is off limits for one week.

Age 7

• Prepare plan for public-school
  propaganda.

• Speak to your mom kindly or go to your room.

Age 6½

• Praise music fills the home.

• "Those" cartoons & comics
  aren't acceptable in this house.

Age 6

• Praise, prayer, & encouragement

• "Please" gets results.
  "Thank You" gets them again.

Age 5

• Family, church, & Sunday school

• "I'll give you to 1 to come here."

Age 4½

• Family devotions at the table

• "Time out"— screaming is not tolerated.

Age 4

• Christian cassettes & videos

• Don't touch; rare hand slap.

Age 3

• Light Scripture memory begins.

Age 2½

• Bible stories & prayer
  at bedtime

• Defiance gets a spanking.
  What part of "no" don't you understand?

• Prayer at meals
  Mom & Dad harmonious

• "No" means no.

Age 2

• Soft touch.

Age 1

• Hugs and affirmation

• Hugs—soothing voice to all.

Child birth

• Praise, prayer,
  & encouragement

Chapter 10

TODAY IS THE BEST AGE TO START

"And how from infancy you have known the holy Scriptures, which are able to make you wise for salvation through faith in Christ Jesus."   —2 Timothy 3:15

*L*ittle Lori Anne was 14 when she showed up in the nondenominational youth group my wife and I led a few brisk years ago. Though she was one of a hundred or so typical teenagers that night, the patch over her right eye made her face stand out in the rowdy crowd when we sang songs, did goofy skits, and presented the gospel message.

After club that night, I asked a girl who attended regularly who the new kid with the eye patch was. She told me her name and informed me that she had cancer in her face and had recently lost her eye in a radical surgical procedure.

I gulped.

Over the next few months, I made a new friend. Lori Anne was full of questions about God. Though raised in church, she had never experienced the peace and fulfillment of a personal relationship with the Savior. During

71

one of our many talks, she asked Jesus into her heart. From that day on, she had a sparkle in her life that never dimmed.

As the next two years went by, Lori Anne's faith grew as rapidly as her body withered away. All who visited her bedside in her last days on earth walked away changed people, as if they had visited an angel.

A month before Lori Anne died, her team of skilled doctors gathered around her bedside to tell her they had tried everything. Lori Anne looked at them steadily and said, "I appreciate all you've done, but you need to know that I won't die when the medicine runs out; I'll die when Jesus takes me home."

A week before her final breath, I took a superstar recording artist to her room to visit. He was the teen hero of the day. The time together was classic. The next day, a priest visited Lori Anne and said, "Lori Anne, I hear a TV star visited with you!"

Lori Anne quietly responded, "Who's a TV star when you're going to meet Jesus in a week?" She died six days later. Her last words to her mom were, "Mom, I want you to get to know Jesus the way I do."

When does faith begin? The answer is simple. It's always true. *Faith begins today.* Lori Annes are born every day.

*The Effective Faith Trainer
Always Begins Today.*

I was lying in the bottom bunk by my youngest boy the night before his third birthday. His older sister Jamie (age nine at the time) was eavesdropping on our conversation from her perch on the top bunk.

"Cooper," I said, "tomorrow's your birthday, and you'll be three years old." I showed him how to put his three chubby fingers up to announce his age when asked.

Jamie broke into our conversation to announce, "Cooper, now that you're three, it's time you became a Christian."

This will be interesting, I thought. I held my breath and listened curiously as she went on with a nine-year-old's naïveté.

"You see, Cooper, to become a Christian, you've gotta ask Jesus into your heart."

"Umm," Cooper responded. He always soaked in every word his sister said. My, how he idolized that girl!

"Cooper, do you want to become a Christian?" she continued.

"Uh huh."

"Okay, you pray this after me."

Phrase by phrase, Jamie led Cooper through the simple prayer of salvation that she and I had prayed together years before. Though he renewed his faith and asked me to baptize him in the lake when he was 11, he still points to his third birthday as the day his walk with God began.

Tender little sprouts pop up in homes where the soil is rich and cultivated daily.

The soil is fertilized with prayer and tilled with a never-ending sea of encouragement. Weeds are kept from choking the tender sprouts by consistent, firm (not harsh) discipline.

The earliest days are loaded with prayer. I found the following wise thoughts on prayer in my notes last week. I don't know who left them there, but they concisely teach good parents what to do with their minds while their hands are changing diapers.

- Pray that nothing will hinder your children from accepting Christ as their personal Savior early in life (see Matt. 18:6; 19:14).
- Pray that your children will learn to know their God, the true and living God, and will have a deep desire to do His will for their lives (see Ps. 119:27, 30, 34-35).
- Pray that as your children hear stories from the Bible, a genuine love for God and His Word will become such a part of their lives that it will be the basis for all their decision making throughout life (see Ps. 71:17; Eccles. 12:1; 2 Tim. 3:15).
- Pray that your children will develop a keen sense of what's right and wrong—that they will truly abhor evil and cling to that which is good (see Ps. 51:10; 139:23-24; Rom. 12:9).
- Pray that your kids will increase in wisdom mentally, in stature physically, and in favor with God spiritually and man socially (see Luke 2:52). This prayer covers children's total development to their full potential.
- Pray that your children will develop a thankful heart and a fine, confident mental attitude (see Ps. 126:2-3; Rom. 8:31).
- Pray that God will protect your kids from Satan and his wiles in every area of their lives (see Ps. 121:8; John 17:15).

- Pray that God will destroy the enemies in your children's lives, whatever they may be—weaknesses, lying, selfishness, disobedience, and so on (see Ps. 120:2; Phil. 2:4).
- Pray that God will make your kids successful in the work He has planned for them to do (see Ps. 118:25; 139:9-10).
- Pray that your children will have a strong sense of belonging to a family that is loving and dwells together in unity (see Ps. 133; Col. 3:12-14).
- Pray that your kids will respect those in authority over them (see Rom. 13:1; Eph. 6:1-4).
- Pray that their entire lives will be a testimony of the greatness and love of Jesus Christ (see Phil. 2:15-16; 1 Thess. 5:23).

In addition to the above, pray that your kids:

- will be caught when guilty.
- will desire the right kind of friends and be protected from the wrong kind.
- will be kept from the wrong mate and saved for the right one.
- will, along with those they wed, be kept pure until marriage.

ABC's

In America's first 100 or so years, every child in every school learned to read from the *New England Primer*. Every story was laced with scriptural truth. The ABC's were taught like this:

A   "A wise son maketh glad a father" (Prov. 10:1).
B   "Better is a little with righteousness" (Prov. 16:8).
C   "Come unto me all ye that labour" (Matt. 11:28).
D   "Do not this abominable thing that I hate" (Jer. 44:4).
E   "Except a man be born again, he cannot see the kingdom of God" (John 3:3).

Today, all public-school education is stripped of any biblical truth, even though 52 of the 55 Founding Fathers who wrote the Constitution were members of orthodox Christian churches. They were men of great biblical convictions like Benjamin Franklin, who said, "If a sparrow cannot fall to the ground without His notice, is it probable that an empire can rise without His aid? We have been assured in the sacred writing that, 'Except the Lord build the house, they labor in vain that build it.' "[1]

In elementary science textbooks, children are assured that the universe was formed by naturalistic causes and that man came into being as a product of sheer accident rather than through the design of a Creator. In the area of ethics, kids are taught with various New Age curricula like "Children of the Rainbow," which asserts that gay and lesbian couples are every bit as capable of building stable families as monogamous husband-wife relationships.[2] In health (as early as fourth grade), kids are being taught that sex is for any age if it is "safe" and condoms (available free of charge from the school nurse—in school colors, no less) are used. In government, kids are taught that the Constitution was written to keep God out of the American system rather than the truth that its writers carefully designed it to put God and His Word *in the middle* of our governing structure.

George Washington said, "Of all the dispositions and habits which lead to political prosperity, religion and morality are indispensable supports. In vain would that man claim the tribute of patriotism, who should labor to subvert these great pillars of human happiness."[3]

Thomas Jefferson claimed, "Of all the systems of morality, ancient or modern, which have come under my observation, none appear to men so pure as that of Jesus. No power over the freedom of religion is delegated to the United States government."[4]

Benjamin Franklin said, "He who introduces into public affairs the principles of primitive Christianity will change the face of the world."[5]

I'll never forget the tears I shed the day the big yellow monster (school bus) came by to pick up my older daughter for her first day of school. Ouch! That hurt!

Knowing that she'd be learning a new form of the ABC's and that school days were no longer the "Golden Rule" days, my wife and I buckled up for a defense of our beliefs at home. Some of you will be fortunate enough to have a good Christian school or even a good home-schooling opportunity. I applaud you! However, if Mom or Dad is building a strong biblical environment at home, any of the three learning systems can work and turn out wonderful kids. But if the home environment doesn't reflect the biblical truths your kids are learning, none of the three systems will work.

I've met too many out-and-out rebels who are the product of Christian schools and home schools where the moms and dads left the Bible in the classroom. By the same token, I've met some neat teen saints in the public schools whose moms and dads did their homework from 3:30 P.M. until the yellow monster came to the bus stop the next morning. We've tried all three approaches in our home and have seen the benefits of each. The common denominator of solid kids is at least one parent (hopefully two) who takes biblical education at home seriously and threads it into a lifestyle that is winsome, positive, and enthusiastic.

During elementary-school days, homemade Christian education (3:30 P.M. to 8:00 A.M.) should always have four main ingredients:

1. Devotions at the breakfast or supper table
2. Scripture memory at the bedside at night
3. Conversations, storybook reading, videos, and so on with age-appropriate biblical content
4. An atmosphere without TV smut, and parenting models loaded with fun, encouragement, fair and firm discipline, hugs, and words of affirmation

Resource B offers a list of books, cassette tapes, and ideas to continue to sprinkle the small, fertile minds of your children in the toddler-through-grade-school days. These are tried and tested true. They're as close to you as your telephone. A steady diet in the early years—*starting today*—will build a foundation under your kids' feet that the fierce peer pressure of junior high and high school won't be able to erode.

Note that in his letter to his spiritual son Timothy, Paul did not waste any time in getting to the exhortations he knew the young man needed to hear: "Fan into flame the gift of God, which is in you. . . . So do not be ashamed to testify about our Lord. . . . But join with me in suffering for the gospel" (2 Tim. 1:6, 8). Those words came right at the beginning of the letter, following only Paul's warm, fatherly greeting. He wanted to make every word count; he wanted to see Timothy's life begin to change right away. There's an urgency in Paul's writing, because he understood that every day counts.

Today is the day, parents, for us to become better, more-committed faith trainers. Today is the day for our children to grow closer to the Lord.

Chapter 11

THE TABLE-SIDE CHAT

"What you heard from me, keep as the pattern of sound teaching, with faith and love in Christ Jesus." —2 Timothy 1:13

*H*alf of girls have had sex by age 17; half of boys by 16."[1] "Between 1970 and 1986, the suicide rate for those aged 10 to 19 rose by 80%."[2]

"The average age at which children first try alcohol or marijuana is 12."[3]

I'm weary of all the statistics and reports of a "rapidly deteriorating" youth culture in every category. Many cultural scientists point to the deteriorating family as the leading cause of our moral weakness. (You don't need a Ph.D. to see that!) But some insightful experts have determined that the lack of time at the table as a family is one of the greatest losses to kids in our country. In days gone by, we held hands and learned to pray together at the dinner table. That's where Americans developed reverence for God and built relationships that would span the generation gaps. The table was no less than the taproot of true education.

McDonald's, Wendy's, and Burger King have long since taken over the family altar. Our Bibles have been traded in for fast-food menus, and our devotional books have been lost in the pile of burger boxes and french fry wrappers.

I'm a stubborn, hardheaded, old football player, and when it's fourth and one, your toes are dug into your own end zone, and the national champions are trying to take over that precious territory you call home, I've learned to root in groundhog style. I'm determined that for at least one meal a day, my family will circle the wagons around the table and devote some time to discovering God's Word together.

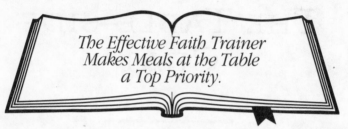

The Effective Faith Trainer Makes Meals at the Table a Top Priority.

Deuteronomy 6 exhorts us dads and moms to teach our kids the Word (not *about* the Word but the Word at its core). My dear mom (neighborhood kids flock to her door) has developed a dinnertime devotional guide for your family (for kids about four to eight years old) from the book of Mark to get you started. Here's a sample of how this adventure can thrill you in the next month or two. (You'll find the complete study in Resource C.)

The ground rules to magnify this devotional adventure are simple.

1. Read the Scripture passage first. If you have time and your kids have the attention span, read the entire chapter (for context) and then reread the focal verses.
2. Let anyone who can read do part of the reading. This keeps everyone interested.
3. Read the devotional story. (A new reader makes it even better!)
4. Ask the discussion questions to as many family members as you have time for.
5. Green-light thinking! Don't squelch answers! Let 'em talk! Agree as often as possible. Encourage any answer that isn't scripturally off base.
6. Mom and Dad, get involved. Reveal your struggles. Be real, be open, and most of all, be excited!

7. The "Lifeline" is a thought for the day that you can all hold each other accountable to (gently!).

BE WILLING
Mark 14:36

A story is told about a seven-year-old boy whose younger sister had a disease that would take her life if she didn't receive blood from a family member. It had to be the same blood type to match hers. All her brothers, sisters, father, and mother lined up for the doctor to take blood samples. Only one had the right type to match the dying girl's—her seven-year-old brother. The doctor explained to the brother how the blood would be taken and transferred to his little sister's arm. The brother was courageous and willing to do this for his sister because he loved her very much.

He lay on a hospital bed close to his sister's, their hands touching while the blood was drawn and transfused. After a long while, as the blood was still being drawn, the brave little boy looked into the eyes of the doctor and asked, "Am I nearly dead yet?"

He had not confided this fear to anyone before, but he had thought all along that when his blood was given to his sister, he would die and his sister would live.

Yet he was *willing!*

Jesus knew the horrible and humiliating death He would go through on the cross. He who had never sinned would be taking on the filthy sins of the whole world when He hung on the cross. Yet He was *willing* to do God's will.

QUESTIONS

1. Why was it God's will for Jesus to die on the cross?
2. How do you think the seven-year-old boy had the courage to give blood for his little sister?
3. Why was Jesus agonizing about the death facing Him?
4. What would you do if you faced a situation like the one confronting the seven-year-old boy? Would you be willing to lay down your life for someone in your family?

LIFELINE

The little sister lived, thanks to her brother. We who trust in Jesus will live forever, thanks to the God who loves us so much that He gave Jesus to be our Savior.

Resources C and D will get you and your little ones well under way; besides the Mark devotional, you'll find studies for the books of John and James. Writing those studies for you and your kids has been just about the most fun I've ever had. My wife and I have tried them out for years on our kids and the kids who come to our camps. How exciting it is when their eyes get opened to the Word! Our first goal is that when your children are under the greatest pressure to break their moral code, this table-side adventure into the Word will make their hearts strong like steel so a hearty *No!* will fly from their consciences with confidence and security. Our second goal is that they will "know the love of Christ which surpasses knowledge" (Eph. 3:19, NASB) and will be able to make Him known to their friends.

One of the greatest tragedies of our day is that almost all parent-child devotional activities are done between parents and little ones. Most moms and dads get discouraged or too busy when their children land on the planet called puberty and the kids' needs for the Word and parents to teach it are most acute. The youth director or Sunday-school teacher is relied upon to do this all-important task, and the teens avoid the Word in droves. The Word has been and always will be relationship given! The responsibility for doing that rests firmly on the shoulders of the parents!

Like a magnet, this all draws us back to the stellar example of Paul and the fatherly counsel that jumps off the pages of his inspired writings.

> *I solemnly charge you in the presence of God and of Christ Jesus, who is to judge the living and the dead, and by His appearing and His kingdom: preach the word; be ready in season and out of season; reprove, rebuke, exhort, with great patience and instruction. For the time will come when they will not endure sound doctrine; but wanting to have their ears tickled, they will accumulate for themselves teachers in accordance to their own desires; and will turn away their ears from the truth, and will turn aside to myths.* (2 Tim. 4:1-4, NASB)

The teen years are the time when sound doctrine is stolen from our kids by our politically correct society! The teachers that tickle their ears are the TV set, the humanistic textbooks, and the boom box.

Never stop teaching the Bible at home, moms and dads. There's nothing under the sun more exciting than seeing your teen get hooked on God's compelling Word. Resource D can rest on the edge of your table for the next two to three months to aid in your family's pursuit of the Bible's truths. My hope is that those studies will become the highlight of your mealtimes together.

Chapter 12

FOOD FOR TEENAGERS: 100% PURE BEEF

"There will be terrible times in the last days."
                                        —2 Timothy 3:1

*I*f you have a child who is anywhere from 12 years old to 18, I probably don't need to convince you that it's a cruel world to grow up in right now. I speak to thousands of adolescents annually in youth rallies, camps, and public- and private-school assemblies, and I hear their cries in one-on-one counseling sessions every day.

Our kids are hurting.

Our kids are in a war.

"Seventy percent of girls and 80% of boys are sexually active (churched and non-churched; public school and Christian school) by the time they are 20 years old."[1] The others are challenged mentally every day by the media and peer pressure in a grueling manner unparalleled in history. In 1988, for the first time, a million of America's kids got pregnant before the wedding bells rang.[2] The current trend shows that 40 percent of those who become pregnant each year will end up in an abortion clinic.[3] The kids I speak to don't blink when they tell me that "everybody's doing it." Now they are instructed and equipped in school. And cases of teenage AIDS double every 14 months.[4]

Furthermore, 80 percent of our kids are drinking sometime before they leave high school.[5] As for our college kids, "As many as will earn post-graduate degrees will die from drinking."[6]

Ten percent of teen boys and 18 percent of teen girls have attempted suicide.[7] "Forty-four percent of high school seniors report having used illicit drugs—including cocaine, marijuana and heroin."[8]

Some say that America hasn't had to fight a world war on its own soil. I flatly disagree. Our teenagers are in the most ruthless battle the world has ever known in every small town and city. The drugs pour in from Asia, South America, and Europe like fire ants. Perversion is everywhere. Our kids are falling in battle more tragically than any army of American soldiers who have ever fought under the Stars and Stripes.

It's mean to be a kid nowadays!

Kids are having sex in the high-school parking lot at lunch and on church youth-group retreats. Christian kids listen to sex-and-drug music artists like Guns 'N Roses, Slayer, Motley Crüe, Madonna, Michael Jackson, and Kriss Kross the way children eat cotton candy at a carnival.

But well-prepared kids are still saying no. Properly parented kids are still saying no. Intellectually and emotionally trained kids are still saying no. Parents who have done their job teaching the faith rigorously can have kids who say no. I've interviewed hundreds and have four of my own who delight in going against the flow, swimming upstream, rebelling against the sex-pop culture, and saying *no!* This chapter is dedicated to the parents of those teenage warriors who want to pass out the battle armor. It's for the parents of the just-say-no kids. It's for the parents of kids who can swim upstream.

This one is beef. Pure steak—100 percent nutrition.

The Effective Faith Trainer Prepares His Kids for War.

The day is long gone when we can leave the job to the public-school system or Sunday-school teachers. Successful kids (almost without exception) come from homes where a mom or a dad is teaching the basics of the faith daily, diligently, persistently, and lovingly until the time that parent is seen in the rearview mirror of a grown-up child honeymoon-bound on a happy marriage adventure.

Warning: Folks, this stuff will take work and lots of it. I've written the following shields of armor in the environment of teenage battlefield skirmishes. This is no ivory-tower intellectualism. This is required hand-to-hand combat basics. If you'll study it hard with your kids, you'll watch their eyes open wide with delight as they see that their faith is intellectually sound. Your kids (as with thousands of others I've taught) will be able to stand up in biology class and refute the humanistic Darwinism (now a religion I call *Darwintarianism*) they'll face every day. They'll be equipped to write term papers on the subjects that confront their biblical faith and challenge their peers and teachers on the reliability of Scripture and all it contains.

Most importantly, they'll know their God, and they'll know that they know their biblical faith is their own faith. No critic, cynic, or unbelieving professor alive will be able to take it away from them.

BEEF—PHASE 1

We'll begin this all-important parent-teen study where God began. As the grass grows thinner each day on the pathway to my counseling office, worn down by the feet of teens caught in the waves of emotional crisis, I believe with all my heart that the most important things parents can give kids are *roots* and *wings*.

Our faith is rooted in Genesis 1: "In the beginning . . ." The textbooks in junior high, high school, and college say, "In the beginning—*bang.*"

Our Bible says, "In the beginning God."

From Genesis 1, we get our entire foundation of God's deity, the sanctity of life, the holiness of marriage, Satan's trap of sin, and God's plan of redemption. If Darwin were able to take away or humanize Genesis 1, the New Testament would be built on quicksand.

Fortunately, mountains of discoveries in the last 20 years have given keen-eyed, open-minded scientists reliable documentation that has put biblical creation soundly in the forefront of scientific origins.

Get ready for one of the most enjoyable studies of your life! While our kids' textbooks assure them that our origins are purely accidental, the fossils (and some of today's greatest scientists who study them) clearly say that's impossible. My daughter's ninth-grade science teacher's face turned pale when I told him that Dr. Colin Patterson (chief paleontologist for the British Museum of Natural History and the most respected fossil scientist in the world) spoke the following shocking words to several hundred of America's leading evolutionists only a few years ago in the American Museum of Natural History:

> The explanation value of the evolutionary hypothesis of common origin is nil! Evolution not only conveys no knowledge, it seems to convey anti-knowledge. How could I work on evolution ten years and learn nothing from it? Most of you in this room will have to admit that in the last ten years we have seen the basis of evolution go from fact to faith! It does seem that the level of knowledge about evolution is remarkably shallow. We know it ought not be taught in high school, and that's all we know about it.[9]

With no Creator, there are no moral absolutes. With no Creator, there is no Savior. As textbook writers have carefully filtered God out of the classroom, it now takes metal detectors in school doorways to filter the guns out of the high-school hallways.

Resource E promises to be a great experience in team study for you and your child. It will help give teens intellectual support for their faith in God's creative hand. May you be able to see why Dr. S. Lovtrup reported in 1987,

> Micro mutations do occur, but the theory that these alone can account for evolutionary change is either falsified or else it is an unfalsifiable, hence metaphysical theory. I suppose that nobody will deny that it is a great misfortune if an entire branch of science becomes addicted to a false theory. But this is what happened in biology: . . . I believe that one day the Darwinian myth will be ranked the greatest deceit in the history of science. When this happens many people will pose the question: "How did this ever happen?"[10]

BEEF—PHASE 2

Recently, a wonderful young friend named David came by my office. Only six months before, David's faith was fresh, childlike, and solid. David's father is a pastor of a strong Christian church. David cut his teeth on his father's teachings. But now David was confused. The peace was gone. His eyes wandered with questions and doubts. In his college environment, his religion teachers threw him a curve. David had a faith of feelings and habit. Like eight of ten other Christian kids who abandon the faith in college, David didn't have the intellectual braces to support his fragile childhood beliefs and withstand the incredible humanistic pressure of the collegiate environment.

Two primary questions remain unanswered in the minds of the thousands of high-school and college kids I talk to annually:

1. How do we know the Bible is God's Word?
2. How can we be sure that Jesus is who He said He was?

Our kids are taught in school today that Jesus was a historical figure of questionable reliability and that if He truly even existed as portrayed in the Bible, He was, at best, a religious figure on a par with Buddha, Confucius, and other spiritual leaders.

The Bible, considered unconstitutional in today's educational setting, is regarded as one of a variety of religious works, full of error, of questionable historical value, and useful only in religious settings.

Nothing could be further from the truth!

Does your teen know that the *Encyclopaedia Britannica* says (in its 20,000-word discourse on the historical Jesus of Nazareth), "These independent accounts prove that in Ancient times even the opponents of Christianity never doubted the historicity of Jesus"?

When your child is getting shot down by a professor or peer for carrying his Bible or referring to it, will he know that the *Handbook of Classical Literature* (the leading collegiate study guide to secular historical literature) points out that the Bible is the most historically supported piece of literary work ever published? According to the *Handbook,* the Bible is more historically reliable than the next ten most reliable literary works combined![11]

Resource F will give your child great confidence and tie his faith and intellect together like part A and part B of epoxy glue.

Not long ago, my 18-year-old daughter was given a term-paper assignment in her twelfth-grade college-prep English class. She had great fun using the information in Resource G to write a paper that was historically accurate about the Savior and His Word that she loves so dearly. Your study of that material with your teen will equip him or her to do the same.

BEEF—PHASE 3

"Just as Jannes and Jambres opposed Moses, so also these men oppose the truth" (2 Tim. 3:8).

"You too should be on your guard against him [Alexander], because he strongly opposed our message" (2 Tim. 4:15).

"[Hymenaeus and Philetus] have wandered away from the truth" (2 Tim. 2:18).

As Paul warned Timothy, so I warn my four teenagers. Folks, there are lions out there in the peer jungles our kids are in. We Christian parents had better quit turning our heads and ignoring the many cults and false prophets that are luring our kids away from their roots to the tune of 700 to 5,000 false religious cults in America today, including 100,000 pagan worshipers![12]

No wonder Paul warned the parents of the late twentieth century, "Evil men and impostors will go from bad to worse, deceiving and being deceived" (2 Tim. 3:13).

Five of our summer sports camps serve 8,000 of America's everyday kids from 49 states. They are mostly suburban kids from, for the most part, Christian homes. Two of our camps are built to exclusively serve 4,500 street kids from our cities' toughest ghetto neighborhoods. These inner-city kids have been robbed of hope, but they often have the most tender, huggable hearts. A few are hardened by gang violence and street crime.

To my great surprise, the few suburban white kids who have been lost to cults and who occasionally slip into our camps are far tougher to crack than the Crips and Bloods of the inner city. Kids need to be staunchly prepared for the onslaught of cultic activity that awaits them on every high-school and college campus in America.

Satan portrays himself as an "angel of light" (2 Cor. 11:14). He appears disguised in pop, country, and rock music; in TV and movie scripts; and in magazine racks in every grocery store in the country.

Here are samples of just a few of the anti-Christian religions that are flourishing in the 1990s:

- Mormon founder Joseph Smith said, "Man is co-equal with God Himself."[13]

- The New Age movement insists that the map of your life is in the lines in the palm of your hand, your daily plan is in the stars, and God is in everything—good and evil. As Shirley MacLaine, a leading New-Age advocate, proclaimed, "I know that I exist, therefore I AM. I know that the God-source exists, therefore It IS. Since I am part of that force, then I Am that I AM."[14]

• The Jehovah's Witnesses travel from door to door in neighborhoods and college dormitories to proclaim the teachings of *The Watchtower*, which states that Jesus was a created mortal unequal with God: "Jesus' birth on earth was not an incarnation."[15]

• The Muslims believe it is blasphemous to call Allah—their name for God—your father.[16]

• The Buddhists deny a personal God and ultimate creator.[17]

Anna grew up in a wonderful Christian home. She was one of our best campers, and she modeled the Christian life like few kids I've ever known. Her faith was strong. But like most American Protestant youth, her intellect was unprepared for life on a humanistic university campus. Her freshman year at a large university, her religion professor shot her faith to pieces and plunged Christianity, in her mind, to a level equal to the other world religions. After a great deal of healing and months of searching, Anna recovered. Unfortunately, all too many ill-equipped college freshmen never recover from those attacks on their faith.

Walk with your teen through the study in Resource H to give him or her the intellectual armor that will serve as a shield against the barrage of cultic missiles to be faced in high school and college.

BEEF—PHASE 4

In the spring of 1994, an enthusiastic friend with a strategic, global mind called me moments after returning from a breathtaking trip to Russia. "Joe," he said, bubbling with enthusiasm, "do you realize there is a lost generation of kids over there? I have just seen the most confused, searching teenagers on this globe! But I think we can reach them."

"How?" I asked.

"Well, there are 20,000 empty youth camps over there that you need to turn into Christian camps. You see, in the days of Lenin and Stalin, the Communist Party brainwashed the children in those camps and changed an entire nation from Christianity to atheistic socialism."

I thought about the American kids I talk to in public-school assemblies and youth gatherings—equally brainwashed, equally confused, even more immoral than Russian kids.

With 18 years of the average American youthful diet of television and music under their belts, our kids leave high school having witnessed, audibly and visually, over one million messages suggesting that premarital sex is okay if it's "safe," abortion is politically correct, pornography is satisfying, and God is irrelevant to daily life.

That dosage of misguided education would have delighted Lenin beyond his wildest imagination. He couldn't possibly have been that convincing, because he didn't have the magic of Hollywood at his disposal. No generation of kids in history has been asked to weather a more dangerous hurricane of decadent information than the American teen of the closing years of the twentieth century.

The six greatest issues of difficulty for teens today are alcohol and drugs, pornography, "safe" sex, abortion, homosexuality, and the disappearance of God from American public education. Every kid has to deal with one or all of those. Most kids will fall into the painful trap that Time-Warner, Paramount, Universal Studios, RCA, Capitol, and their colleagues have laid.

Together, let's discover why Proverbs 23:29-35 says,

> *Who has woe? Who has sorrow? Who has contentions? Who has complaining? Who has wounds without cause? Who has redness of eyes? Those who linger long over wine, those who go to taste mixed wine. Do not look at wine when it is red, when it sparkles in the cup, and when it goes down smoothly; at the last it bites like a serpent, and stings like a viper. Your eyes will see strange things, and your mind will utter perverse things. You will be like one who lies down in the middle of the sea, or like one who lies on the top of a mast. "They struck me, but I did not become ill; they beat me, but I did not know it. When shall I awake? I will seek another drink." (NASB)*

Let's help our kids understand what Jesus really did when He turned water into wine.

Let's discover why pornography is responsible for much of the child abuse, rape, and premarital sex that pervades our culture.

Let's learn with our kids what "safe" sex really is and isn't. Let's discover the five ways condoms don't work.

Let's uncover the facts about abortion. What does the Bible say about it? Is a fetus a child?

Let's learn about the new religious order that undergirds the textbook writers of modern education.

Resource I is designed for a most interesting teen-parent study that will be strong preventive medicine for all of those six areas of great challenge to your children.

The resources referred to in this chapter were developed in the foxhole of the teen battlefield and have been presented to hungry audiences for several years. They will help to prepare your kids to face a hostile world with confidence and strength. Use them regularly; do the studies together. Then your children will be ready to fulfill the same instruction Paul gave to young Timothy: "Retain the standard of sound words which you have heard from me, in the faith and love which are in Christ Jesus" (2 Tim. 1:13, NASB).

Chapter 13

ICING ON THE CAKE

"At my first defense, no one came to my support, but everyone deserted me." —2 Timothy 4:16

When my children were young, I received the greatest piece of advice from a mentor. He stressed his point so that I couldn't forget it. "Know your kids' friends," he insisted. "Know everything about them. Specialize in their lifestyle, their home life and church life. Don't tolerate any friends who aren't good for your kids."

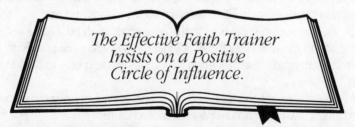

The Effective Faith Trainer Insists on a Positive Circle of Influence.

The Bible states plainly that "bad company corrupts good character" (1 Cor. 15:33). I'm amazed how quickly a bad boyfriend can pull a Christian girl down or vice versa.

As early as age five or six, some kid from school would ask one of my pups to spend the night. If we didn't know the child well, we'd say no. Sometimes we allowed that child to come over and spend the night with us. Looking back, I see the value of such early discipline in the area of friends. Our kids got used to the idea that Mom and Dad are very involved in friendship decisions.

When our children were in early junior high, "everyone" went to the movies. Our kids didn't go often unless we knew who "everyone" was and exactly what they were watching.

By high school, our kids became skilled at choosing good friends. That was payoff time.

During Jamie's ninth-grade year, I looked at the boys in her class that she might date or have for friends, and I noticed a lack of seven-days-a-week Christians. At first, I was depressed and critical of the possibilities. Then I decided to do something about it.

I prayed during the fall semester for a small group of ninth-grade boys to disciple. The Lord answered my prayer abundantly. I began with one solid Christian named Jason. He invited four others. Two others called to join, and finally we added an eighth. Every Friday morning, we'd meet at my grandmother's house before school for donuts and Bible study.

The first year was awkward, but the momentum grew. One by one, they embraced Christ as Savior. They made a pact not to drink or do drugs, and they monitored one another's dating lives. We studied the resources at the back of this book. During their senior year, each boy did his own Bible study using Resource J. We'd discuss their journals at each breakfast together.

Guess who Jamie got a major crush on her senior year? You guessed it—one of the guys in that group. They dated for months and remain close friends today. I can't thank God enough for giving that boy a couple of hundred Friday-morning Bible studies with his friends and me!

By their junior year, the boys in the Bible study each adopted a seventh-grade boy to mentor. Now those original ninth-graders are in college, and their seventh-grade disciples are a new ninth-grade group to lead for the next four years.

My daughters got the hint, and each one started her own small-group Bible study. Two women volunteered to lead them.

Every high-school kid needs a small-group Bible study. It will surprise you how many kids desire one, but there's no one to lead it. "The harvest is plentiful but the workers are few," Jesus said (Matt. 9:37). Initiate a small group for your child, and ice the cake with rich and creamy frosting—love, encouragement, and the deep truths of God's Word. Help those kids develop into a group of friends who will stand together in life's most challenging moments—who will never find themselves, as Paul had to say to Timothy at the beginning of this chapter, feeling deserted and alone as Christians.

Chapter 14

A Soldier, an Athlete, and a Farmer

"I have fought the good fight [the soldier], I have finished the race [the athlete], I have kept the faith [the farmer]."
—2 Timothy 4:7

*T*he one memorable season that I coached football at Texas A & M under Gene Stallings was an experience I could repeat many times over. I left that south-Texas gridiron with a valuable mentor and friend.

The seasons have flown by since then. My friend Gene (still "Coach" to me) moved from A & M to the Phoenix Cardinals to the Alabama Crimson Tide. In 1992, he won his first national championship and was selected national coach of the year.

When the award was announced, I called to say I was proud of him. He rebuffed the praise with typical humility. "If you want to measure my success as a man," he said, "don't look at my win-loss record. Look at my kids, and see how well they're doing with the Lord."

He's a national champ there, too. Much of the credit goes to his wife, but those five children (all over age 20 now) rise up and call their daddy their hero. All lead godly lives and have made godly homes. (His boy Johnny has Down's syndrome, but he also portrays the faith legacy.)

In the language of 2 Timothy 4:7, as a farmer, Coach constantly planted the seeds of faith. As an athlete, he taught his kids to play by the rules of God's Word. As a soldier, he prepared them for battle.

"Measure my success by the depth of my kids' faith."

I quickly recalled a conversation Coach and I had when he was with the Dallas Cowboys a few years ago. He asked me that day what my goal in life was. I told him it was to live for Christ.

He replied abruptly, "That's not mine."

I said, "What is yours then?"

He took a pencil and wrote down the following numbers: 29, 30, 31. Then he shoved the paper to my side of his desk and explained, "When my kids are 29, 30, and 31, I want them to be godly people with godly kids in godly homes."

Doesn't that sound good? The older I get, the more wisdom I see in that unusual goal. Goal setting and training win national championships. They also build solid kids.

Each year, thousands of kids of all ages come to our sports camps. Our highest honor for a teenager is called The Victor's Crown. In a giant campfire ceremony, we award it to the campers who have completed a one-year study of God's Word.

Many kids begin the study. The ones who have a mom or dad or strong friend to do it with them usually complete the task. It changes their lives forever. But the majority of those who try to do it on their own fall by the wayside.

The study takes only five to 15 minutes a day. The results alter a lifestyle for a lifetime.

Amy was a picture-perfect teenager. Her lovely brown eyes twinkled like stars in the night sky. She and her family were close to each other and close to God. Then one afternoon when she was 16, as she was leaving school, Amy suffered an assault that measured at least 8.6 on the emotional Richter scale and would have haunted most teens for years to come.

As she was walking home that day, a drunken street man attacked her, beating and almost raping her. Broken bones and bruises put her in the hospital.

Amy had been one of our campers, and as soon as I heard what had happened to her, I called her in the hospital. I'm happy to report that though her body was battered, her emotions rested calmly. Her heart held no bitterness toward her attacker; she had already forgiven him. She even quoted a favorite passage from Psalms to me. Clearly, her physical trauma had not produced emotional or spiritual trauma.

Why was Amy able to respond to horrible circumstances in such a genuinely healthy way (she wasn't just stuffing negative emotions)? I believe it's because at camp and at home, she had established a habit of daily quiet times with God. She read a chapter from Proverbs and one of the psalms every day. Over the previous three years, she had done The Victor's Crown Bible study. As a result, her feet had been firmly planted on the rock of God's Word, and she had been prepared by it for even life's most terrible storms.

In short, Amy was a living illustration of Jesus' words in Matthew 7:24-25: "Therefore everyone who hears these words of mine and puts them into practice is like a wise man who built his house on the rock. The rain came down, the streams rose, and the winds blew and beat against that house; yet it did not fall, because it had its foundation on the rock."

You can be sure you have passed the faith baton most successfully if your children are having their own daily quiet time with God and are growing in their knowledge of and trust in Him. Anything you can do as a parent to encourage or reward that is well worth it!

Resource J gives you that one-year study that we designed to challenge, motivate, and meet the needs of today's teenagers.

To do the study, just copy the outline pages once for each day of the year and put them in a notebook. Follow the instructions, and embrace the most basic and vital elements of teens' faith so that they can some day say, *"I have fought the good fight, I have finished the race, I have kept the faith."*

Chapter 15

GRACE GIVING

---

*"The Lord will rescue me from every evil attack and will
bring me safely to his heavenly kingdom. To him be glory
for ever and ever. Amen."* —2 Timothy 4:18

A little tyke ran enthusiastically out the front door to greet his daddy
as he came home from work late one afternoon. As the lad cleared
the doorway, two pennies and a dime flew from his overloaded fist, which
was clenched around the entire contents of the piggy bank he had emptied
moments before.

"Look, Daddy!" he said. "Look at all my money!"

"That's great, son," the father replied. "Sure is a lot of cash there!"

"Dad, I emptied my piggy bank. It's all my savings for the last six months.
See!"

"Yeah, sure, I see it."

"Hey, Daddy, I've got $7.63 in here."

"Wow, okay! $7.63!"

The boy stopped in his tracks and looked into his dad's eyes. "Daddy," he said, "I'll give it all to you if you'll stay home and play with me just one afternoon this week."

Kids beg for our time every day. They say it with a bag of marijuana stuffed in the top drawer; a condom buried deeply in a purse; a tattered, sensuous love letter lost in the laundry; an *F* on a report card.

We fret over the way life pulls us in eighty jillion directions. Our job is demanding; the bills are skyrocketing; the kids' peers are prowling the neighborhood like a pack of wolves.

We clutch our heads under the pressure. Being a parent is hard, hard, hard work. Donahue, Oprah, and Geraldo have all the answers. Their methods don't work, but they have a new way to parent almost every day.

Where do we go? How do we succeed? Somebody help me make some sense out of this crazy mess!

I run to the Word. Daily, I get out the pick and shovel and dig for answers with the fierceness of a California gold miner. I find the Word staunchly reliable. It tells me I'm forgiven. It tells me I'm okay even if I'm not perfect as a dad. It tells me I can take my failures to the Cross. My inner-city friends teach me lessons about God and His Word each summer.

Three hundred teenagers from urban projects, gangs, and city streets listened with all sorts of question marks in their eyes at our summer camp for forgotten kids as I tried to explain the miracle of the Man who died on the cross. With a large ax, I hacked a 15-foot elm tree into a cross. Huge wood chips flew through the air into the silent crowd of ever-huggable kids. As I completed the life-size cross, I challenged all the kids to write their sins on a piece of paper and, one by one, nail those sins to the cross.

The atmosphere grew somber and pensive as each kid made his way to the cross with hammer and nail. The paper display of unknown burdens soon filled the cross, but then a teenage boy stopped at my feet—troubled, scared, confused. His paper was covered with hurts and sins that only a Savior could bear. A dear-hearted street pastor put his arm around the teen's shoulder and simply said, "What's wrong?"

The boy mumbled, "I dunno."

The pastor wisely pointed to the sin-filled paper, then to the hammer and nail, and finally he motioned carefully to the cross. "Just take it there, put it there, and leave it there," he said.

"That's it?" the boy queried.

"That's all there is to it. Take it there, put it there, and leave it there."

God's Word tells me I can give that same forgiveness to my wife and kids as they, too, fail each day. God doesn't hold grudges; I don't need to hold grudges.

God's Word also tells me I'm a personal recipient of His amazing grace. That grace gives me courage to go home to my kids and give them the best of my day.

Last spring, in an effort to kindle afresh my son's dwindling dreams of personal success in a game called basketball, I took him on a father-son expedition to see the Chicago Bulls play the San Antonio Spurs. We had a ball together! (Excuse the pun.)

The next day, in a Chicago taxi, we got lost. The ride grew real expensive as the meter flew through the quarters. I asked God why this was happening, and He turned my heart to the driver, a Syrian Muslim named Imad.

Imad and I cut up and told stories as we searched Chicago for the house where we were staying. Sixty dollars later, we found it! Wow—$60 is a lot of "fun" in a taxi!

As we entered the driveway of our lodging, I looked toward Imad with great care and concern. "Imad," I said, "tell me something if you please. When you die, what will happen to you?"

"Well," the Syrian began slowly, "when I die, according to my Muslim faith, I'll go before God, and there will be a judgment." He paused. "Then God will examine my deeds to see if there are more good ones than bad ones."

"What if there are more good ones?" I asked.

"Then I suppose I'll go to heaven."

"And," I asked, "if your bad deeds outweigh your good ones?"

His eyes looked into mine with pensive concern. "I suppose I'd go to hell," he concluded.

I was filled with sympathy for this new friend who had been brought into my life by most unusual circumstances. "Imad, that really scares me for you," I said. "To think that one could live his life only to grow one day closer to a judgment like that where someone's keeping score of your good and bad deeds. I . . . I . . . I'd be most afraid!"

He responded as if scripted by a Broadway playwright, "And what does your faith teach you?"

"Well, sir, my faith clearly teaches me that there will be a judgment at the end of my life. But Imad, when I meet God, He will see only the righteousness of His Son in me, because His Son lives in my heart. That's the pure essence of the Christian faith."

"Joe, I grew up in a Christian school in Syria for my first six years, and nobody ever told me that," he said. He paused to pick up a pencil and paper, and then he asked, "Where are you going to church tomorrow?"

"Willow Creek."

"How do you spell that?"

"W - i - l - l - o - w . . ."

He carefully took note.

Amazing grace, isn't it?

That's the grace I can give to my kids. That's the grace I can come home to. That's the grace that helps me fill the air with phrases of grace to my kids—"Way to go!" "I'm proud of you!" "You're awesome!" "Super job!" "That's incredible!" "What a champ!" "My buddy!" "What a player!" "You are so special to me"—rather than with criticism and faultfinding.

My wish for you and your home is that Paul's words to Timothy will infect your inner being with a drastic case of baton-passing, grace-giving, intellect-building, family-fellowshiping, kid-hugging, knee-praying, Bible-learning *fun* that will consume every cell in your body until the last high-school diploma is received and the last of your offspring walks the aisle into a "happy ever after."

Take 2 Timothy by storm this year. Absorb the secrets that jump off its pages. See and experience how a parent *pushes*, *pulls*, *practices* what he preaches, and *presents* sound teaching. Following are a few of the diamonds and gold pieces I found. Cover your family and yourself with the precious gems and nuggets of the Word.

FATHERLY EXHORTATIONS IN 2 TIMOTHY:

A parent pushes

1. *Kindle afresh the gift of God within you (1:6).*
2. *Do not be ashamed of the testimony (1:8).*
3. *Retain the standard of sound words (1:13).*
4. *Guard the treasure within (1:14).*
5. *Be strong in grace (2:1).*
6. *Entrust the Word to faithful men (2:2).*
7. *Suffer hardship (2:3).*
8. *Consider what I say (2:7).*
9. *Remember Christ Jesus (2:8).*
10. *Remind them of the basics of the faith (2:14).*
11. *Charge them not to talk foolishly (2:14).*

12. *Be diligent to present yourself approved to God* (2:15).
13. *Flee from youthful lusts* (2:22).
14. *Refuse foolish speculations* (2:23).
15. *Don't be quarrelsome* (2:24).
16. *Realize the struggles in the last days* (3:1).
17. *Avoid godless men* (3:5).
18. *Continue the things you have learned* (3:14).
19. *Preach the Word* (4:2).
20. *Be ready in and out of season* (4:2).
21. *Reprove, rebuke, exhort* (4:2).
22. *Be sober in all things* (4:5).
23. *Endure hardship* (4:5).
24. *Do the work of an evangelist* (4:5).
25. *Fulfill your ministry* (4:5).
26. *Be on guard* (4:15).

FATHERLY ENCOURAGEMENTS IN 2 TIMOTHY:
A parent pulls his child toward himself

1. *My beloved son* (1:2).
2. *Grace, mercy, and peace to you* (1:2).
3. *I thank God for you* (1:3).
4. *I pray for you night and day* (1:3).
5. *I long to see you* (1:4).
6. *I recall your tears* (1:4).
7. *You bring me joy* (1:4).
8. *Your faith is sincere* (1:5).
9. *You followed me faithfully* (3:10).
10. *Come to me soon* (4:9).
11. *Come before winter* (4:21).
12. *The Lord be with you* (4:22).
13. *Grace be with you* (4:22).

FATHERLY EXAMPLES IN 2 TIMOTHY:
A parent practices what he preaches

1. *I'm an apostle* (1:1).
2. *I'm thankful* (1:3).

3. *I have a clear conscience (1:3).*
4. *I suffer for the gospel (1:8).*
5. *I'm a preacher, an apostle, and a teacher (1:11).*
6. *I'm not ashamed (1:12).*
7. *I'm lonely (1:15).*
8. *I suffer, but I endure (2:9-10).*
9. *Persecutions I endure (3:11).*
10. *I'm being poured out (4:6).*
11. *I've fought a good fight, I've finished the race, I've kept the faith (4:7).*
12. *His crown is waiting for me (4:8).*
13. *I have a forgiving heart (4:16).*
14. *God is my strength (4:17).*
15. *I want all Gentiles to hear the gospel (4:17).*
16. *God delivers me (4:17).*

FATHERLY EDUCATION IN 2 TIMOTHY:
A parent presents sound teaching

1. *The Word taught through one's childhood will stick with you throughout your lifetime (1:5; 3:15).*
2. *The Holy Spirit gives you power, love, and discipline (1:7).*
3. *We have a holy calling (1:9).*
4. *Real friends are faithful friends (1:16).*
5. *Real friends are greatly rewarded (1:18).*
6. *A soldier avoids worldly traps and pleases his master (2:4).*
7. *An athlete obeys the rules and wins the prize (2:5).*
8. *A farmer who works hard gets the first fruits of the field (2:6).*
9. *Personal sacrifice brings perfect salvation (2:10).*
10. *Handling the Word accurately brings great rewards (2:15).*
11. *Foolish talk leads to strife and ungodly character (2:16).*
12. *God is a good, faithful Father (2:19).*
13. *A sanctified man is like a gold vessel in a home (2:20-21).*
14. *The end times will be filled with wickedness (3:1-7).*
15. *Persecution is inevitable (3:12).*
16. *The Word is God's breath. It's reliable. It will save you in the heat of battle (3:16-17).*
17. *The crown of life is for all sincere believers (4:8).*

Fellow Christian parent, study those truths for yourself. Put them into practice in your family. Savor every opportunity, and watch your most cherished dreams come true!

PART 2

THE TOOLS

———

365 Ways to Tell Your Child "I Love You"

(Without Saying the Words)

---

1. When your child is participating in an athletic event or musical performance, be there watching.
2. Help your son or daughter learn a new skill, such as riding a bike, making a cake, fixing a flat tire.
3. Walk together with your child some morning all the way to the school bus stop.
4. Leave an "I love you" note in your child's school lunch box.
5. Read a chapter together from your child's favorite book.
6. Memorize a verse in the Bible together.
7. Share a devotional time with your child some morning before school.
8. When the school bus brings home your child, be there at the curb with a "welcome home" smile.
9. Talk together about your favorite memories growing up.
10. Find a new way to trust your child by granting a new area of responsibility that he or she would both enjoy and benefit from.
11. Have a family picnic on a Sunday afternoon.
12. Sit in church together.
13. When your child is being punished, undergo the punishment with him or her (occasionally).

14. After your teenage son or daughter comes in from a date, have popcorn together by the fireplace.
15. Go out in the snow together and throw snowballs at a target (even a few at each other).
16. Wait up some weekend until your son or daughter comes home (no matter how late).
17. Give your child a back rub.
18. Walk in the rain and jump puddles together.
19. For a time of reflection together, ask your child, "When you pray, how do you think of God?"
20. Listen to your child—with all your attention.
21. If your child goes on an overnight trip, leave an "I love you" note in his or her bag.
22. Sit down together and watch your child's favorite TV show.
23. Snuggle in bed together as you tell a good-night story.
24. Have a water-pistol fight (let your kids drench you).
25. When your child expresses a fear, try to remember in your own childhood when you had that same fear, and talk together about it.
26. Skim rocks together on a lake, pond, or river.
27. For your eyes only, write down on a slip of paper any unloving attitude you may have felt recently toward your child—perhaps irritation or anger that came too easily about something . . . a slowness to offer heartfelt forgiveness for some failure . . . or a lingering focus on something you perceive as negative in your child's behavior or personality. Then shred or burn that slip of paper, offer your feelings to God in a prayer of confession, ask for His perspective, and commit yourself to living and thinking a stronger love, by God's grace and power.
28. Reminisce about your child's toddler days, and say what a wonderful baby he or she was.
29. On the first cold day of autumn, make and drink hot chocolate together.
30. Have milk and cookies together after school.
31. Say, "I'm proud of you."
32. Prepare your child's favorite dinner menu twice in one week.
33. The next time you take a child to an athletic practice, stay and watch from a distance.
34. Help your child make his or her bed (occasionally).
35. Help your child clean his or her room (occasionally).

36. Let your son or daughter select where you eat out (even if it's McDonald's again).
37. Allow (but don't force) your child to share in the cost of some major item the whole family wants. Let your child also be a part of the decision-making process (e.g., helping select the color, brand, features, and so on, of an item).
38. Catch fireflies together and make a living lantern.
39. Go rowing or canoeing together.
40. Tell your child about the things you appreciated most about your own parents.
41. Ask your child, "What is your favorite passage in the Bible, and why is it your favorite?"
42. Build a small animal or insect cage together; then go hunt together for something to put in it.
43. The Bible's love chapter says that love "is patient" (1 Cor. 13:4). Have you recently failed to be patient in some way with your child? If so, confess that failure to God and ask for (and expect) His help in overcoming impatience. Obey His Spirit's prompting whenever He reminds you not to be so uptight and demanding.
44. Have a family worship time after a meal—sing together, pray together, read Scripture together.
45. Make up and tell stories with your kids as the heroes.
46. Write a crazy poem together—take turns writing the next line (make sure it rhymes!).
47. Bring home your child's favorite candy bar.
48. Make up and sing songs to your kids about how much you love them.
49. Dream together about a round-the-world, as-long-as-you-like, all-expenses-paid vacation. Talk about the favorite places you would like to see and what you would do in each one.
50. Take an evening walk together.
51. Make a telephone call to your child, just to say you're thinking of him or her.
52. Have a pillow fight together some night at bedtime.
53. Play games together (e.g., Old Maid, Concentration, Candyland, Sorry, Pictionary).
54. Rake leaves together—then jump in them.
55. Have a family water-balloon fight (with you as the prime target).
56. The Bible's love chapter says that love "is kind" (1 Cor. 13:4). Think of a special way you can show kindness to your child today.

57. Go apple or berry picking together; then take some to neighbors.
58. At the beach or in a park sandbox, play ticktacktoe in the sand.
59. Make cookies together; then put them on neighbors' porches, ring the doorbell, and run.
60. Make homemade ice cream together.
61. Talk together about your favorite characters in the Bible. Why do you admire them? In what ways do you identify with them?
62. Ask your child, "If you could live inside an animal for a day, what animal would you choose? Why?"
63. Plant trees in your yard in honor of your kids (one for each kid).
64. Take nature hikes together, and collect leaves, acorns, rocks, moss, sticks, and whatever.
65. On a hot day, hook up a water hose and sprinkler in the backyard and run through the water together.
66. Give everyone a dollar (or some other prudent amount) and go shopping together just for the fun of it.
67. As a family, have a make-your-own-peanut-butter-specialty-sandwich party. To start, spread peanut butter on bread; then add toppings, such as apple and banana slices, chocolate chips, marshmallows, and raisins.
68. Roast marshmallows together in the fireplace.
69. Make caramel-covered apples together.
70. Shop together for a model plane or ship; then build it together.
71. The Bible's love chapter says that love "is not proud" (1 Cor. 13:4). If some unwanted "distance" has recently come between you and your child, ask yourself if any pride on your part is hindering a quick return to closeness.
72. Spend a special time praying together for others—for the leaders and teachers in your church, for government officials, for any missionaries your child knows, for neighbors, for friends, for family members.
73. Imagine together that you had a time machine and could go back to any era in history. What time period would you most want to visit? Why?
74. Make a tree house together.
75. Say (with a big hug), "You're my favorite son [or daughter]." When he (or she) says, "But I'm your *only* son [or daughter]," answer, "But you're still my favorite."
76. The night your child says he or she is running away from home, fix his or her favorite dinner.

77. Listen appreciatively as your child practices his or her first trumpet lesson.
78. When you sense something is troubling your child, make a reason for a trip in the car alone together.
79. Plan and carry out a treasure hunt—at home, in the backyard, in the neighborhood, at the park, or all of them combined.
80. Press your child's band uniform before each performance.
81. Go to court with your child when he or she pays his or her first speeding ticket.
82. Have fun together answering this: What would be the most exciting surprise that could happen to you tomorrow?
83. Pretend you're a team of television writers asked to develop a new TV adventure series. What would be the setting for the series, what would the major characters be like, and what would you name them?
84. Stay up to talk together after your son's or daughter's first date.
85. Keep a scrapbook of your child's awards, newspaper clippings, photos, and so on. Get it out often and look at it together.
86. If your child is participating in the Christmas parade, be there on the cold street to watch.
87. Look together at a road atlas, write your initials on each state you've visited, and talk about your memories of those visits.
88. Let your child teach you to roller-skate.
89. The Bible's love chapter says that love "is not rude" (1 Cor. 13:5). Have you in any way failed to show the right respect and simple courtesy to your child? Ask God to remind you of any failure in this area, and if you've been guilty, confess the sin immediately and go as soon as possible to ask for forgiveness from your child.
90. Invite your son's or daughter's friends to your home to spend the night.
91. Know when report card day is, and ask to see it.
92. Show genuine concern when your child says he or she is sick and can't go to school that day. Take his or her temperature, and ask if you should make an appointment with the doctor.
93. Take a half-hour, silent walk through a park or through the woods together; when the half hour is over, talk together about what you observed and what you were thinking.
94. Have fun together answering these questions: What famous person living today would you most like to meet and talk with? Why?

95. Build a "Faith Growth Chart" on which you list prayers and answers in one column and memorized Bible verses in another. See your child's faith grow!

96. After a family picnic in the park, have everyone browse and explore to find something that represents some aspect of God. Then come together and take turns telling what you found and what it means to you. (An example: A black-eyed Susan illustrates how God wants to be the center of our lives—like the flower's black center. When we have Him truly at the center, all the parts of our lives form a beautiful and orderly whole—like the arrangement of the flower's petals in a perfect circle.)

97. When you shop for clothing for yourself, take along your child and ask for his or her opinion of what looks best on you.

98. Taking cameras for each child, go on a scavenger hunt to find and take pictures of God's many different creations. Make a scrapbook or poster with the photographs; then show them in an after-dinner presentation for grandparents and friends.

99. Make popcorn, curl up together on the couch, and watch your son's or daughter's favorite video.

100. Have a surprise make-your-own-sundae ice-cream party, making sure your child's favorite toppings are served.

101. As you do household chores, let your child help in everything—even if it takes four times as long to complete them.

102. After a scolding, tell your child, "Did you know I love you even when you're naughty?" Then give him or her a hug.

103. The Bible's love chapter says that love "is not easily angered" (1 Cor. 13:5). Is it truly difficult for you to become angry with your child? Or is it far too easy? For your own benefit as well as your child's, evaluate yourself honestly in this regard.

104. Ask for your child's opinion on a big family decision.

105. Show your child where you've kept for a long time a special card or picture he or she has given you.

106. Never say, "I'm too busy."

107. Pretend together that you were chosen to join a space voyage to another galaxy, a trip that would take several years. What would you take with you?

108. For your spouse's birthday or for Mother's Day or Father's Day, be a partner with your child in planning and making (or doing) something special for your spouse. Offer suggestions and assistance, as appropriate, to help make it a successful creative experience for your child.

109. With every "good morning" and "good night," give your child a hug.
110. Give your child your full attention when he or she tells you what happened at school today, and provide a thoughtful response.
111. Volunteer to be a homeroom mom or dad on a special day at school.
112. Make pancakes shaped like animals, footballs, flowers, your child's initials, and so on.
113. Buy a box of paper clips, and have a contest to see who can make the longest chain in one minute. (If you need to handicap yourself to make the contest fair, put your pile of paper clips in the next room, and allow yourself to get only one at a time to bring back and add to your chain.)
114. Have fun together answering these questions: If you could go back in time, what famous person in history would you most like to meet and talk with? Why?
115. Compliment your child's attempt to keep a tidy room.
116. The Bible's love chapter says that love "keeps no record of wrongs" (1 Cor. 13:5). Have you learned to let go of your child's past failures?
117. Show your child one of his or her baby pictures and tell why it's one of your favorites.
118. Help your daughter fix her hair in a special way.
119. Take a winter's afternoon off and put a jigsaw puzzle together.
120. Make your child's favorite cookies or snack.
121. Ask your child—with genuine and obvious sincerity—how his or her day was.
122. Occasionally include your son or daughter when doing something with your adult friends.
123. Take your child out to breakfast (just the two of you) before school.
124. For a temporary but fun change in your home's decor, cover a wall with paper (a roll of butcher paper is great for this); then work together to make a "big scene" using colored markers or poster paint. Add into your artwork some "I love you" messages to your child.
125. Before a big event in your child's life—a birthday, a competition, a big test at school—decorate his or her room with crepe paper and posters.
126. Allow your child to plan the day for your family.
127. Send your child a fun balloon-o-gram at school.
128. In a relaxed time together, get out your high-school or college yearbook and talk about your "school days" memories. (Be sensitive to focus on the things that your child seems most interested in.)

129. Have fun together answering these questions: If you were a brilliant scientist, what new process or product would you like most to invent? Why?
130. The Bible's love chapter says that love "always protects" (1 Cor. 13:7). Think of a new and positive way you can truly offer protection to your child.
131. Take your child out for a $20 or $30 after-school shopping spree.
132. Buy a guidebook to the trees and wild plants of your region, and take a nature hike to identify as many different kinds as you can. Take a notepad along to list your discoveries.
133. Go on a bike ride together around the neighborhood.
134. Take your child out for bowling or miniature golf, and dinner afterward.
135. Write your child a short poem and stick it in his or her pocket or lunch box before school.
136. Honor your child with a "just because" party ("just because I love you") and invite his or her friends.
137. Prepare a special dessert that's just for your child.
138. Have a family slumber party in the family room in front of the fireplace (complete with treats and classic-movie videos).
139. Buy a children's crossword puzzle book, and do one puzzle together each night until you complete the book.
140. Pretend you're a team of movie producers, and plan the plot and scenes for your next production.
141. Plan a family scavenger hunt around the house, with prizes for all.
142. Cut out pictures from magazines and make a collage illustrating your child's talents, interests, and favorite activities.
143. Dry and brush your child's hair after a shower, and have a neat chat while you're doing it.
144. With an Etch-a-Sketch toy, do a "silent partners" drawing together: Take turns adding a single line to the drawing, but don't tell one another what you're trying to draw. See what you come up with!
145. Always display (on the refrigerator or in another prominent spot) the artwork or other creations your child made at school, Sunday school, and so on.
146. The Bible's love chapter says that love "always trusts" (1 Cor. 13:7). Think of a specific way you can grow in trusting your child.
147. Say "please" and "thank you" each time you ask your child to do something.

148. Let your children sleep in your bed with you when your spouse is out of town. (You may not get much sleep, but they'll remember it forever.)
149. Reward your son or daughter for getting good grades.
150. While you're driving your child somewhere, hold and squeeze his or her hand.
151. Tell your spouse how proud you are of your child for something he or she did, and let him or her overhear your remarks.
152. As you notice your child making or doing something creative, call other family members to come and see.
153. Make a special greeting card for your child that in your own handwriting says "I love you" in as many different languages as you can find the words for. (You'll probably need a trip to the library for this one!)
154. Give your child a hug when he or she is feeling down.
155. When your child is sick, stay up with him or her at night.
156. Discuss these questions: If you were asked to appear before Congress to tell what three new laws you think our country needs most, what would you say? Why?
157. Do this fun and challenging project together: Draw and color a map of your house, and do your best to draw it to scale.
158. Take sack lunches for you and your child, and enjoy them together at a local park.
159. Volunteer to give your daughter a perm or to help fix her hair in some other way.
160. Smile when you're together, and be ready to laugh when your child does.
161. When your child is upset or hurt, make listening your first response.
162. The Bible's love chapter says that love "always hopes" (1 Cor. 13:7). Are you keeping in mind an exciting view of your child's greatest potential? Think of a way you can grow in your hope for your child.
163. Plant flower or vegetable seeds with your child. As you together see the plants sprout and grow, talk about your child's own growth—physically, intellectually, socially, and spiritually.
164. Go shopping for clothes together.
165. Talk about what you believe about God.
166. With help from friends and others in the family, prepare a "This Is Your Life" skit to honor your child on a special occasion.
167. With your child, talk openly about your most significant convictions, and ask for his or her opinions in response.

168. Kiss your young child's hurt when he or she falls down.
169. In a relaxed moment together, talk about favorite memories. (Even younger children enjoy this—their "past" may be short in years, but relative to their ages it seems just as long as ours.) Talk about favorite gifts, favorite toys, favorite surprises.
170. Build and fly kites together.
171. Always welcome your child's friends to your home, and practice hospitality toward them.
172. Roast some nuts together, and then shell and eat them by the fire.
173. Say to your child, "Let's spend some time together, just you and me."
174. Give your child positive nicknames. (In our house, we've used "Super Cooper," "Little Buddy," and "Rocky-Pop.")
175. Listen to your child with "unconditional ears."
176. The Bible's love chapter says that love "always perseveres" (1 Cor. 13:7). Commit yourself today to never let up in your love for your child. Keep going and growing!
177. Give your child the freedom to fail. Remember, mistakes are rarely fatal.
178. Encourage your child often to be himself or herself. Tell him or her, "I like you for who you are."
179. Tell your son or daughter, "I'll never give up on you."
180. Write a funny poem—the crazier the better—to your child.
181. In a relaxed moment together, ask your child, "What do you think is the most challenging thing you've ever accomplished?"
182. Be honest. If you have wrongly withheld or distorted something in the way you've talked with your child, confess your dishonesty and tell your child the truth.
183. Share your life with your child; let him or her into your world. Tell him or her the things you like most about your life and work, and talk together about some of the frustrations as well. Talk about your hopes and dreams in every area of your life.
184. When you and your child are around other adults, include him or her in your conversations with them.
185. Buy a pack of chewing gum to give to your child, but first slip a note inside the outer wrapper of each piece. In each note, list one of the qualities of your child that you most admire: "I love you because you're so _____."
186. Without being preachy, talk openly with your child about the dangers of substance abuse.

187. On your child's birthday, prepare your own greeting card with a poem to your child.
188. Leave a note of encouragement inside your child's favorite pair of shoes.
189. As often as possible, let your child hear you tell your spouse, "I love you."
190. Talk frequently with your child about spiritual lessons you're learning. (Invite his or her observations about how well you're learning them.)
191. During an enjoyable time when you're talking together, ask your child, "What are the most important decisions you've ever made?"
192. The Bible's love chapter says that love "never fails" (1 Cor. 13:8). In a quick but sincere prayer, thank God now that His love for both you and your child is everlasting, and ask Him to continue teaching you about love. Then think of a special way to tell your child today, "I will always love you."
193. Write a note of encouragement to your child and have it published in the classified ads of your local newspaper.
194. Out of the blue, send your child a greeting card (either bought or homemade) and include a signed photograph of yourself.
195. Prepare a dinner or lunch in which the name of every item served starts with the same letter as your child's first name (don't worry about whether it's a balanced meal). When your child asks the reason for the strange menu, let him or her guess.
196. Paint your fence together.
197. If your child is sick in bed, read from his or her favorite books.
198. Make your child fortune cookies with notes of encouragement inside them.
199. Build a scarecrow together, whether you have a garden or not.
200. Buy your child a recording by his or her favorite performing artist (if you approve of the music).
201. Ask for your child's suggestions in planning your family vacation.
202. Go canoeing or rowing on a peaceful stream or lake, and enjoy the peacefulness together.
203. Enter together in a local race for amateur joggers.
204. Listen to your child even when you don't feel like listening.
205. Hike up a mountain together.
206. Make it a special project one day to listen intently to every word your child says.

207. Attend every open-to-parents function at your child's school.
208. Get up early on a clear morning, find a quiet spot outdoors with a clear view to the east, and watch the sunrise together.
209. Talk frequently with your child about the truths in the Bible that you're enjoying in reading and meditation.
210. Sometime when you're enjoying being and talking together, ask your child, "In what area of life would you most like to improve in the next year?"
211. Go on a train or bus ride together.
212. Take up a new hobby or craft together—one that's new to both you and your child.
213. Teach your child a special skill that you know (woodworking, needle-point, etc.).
214. When your child shows particular interest in a national or world news item, talk about it together, discuss the media's presentation of it, and look at a map together to find the location where the event occurred.
215. When you're watching TV together and see questionable scenes and dialogue presented, turn it off and talk together about what you find questionable and why.
216. Go to the library together and find all the information you can about one of your child's current interests—a hobby, hero, skill, or whatever.
217. On an otherwise ordinary evening, serve the family dinner with candlelight and fancy place settings.
218. Review together the lyrics of the recordings that both you and your child own or the songs you listen to on the radio, and talk about how honoring they are to God and how edifying they are to those who hear them.
219. Encourage your son or daughter to bring friends over to visit, and talk with them to get to know them better. Always be polite.
220. On the first crisp Saturday of the fall, pass around the football together in the front yard.
221. Paint the trim on the house together.
222. On a "rough" day for the child, let a small forgotten chore go "unno-ticed."
223. As an exercise in helping you be more sensitive to your child, ask your-self, "What are the most challenging or difficult issues in my child's life? What concerns weigh heaviest upon him [or her] at this time?"
224. Enjoy talking together about your answers to this question: What are your biggest dreams for the future?

225. Talk with your child about the most significant prayer requests you have—and pray for them together.
226. Join your child in his or her room and build a fort with mattresses and sheets.
227. Play basketball together.
228. Ask your child what special needs in his or her life you can pray for.
229. Have a snowball fight (let your kids cream you).
230. Serve your child breakfast in bed.
231. Play dominoes, checkers, chess, or backgammon together.
232. Wash windows as a team: At each window, one of you cleans the inside while the other does the outside. Promise yourselves something special when you're through.
233. Bring your child along when you go to assist a friend or neighbor in need.
234. Let your child see and hear you explaining the gospel to non-Christians. Talk together about it afterward.
235. On Halloween, instead of trick-or-treating or getting into the witches-and-goblins scene, get together as a family and cut crosses into pumpkins; then set candles in them to symbolize Christ's complete victory over death and evil.
236. Go through old boxes in the attic together.
237. Something to think about: When you consider the biblical command "Love the Lord your God with all your *heart*," what relevance could it have for the way you love your child?
238. Don't be afraid to admit to your child when you're wrong.
239. Go swimming together.
240. When the weather turns stormy, sit together at a picture window and watch it.
241. Tell your child how you most want to improve in your life in the coming year, and ask him or her to pray for you.
242. Discuss this question: If you could design and build your own mansion, what would it be like?
243. Look at old photograph albums together.
244. Think about what you would like your life to be like at age 40, 50, 60, and 70. Then talk about your dreams and desires with your child.
245. Give your child something you like (your favorite sweatshirt, your dessert at dinner).
246. Go horseback riding together.

247. Laugh together.
248. Cry together.
249. "Bury" a prize somewhere in your house or yard, put together a map and some cryptic clues, and help your children conduct a hunt.
250. Climb a tree together.
251. Treat your child like a fishing line: Give some slack, but don't let him or her run away or get tangled up.
252. Something to think about: When you consider the biblical command "Love the Lord your God with all your *soul*," what relevance could it have for the way you love your child?
253. When your child makes mistakes, instead of condemning, work together toward a solution.
254. As you think about your way of life and the example you provide for your children, ask God to empower you to live out the gospel of Christ (the greatest love of all).
255. Remind your child often that he or she is created in God's image.
256. Worship together at church and at home.
257. Celebrate your children's achievements and victories, but don't let them feel they have to "win" in order to be loved. Accept and love them at all times, and communicate that your greatest joy is because of who they are, not what they do.
258. Tell your child, "You contribute so much to this family."
259. Ask your child to tell you about any special prayer requests and needs for his or her friends, and then pray together for them.
260. Tell your child, "You have many special friends who think you're wonderful."
261. Tell your child, "You're the apple of my eye."
262. With toy building blocks, work together to make the tallest object you can.
263. When your child feels like a failure, reassure him or her by saying, "I believe in you; I know you can do better next time."
264. When you must punish, give an explanation: "I had to punish you this way because I care for you and want the best for you."
265. Something to think about: When you consider the biblical command "Love the Lord your God with all your *mind*," what relevance could it have for the way you love your child?
266. On a day when the weather is adverse, offer to help your child with his or her paper route.

267. Make popcorn balls together.
268. With sticks or straws, string, and paper cutouts, make mobiles together.
269. With your child, take turns answering this question: What is the funniest thing that has ever happened to you?
270. Allow your son or daughter to go to work with you and be your helper.
271. After punishing your child for striking a match in an unsafe place, take him or her to a safe place and together light a whole box of matches.
272. Help your child with a school project. Encourage creativity.
273. Put up a tire swing in the tallest tree around, and swing together.
274. Play marbles together.
275. Imitate animals together on the family room floor.
276. Find extra work projects your child can do to earn money.
277. Make a bug collection together—or work together on any collection (e.g., baseball cards, dolls, old coins).
278. Something to think about: When you consider the biblical command "Love the Lord your God with all your *strength,*" what relevance could it have for the way you love your child?
279. Invite your child's friends over, build a mountain on a tray out of ice cream scoops and whipped cream (with all the toppings), and then eat it.
280. Make a wildflower collection together.
281. If your child breaks something, help him or her fix it.
282. When you're enjoying being and talking together, ask your child, "What have been the toughest and most discouraging things you've ever had to work through and overcome?"
283. Have a game night together.
284. In a moment when you and your child are relaxed and enjoying each other's company, tell your child about your spiritual past—your wonderings and wanderings, how you found Christ, and how Christ changed your life.
285. Have an "open forum" sharing time at dinner, and let your children express themselves fully.
286. Plan a day each month that is your child's special day, and do the things he or she enjoys.
287. Have your child help with your daily activities at home—cooking and baking, cleaning, mowing, repairing, and so on. Use this time to teach: Don't just assign tasks; help your child accomplish them.

288. Be consistent in your discipline. Establish guidelines, and follow through with what you say you'll do.
289. In love, challenge your child to make goals (to stretch himself or herself) and to strive for them ("Press on!").
290. Always take photographs on your child's special occasions.
291. Take your child out for ice cream after school.
292. Compliment your children for their truly distinctive qualities. Let each child know that he or she is unique, and make each one feel special for who he or she is.
293. Walk the dog together.
294. Cook breakfast together on Saturday morning.
295. Help your child wash his or her bike (or tricycle).
296. Ask your child, "What have been the most encouraging things that ever happened to you—things that really helped you grow in confidence?"
297. As you think about your responsibility in raising your children wisely, ask God to empower you to "bring them up in the training and instruction of the Lord" (Eph. 6:4).
298. Build a snowman together.
299. Volunteer to help with your son's or daughter's youth group at church.
300. Say something encouraging about your child in front of his or her friends.
301. Mow the lawn occasionally when it's your child's turn.
302. Sit outside some night and talk together as you watch the moon and stars.
303. Talk about your favorite hymns and why you like them.
304. Go all out to celebrate your son's or daughter's birthday.
305. Make up a secret code language, and write messages to one another.
306. Put your child's school pictures up on the refrigerator.
307. Make a photo gallery somewhere in your home, and display your children's school pictures from each year.
308. Go jogging together.
309. Take binoculars and go bird-watching together.
310. Play hide-and-seek with your children (don't find them too quickly).
311. Take a day off from work and spend the whole day doing things your child enjoys.
312. Ask your child, "What encouraging comments from others have been most meaningful to you?"

313. Take your child and some of his or her friends out for pizza.
314. Talk with your child about what you're learning personally about Jesus Christ.
315. On occasion, allow your son to use your credit card for a dinner date.
316. If your child has a car, help him or her wash it.
317. Do exercises (such as jumping jacks, push-ups, sit-ups) together.
318. Help your child learn his or her spelling words or multiplication tables. Make it a game.
319. If your child is into skateboarding, build a slalom course together.
320. Take your child with you on a business trip.
321. Go to the state or county fair together.
322. Stay up as a family till past midnight on New Year's Eve, playing games, performing skits, singing songs, and just being zany.
323. Start praying now for the spouses your children will have someday. Pray that their marriages will be strong and Christ-centered.
324. Ask your child, "If you were stranded alone on an island for a year, what would you like most to have with you, besides adequate food, water, and clothing?"
325. Drive the speed limit.
326. Fasten your seat belt when you're in the car, and insist that your children do, too.
327. Lead the family devotions at breakfast.
328. Help your son or daughter prepare to lead a family devotional time.
329. Have lunch together in the school cafeteria.
330. Turn off the TV and play a game together.
331. Take advice from your kids, and encourage them to give it freely, even when it is confronting and personal.
332. Volunteer to help out when your child's class at school takes on a special project.
333. For a time of reflection together, ask your child, "What qualities do you most value in a friend?"
334. Say "I love you" even after your child has volunteered you to make all the costumes for his or her class in the Christmas play at school.
335. When your child finishes last (or not much better) in a race or other contest, make a big display of encouragement and approval, because you know he or she was doing his or her best.
336. Smile at your child.

337. When your child's friends need an adult (besides their parents) to talk to, be there.
338. Take time to make today special.
339. Make smiley-face pancakes.
340. Select a mentally challenging book (for both of you), and read it through together, pressing ahead to the end no matter how difficult.
341. Keep updated photos of your child around your home and office. Point them out to him or her often, and remark how you smile inside each time you see them.
342. For a time of reflection together, ask your child, "Whom do you consider your greatest heroes?"
343. As you're working on a project that must be done by an adult, provide a scaled-down version of it that your child can do alongside you. Compliment your child for the "good hands" God gave him or her.
344. The next time you make a special meal, allow your child to prepare one of the dishes (on his or her own, as much as possible). Serve and enjoy it, with sincere praise for this young one's developing skills.
345. Talk with each other about your favorite books and why you like them.
346. When your child talks to you, be quiet and use total concentration to listen. Put down what you're doing and look into his or her eyes. Maintain an encouraging expression, and when you speak, make your comments positive.
347. At your very next opportunity, give your child a hug. If your child is young, pick up and hold him or her.
348. When your child says, "Watch me!" watch. Clap and cheer, and say, "Great job!"
349. Take regular ten-minute walks outdoors with your child—daily, if possible, or at least once or twice a week. Allow the sense of wonder in his or her heart to unfold as together you observe God's creation.
350. Each time you greet your child, do it eagerly and warmly.
351. Ask your child, "What new hobbies would you most like to try getting into?"
352. Write to your children whenever they're away. Send cards with messages of encouragement.
353. Make personalized Christmas tree ornaments together.
354. Save ten percent of your energy from your workday and take it home with you to spend on your children and spouse. Offer your best to your family.

355. If your child especially dislikes one of his or her chores, think of a surprising way to make it more fun.
356. Listen very hard—even when your ears are tired!
357. Treat your children's friends the way you treat your own kids.
358. Be a "note fairy": Place an encouraging note under your child's pillow while he or she sleeps, to be found in the morning.
359. Ask your child what achievements and accomplishments in life he or she is proudest of.
360. For your daughter, make a special outfit (Easter is a great occasion for this) instead of buying something new.
361. Color Easter eggs together, and make each egg a personalized masterpiece.
362. Climb the roof together to get a good view of your city's Fourth of July fireworks display.
363. Help your child raise a farm animal.
364. For a time of reflection together, ask each other, "How do you picture heaven?"
365. As you talk to your children today, say the three magic words: "I LOVE YOU." You've earned credibility, and they'll believe you!

TOOLS FOR
SMALL CHILDREN

(Available at Your Local Christian Bookstore)

BOOKS

The Accidental Detectives Series (4-book set), by Sigmund Brouwer (Victor)

Adventures in Odyssey Series (5-book set), by Paul McCusker (Focus on the Family)

Adventures in the Big Thicket, by Ken Gire (Focus on the Family)

All About God, by Mary Rose Pearson (Tyndale)

The Book of Virtues, by William Bennett (Simon and Schuster)

Cottontale Series, by Pamela Kennedy (Focus on the Family)

The Daring Family Adventure Series, by Peter Reese Doyle (Focus on the Family)

The Environmental Detective Kit, by Doug Herridge and Susan Hughes (Harper Collins)

The Focus on the Family Clubhouse Collection, edited by Ray
Seldomridge (Focus on the Family)

Forest Friends (4-book set), by Danae Dobson (Word)

Friends of God, by Sally Lloyd Jones (Standard)

The Hardy Boys Series, by Franklin W. Dixon (Grosset & Dunlap)

Here Comes Ginger, by Elaine L. Schulte (Chariot Books/David C.
Cook)

How to Survive Middle School, by Rick Bundschuh (Zondervan)

Just in Case You Ever Wonder, by Max Lucado (Word)

Kids' Praise! Adventure Series, by Ken Gire (Focus on the
Family/Maranatha! For Kids)

The Ladd Family Adventure Series, by Lee Roddy (Focus on the Family)

Mr. Marble's Moose, by D.J. May (Word)

Precious Moments Bedtime Stories, by Samuel J. Butcher (Baker)

Read and Grow Picture Bible, by Libby Webb (Word)

Rebecca of Sunnybrook Farm, by Kate Douglas Wiggin (Scholastic, Inc.)

Seek and Ye Shall Find New Testament, by Michael Berry and Nora
Berry (HSH Educational Media Co.)

Tell Me the Secrets, by Max Lucado (Crossway)

There's a Duck in My Closet, by John Trent (Word)

The Very Best Book, by Christy Weir (Regal)

Watercolour Ponies, by Wayne Watson (Word Kids!/Word)

Who Am I? by Katherine Paterson (Eerdmans)

Woof and the Big Fire, by Danae Dobson (Word)

Woof and the Haunted House, by Danae Dobson (Word)

Woof and the Midnight Prowler, by Danae Dobson (Word)

Woof Finds a Family, by Danae Dobson (Word)

Woof Goes to School, by Danae Dobson (Word)

Woof Series #2 (2-book set), by Danae Dobson (Word)

Woof Series #3 (2-book set), by Danae Dobson (Word)

Woof Series #4 (2-book set), by Danae Dobson (Word)

Questar Publishers offers the following classic children's books by my talented friend Mack Thomas.

The Bible Animal Storybook

The Bible Tells Me So

From God with Love

In His Hands

My First Step Bible

What Would Jesus Do?

Here are some other books from Questar Publishers.

The Amazing Book, Vol. One: A Bible Translation for Young Readers, by John R. Kohlenberger III and Noel Wescombe

Barely There Series, by Stephen Cosgrove

The Beginners ABC Bible Memory Book, by V. Gilbert Beers

The Beginner's Bible: Timeless Children's Stories, by Karyn Henley

The Beginners Bible Question & Answer Book, by Mack Thomas

The Beginner's Devotional, by Stephen T. Barclift

The Best Bible Word Book Ever, by Stephen T. Barclift

Children of Courage Series, by Doris Sanford

Destination: Moon, by James Irwin

The Early Reader's Bible, by Gil Beers

The Great Alphabet Fight and How Peace Was Made, by Steven Jensen and Joni Eareckson Tada

The Guardian Series, by Janifer De Vos

He Is My Shepherd: The Twenty-Third Psalm for Children, by David Haidle and Helen Haidle

Hurts of Childhood Series, by Doris Sanford

In Our Neighborhood Series, by Doris Sanford

I Wonder Series, by Mick Inkpen and Nick Butterworth

The Littlest Shepherd, by Ron Mehl, Jr.

Loving One Another, by Neta Jackson and Anne Gavitt

Someday Heaven, by Larry Libby

Teach Me About God: Includes Special Tips to Help Parents Explain Big Truths to Small Children, by L.J. Sattgast

The Wonder Bible, by Mack Thomas

AUDIOCASSETTES

Adventures in Odyssey Series (Focus on the Family)

Woof Series, by Danae Dobson (Word)

VIDEOTAPES

Adventures in Odyssey Series (Focus on the Family)

McGee and Me! Series (Focus on the Family/Tyndale)

The New Adventures of McGee and Me! Series (Focus on the Family/Tyndale)

"Noah's Ark by Peter Spiers" (Lightyear Entertainment)

"The Remarkable Journey Begins" (Multnomah)

Woof Video Set #1 (2-video set) (Word Kids!)

DEVOTIONS FROM THE BOOK OF MARK

A note to parents: This devotional guide is meant to be used with younger children. The studies on John and James in Resource D are for older children.

COUSINS
(Mark 1:9-11)

Do you have any cousins? Cousins in most families enjoy being together. Some cousins are grown up, in college or even married, while others are still young. No matter what age they are, cousins like to be together, to play games and to visit.

John the Baptist was the cousin of Jesus. Because each was miraculously born of God, angels looked after them just as your parents, and even baby-sitters or nannies, care for you. When John the Baptist and Jesus grew up, John baptized Jesus just as God had planned. That was the beginning of Jesus' ministry on earth.

Wouldn't you love to have seen the pretty white dove over Jesus when He was baptized? That was God's Gift from heaven to Jesus. And God, the

Father in heaven, called out, "You are my Son, whom I love; with you I am well pleased."

QUESTIONS

1. Why do you think God announced to everyone at Jesus' baptism that He was well pleased with His Son?

2. Would you like to have your father or mother tell you that?

3. What are angels? Did you know that angels take care of you?

4. What about John the Baptist reminds you of Tarzan? Where did his clothes come from? What kind of food did John eat? Where did the food come from?

LIFELINE

When you obey your parents as Jesus did, your parents can say to you, "This is my child; with you I am well pleased."

DREAMS COME TRUE
(Mark 1:17)

When Walt Disney started out to fulfill his dream of Disneyland, he sought men who would be able to follow his vision, men who had the imagination for his dream. Walt first created Mickey Mouse, and then Donald Duck and the other dear characters everyone all over the world loves today.

Jesus had a mission, too, and God sent an angel to Mary and a dream to Joseph to fulfill Jesus' mission here on earth. Jesus said, "Follow me," to Andrew and Simon first; then He selected James and John. The other disciples were chosen soon after.

Jesus, all the while, was performing miracles of healing the sick and destroying evil in people. He and His team were to show people how to know God and enjoy life forever.

QUESTIONS

1. How do you think Walt Disney's and Jesus' work here on earth were similar?

2. Why did Jesus want disciples to follow Him?

3. Why do you suppose Mickey and his friends make everyone all over the world happy?

4. What is the difference between Mickey Mouse's popularity and Jesus' popularity?

LIFELINE

Good dreams can come true because loving Jesus and obeying His words will give us good thoughts and actions.

PRAY EVERY DAY
(Mark 1:35)

Two little girls were walking slowly to school one morning. They were good friends. They lived in the same neighborhood. But as they were taking their time walking, they heard the school bell ring in the distance. The girls were afraid they would be late for school. One girl said, "Let's hurry and run!" The other girl said, "No, let's stop and pray . . . then run!"

Jesus prayed all the while He was on earth. He was very popular, and people wanted to be where He was. Crowds gathered around Him constantly. The sick pushed to get close to Him. Jesus healed hundreds of them. But Jesus also would escape from the crowds and find a quiet place to pray to His Father in heaven. All through the books of the New Testament, there are verses that tell us Jesus prayed often.

After He prayed, Jesus would go back to the people, teaching and heal-ing them as they followed Him on the roads, in the villages, on the moun-tains, and in the meadows.

QUESTIONS

1. What would you have done if you lived back when Jesus was on earth?

2. Why did the people want to get close to Him?

3. How do you suppose the people knew about Jesus?

4. Where did the people come from? Who were the most desperate to get close to and touch Jesus? Why?

LIFELINE

Maybe today you could tell a friend what you have been learning about Jesus.

YOU ARE INVITED TO MEET MY NEW FRIEND
(Mark 2:14-15)

A new family moved into the neighborhood. Justin was a young boy in that family, so he was the new kid on the block. Justin visited the neighbors, and it wasn't long until all of them knew him. Justin was especially good about calling on the older people. He visited elderly Mrs. White often. Sometimes he would bring his brother, Elliot, to visit, too. Once he brought his new friend Miles to meet Mrs. White. Another time he brought two lollipops with him—one for Mrs. White and the other for himself. Justin was good company to his new neighbor.

Mrs. White would write her children and tell them about Justin. She wrote that when they came to see her, she would invite Justin. Then they could see what a neat kid Justin was. She was proud of her new, young friend and wanted to show him off.

Matthew the disciple—also known as Levi—was probably very pleased to be asked by Jesus to be on His team. "Follow me," Jesus said to Matthew. And it changed his life. Matthew wanted everyone he loved to have their lives changed, too; so he invited them to come to his house for a dinner party to meet his special friend Jesus.

QUESTIONS

1. Why do kids like to invite their friends to their houses?

2. How do you treat a friend when he or she visits you?

3. What do your parents do when your friends come to see you?

4. Why do friends invite you to their houses?

LIFELINE

Jesus asks you to follow Him. That means to be kind, love others, share with others, obey your parents, and love Him. Do you love Jesus?

THE SABBATH
(Mark 2:27)

Sunday comes once a week, and that's what the Sabbath means to us. God made the week to be seven days. He created our beautiful world in six days, and on the seventh day, He rested. That is why God tells us, "Remember the Sabbath day by keeping it holy."

Your dad and mom work during the week, and you go to school for five days a week. Saturday is a day to do chores: to empty trash, to clean up your room, to help your mom or dad, to practice sports. It is a busy day. But Sunday is the best day of all. You sleep a little longer, crawl in bed with your parents, and talk and snuggle. Maybe there are pancakes for breakfast. Then you drive in the same car to Sunday school and church. Everyone is together on Sunday. Rest and keep holy the Sabbath. Wasn't God good to plan the week like that?

QUESTIONS

1. What are some things you can do to keep holy the Sabbath?

2. What things could you do to please our Lord?

3. Why should everyone tell friends how to learn about Jesus?

4. What are your favorite things to do on Sunday?

LIFELINE

Jesus healed the sick and helped people in need. He was a good neighbor on the Sabbath. He loved to help people. Do you ever help someone you know—maybe an older person in your neighborhood?

JESUS WAS A POPULAR PERSON
(Mark 3:9, 13)

Many people like to see famous movie stars, athletes, and leaders. They crowd around to shake hands and ask for autographs. Famous people may run into such fans wherever they go.

Jesus was popular, too. People everywhere were hearing about Him and they crowded as close as they could in order to see Him, hear Him, and touch Him.

Jesus often left the mobs of people to go up into the mountains, to walk along the beach, or to sail on the lake. It was the only way He could rest and pray. Jesus talked often to God so that He could know what His heavenly Father wanted Him to do.

QUESTIONS

1. What would you say to a famous person if you saw him or her?

2. Where did Jesus and His disciples go to get away from the crowds? Would you like to be followed all the time by mobs of folks?

3. What would you say to Jesus face to face if you had the opportunity?

4. How can we know what God wants us to do?

LIFELINE

Jesus was once a small child like you. He obeyed His parents and learned His lessons just like you. He grew up and continued to honor His Father in heaven by praying to Him often.

READ ME A STORY
(Mark 3:23)

Do you have a teacher? A Sunday school teacher? Maybe a kindergarten or preschool teacher?

Do you like to have someone read you stories? Wouldn't it be exciting to hear Jesus tell stories? He knew lots of good stories. Most of them were about birds, flowers, trees, water, and fruit. Many were about people. These stories are called parables.

Parables are like "Once upon a time" stories in books with pretty pictures, aren't they? Sounds strange to ask your mom or big sister or brother to "please read me a parable," doesn't it?

QUESTIONS

1. Why do you think Jesus told parables to the people?

2. What do you think about the way Jesus taught the disciples and His followers?

3. Who taught Jesus to be a good storyteller? Where did He learn so much about nature: trees, plants, and seeds?

LIFELINE

The Bible is a wonderful storybook. There are exciting action stories in the Old Testament. Perhaps someone will read to you once in a while.

GOOD SEEDS
(Mark 4:3-8)

When my neighbor's grandsons from Texas were very young boys, they would come visit her several times a year. They knew they were close to their grandmother's house when they saw the big, rocky cliffs and hills. Watching impatiently as the miles rolled by, each boy tried to be the first to see the hills. Then they would scream, "I see them! There's Grandma's rocks!" The Ozark Mountains: those rock piles that go up to the sky! They knew then they were soon to see their grandma.

Out of those rocks grow cedar trees, like tired, rugged old men. It's a marvel how those trees, along with vines and scrubby brush, manage to thrive with so little soil. Fruit trees could not survive there. Just sturdy, hardy vegetation like the cedars.

However, glades and meadows can be found at the foot of the hills and on the hilltops. To prepare that land to plant fruit-bearing trees, vegetables, or flowers, a farmer has to cut down the thick forests and brush. Tons of loose rocks have to be picked up and hauled away. Then good soil must be spread on the barren ground. Seeds can finally be planted, and the farmer blesses the land and prays for occasional rains from heaven.

QUESTIONS

1. What do you know about planting and working a vegetable garden?

2. Who do you know who plants a garden?

3. What do you have to do to make the plants produce? Why does this need to be done?

4. How is the care and attention needed to plant good seed in good soil like the care and attention needed to make good children and grown-ups?

LIFELINE

Think about the seeds Jesus describes in this chapter of Mark. Remember, this is a parable with a meaning to be applied to people. You are a good seed that has been planted. Be the best seed.

TURN THE LIGHT ON, PLEASE
(Mark 4:21)

How old are you? Four, five, six, or close to that? When our neighbor's grandsons were about your age, they wanted to sleep in a tent just as their daddies had done when they were boys. Spring had come, the grass was green, and the nights were warm again. The kids wanted to sleep outdoors by themselves.

The tent was set up in the afternoon, and the sleeping bags were pulled down from the shelf in the attic. The canteens were washed and filled with water. "PB&J" sandwiches and chocolate chip cookies were packed. Finally, new batteries were put in the flashlights, one for each young pioneer. The kids were as excited as they were on Christmas Eve waiting for Santa to come.

It was good and dark when the boys headed for the tent. Their grandparents went along to see that they were settled in. Prayers were said, and then the grandparents kissed each boy good night and returned to the house. As they left, they noticed that the flashlights were left shining by each sleeping bag.

Each time the grandparents got out of their cozy bed that night to check on the grandkids, they noticed that the flashlights were still on. Those "brave" outdoorsmen were not hiding their lights under their sleeping bags; rather, they were letting them shine brightly next to them.

QUESTIONS

1. Why do kids like to spend the night sleeping in a tent?

2. What have you used a flashlight for?

3. What did Jesus tell the people about letting a light shine?

4. What do you think it means to let your light shine?

LIFELINE

Have you ever thanked God that you can see? Some children can't see because they are blind. Jesus said that some people with good eyesight don't "see" things He wants them to see. Does your light shine for Jesus?

I NEED A HUG
(Mark 4:41)

When you were very small and not as old as you are now, did you try to slip into bed with your parents? Doesn't every child? And did your parents try again and again to take you back to your own bed? Were you maybe lonesome or even afraid? Mom and Dad's bed always seems softer, safer, and cozier. Even grown-ups are afraid sometimes.

This verse about the storm is my favorite. Is it your favorite, too? Jesus and His disciples had walked many miles that day. They had been surrounded everywhere by hundreds of people, and Jesus had told them stories to teach them about God and the way God wants us to live. It had been a long day, and everyone was weary and needed rest (just as your mom and dad work all day and need rest in the evening). Jesus wanted to get away from the people, so He said to His disciples, "Let us go over to the other side."

As they were going across the lake, a strong wind came up, and high waters blew into the boat. But Jesus slept soundly. The frightened disciples had to yell as they tried to awaken Jesus because the storm was so noisy. They yelled, "Teacher, don't you care if we drown?" Jesus calmly stood and commanded the wind and waves to stop. And they did! Wow! Jesus can talk to the wind and waves, and they obey Him.

QUESTIONS

1. What do you do when you're afraid? Do you go to your mom or your dad?

2. Why do you run to the comfort and open arms of your parents?

3. What makes you understand that Jesus will hear your cries for help?

4. What does this verse show you about Jesus' power?

LIFELINE

Jesus is in control of all things, big and small.

THE WILD MAN
(Mark 5:6)

A long time ago, when the circus came to town, there were sideshows. These shows would be under tents—one for each sideshow. Outside we kids saw the painted pictures on big boards: "The Tattooed Lady," "The

Two-Headed Calf," "The Biggest Man in the World—500 lbs.," and "The Wild Man from Borneo."

All of us wanted to go inside the tents to see those amazing shows. But our daddies explained that they were not true. It was a trick to get people's money. However, we thought the Wild Man from Borneo sure looked real. And scary, too.

The poor sick man in Mark 5:1-20 was true. Jesus could heal any kind of sickness without medicine. He knew that evil spirits were inside this man. Jesus spoke to the evil in the man, and the man was healed! The evil was driven out because the man knelt in front of Jesus and believed Jesus could cure him.

QUESTIONS

1. How did the sick man know that Jesus was a special person?

2. Why did the sick man run to meet Jesus and fall before Him?

3. What do you understand about this verse?

4. Who can heal you and help you get well (besides a doctor)?

LIFELINE

Keep Jesus in your heart. He is your friend forever.

BECAUSE YOU BELIEVE
(Mark 5:34)

While on vacation in Mexico, four-year-old Lance had a tummy ache. He didn't want anyone to know it. As the family was leaving for breakfast, Lance said, "Wait a minute. I need to go back to the room." His mom quietly followed him to see why he had to return to the room. Lance knelt by the side of his bed and prayed. Then he got up and quickly headed for the door, where his mom was waiting.

"Lance," she asked, "what were you praying about?"

"I had to ask God to make me well so Scott and I could play together today. I'll be fine now, Mom. Don't worry."

Lance had learned early that God is a caring Father Who loves His children and wants them to talk to Him about their concerns and problems. Jesus likes for everyone to "call upon His name."

The woman in Mark 5:21-34 had been sick for 12 years, yet her faith was so strong that she knew she just had to touch Jesus' robe to be healed. She pushed through the crowd, closer and closer, until she could reach out and touch Jesus' garment. Although many people were touching Him, Jesus felt the power go out from Him at this particular touch. He asked who had touched Him. The frightened woman bowed at Jesus' feet. Sweet, gentle Jesus said to her, "Daughter, your faith has healed you. Go in peace and be freed from your suffering."

QUESTIONS

1. What do you do when you're sick?

2. After reading this lesson, what have you learned from the teachings of Jesus?

3. What does it mean to talk to Jesus? Does Jesus want us to pray (talk) to Him?

LIFELINE

Jesus said, "Let the little children come to me" (Matthew 19:14).

MAGIC AND MIRACLES
(Mark 6:12-13)

Mr. Thomas is Brady and Cooper's daddy, and he can do amazing magical tricks. Mr. Thomas has been teaching Brady and Cooper a few of those tricks! When the boys entertain the neighbors with their new tricks, everyone is impressed. The audience knows that the boys had to be good listeners to learn so well; they also had to practice often. Otherwise, the audience would not be fooled by the tricks.

But Jesus could perform miracles with no tricks, no marked cards, no loaded dice. He was for real—the only one who could heal diseases of the body, the heart, and the mind. Jesus spent every day of His three years of ministry on earth teaching the 12 disciples. After much training, and after much time witnessing Jesus' ways with people, the disciples went out in groups of two. They were ready, with His authority, to heal all manner of sicknesses "in the name of Jesus!"

QUESTIONS

1. Why are athletes such as football players and Olympians good at their sports?

2. Would you like to be good at something?

3. How can you learn to be good at something?

4. What does it take to follow instructions?

LIFELINE

Jesus is unique. But when we obey His instructions, with His help, we can accomplish much.

HELPING HANDS
(Mark 6:25-28)

Just as we do today, people in Jesus' time experienced cruel and sad things. That is why God sent Jesus. This verse is a gruesome one. It is important to understand how easily a person can be influenced by evil when he or she is not a Christian. A paid officer in the king's court was made to hand the head of John the Baptist to Herod.

People do good things with hands that serve. Think about the wonderful things hands can do. Here is a list:

HANDS, what great things they can do:
Grandparents' hands writing and sending you letters.
Hands painting pictures and making drawings to give to others.
Warm hands, sewing hands, hugging-and-petting hands.

New baby's hands, soft pink fingers curling around one of yours.

Mom's hands baking bread, cookies, pies, cupcakes, and baked potatoes.

Dad's hands, working, building, buying clothes and food for the family; hands that drive the car, open doors, and shake hands with friends; hands that hold yours while you are walking together.

Little boy's hands flying kites in the springtime, throwing baseballs, holding a football and kicking it, lifting lids off cookie jars; hands getting string or a Boy Scout knife out of a pocket; hands holding a little dead bird, patting a dog, putting worms on a fishing pole hook, building sand castles or little towns for cars.

Little girl's hands playing "house," dressing dolls, loving Teddy Bear, feeding kittens; hands helping Mommy make cookies, setting the table, hugging Daddy, holding the new baby, dressing up and putting a little "makeup" on when Mommy lets her, brushing her doll's hair.

AND THE GREATEST HANDS OF ALL:

GOD'S HANDS, WHICH MADE ALL THINGS, and JESUS' HEALING HANDS.

QUESTIONS

1. What are some things you like to use your hands for?

2. What are some of your favorite things your parents use their hands for?

3. How can you use your hands to serve others?

LIFELINE

Tonight, talk about hands and how they can do good things to make everyone happy and Jesus smile. Remember, train your hands to serve in loving ways. God made hands to serve as Jesus' did!

HONOR YOUR FATHER AND MOTHER
(Mark 7:9-13)

Have you read the stories of Peter Rabbit lately? Peter is such a busy, energetic, and lively rabbit. And he does misbehave often. His hippity-hop has so much bounce in it that it seems to get him into all kinds of trouble. You remember that Mrs. Rufus Rabbit, Peter's ma, had a lot of anxious times getting Peter to obey the rules she had set for her household. She loved Peter. But rules were hard for Peter to keep. He would lie awake after being tucked into bed, and he would think about his stomach and how hungry he was. Then he would slip out of the house to get something to eat from Mr. McGregor's garden. That was the wrong thing to do. Mr. McGregor chased Peter, and Peter hid in a can filled with water. Peter caught a cold because he stayed wet too long, trying not to get caught.

Of course, you know what happened eventually. Peter finally made it back home, sick and wet and feeling very guilty and scared. His mother gave him chamomile tea for his tummy ache and tucked him into bed. Peter was very sorry to have disobeyed his mother.

She had been anxious and worried about him, but she put her soft muzzle against Peter's and rubbed his face. She forgave him, even though Peter dishonored her by disobeying her. Honoring your mother and father is to obey their rules and to love your family and Jesus.

QUESTIONS

1. What do you have in common with Peter Rabbit?

2. Why does it hurt your parents when you disobey them?

3. Why do you suppose God is hurt when we disobey Him?

4. What happens when you are truly sorry for disobeying?

LIFELINE

Because Peter Rabbit did not honor his mother and her rules, does that make you love him less? I love him just the same, because I think he learned a lesson and was very sorry.

WITH ALL YOUR HEART AND MIND
(Mark 7:14-23)

When Sally was a little girl, her mother used to tell her, "Pretty is as pretty does." Sally had been standing in front of the mirror, twirling round and watching herself. She was wearing a brand-new dress for the party. The dress was covered with colored ribbons and ruffles. Sally felt very happy and pleased with the way she looked. She pretended she was a princess, like Cinderella at the ball. She danced around the room like a ballet dancer. Oh, she was pretty!

But Sally knew what her mother was telling her. Being dressed in silks and satins with bows and ribbons did not make her a sweet and good girl on the inside. That depended on what she thought about and how she acted toward her family, her friends, and her neighbors. Sally knew she should be kind and unselfish and not self-centered.

Jesus taught His disciples to have pure hearts and clean minds. He also wants us to feed our hearts, souls, and minds with good spiritual food.

QUESTIONS

1. How do you know when you're not acting "pretty"?

2. What do you do when you hurt someone's feelings?

3. Why are some people snippy and selfish?

4. How can you become better and better day after day?

LIFELINE

Jesus' teachings and sayings are meant for each of us. He is wonderful to show us what is expected of us.

DEAF, MUTE, AND BLIND
(Mark 7:31-37)

When Helen Keller was a two-year-old, she had an illness that left her deaf, mute, and blind. She became angry, irritable, and unruly. Her parents were distraught and sad because they were not able to communicate with her.

They decided to consult Dr. Alexander Graham Bell, the man who had invented the telephone, because he knew so much about sound. But he could not help. At his suggestion, they visited an institution for the blind. The institution sent Anne Sullivan, a 21-year-old lady who had been blind and was operated on successfully, to live at Helen's home and try to help her. After several hard years, Helen became a new person who learned to talk with her hands. She succeeded because Anne Sullivan believed in Helen. She believed Helen could learn. Helen loved Anne all her life. One of the first words Helen spelled out was "T-E-A-C-H-E-R." And that is who Anne always was to Helen: "Teacher."

Helen was the first deaf person to graduate from college. She went on to make speeches all over the world and was famous as a writer and representative for the blind. Helen accomplished all this because someone believed in her and knew that God had a plan for her life. Helen grew to be a beautiful woman—and a Christian.

QUESTIONS

1. Why do we overlook people who are not like us?

2. What can we do to help a handicapped person?

3. How can we show kindness to others not as fortunate as we are?

4. What can you do to be an example like Jesus?

LIFELINE

How interesting that the word Helen loved to spell on her hands was "t-e-a-c-h-e-r"! Jesus was a teacher, too.

HOLDING HANDS
(Mark 8:7)

Norman Rockwell was a famous artist. His many paintings are seen today on the covers of magazines and books and on walls inside houses and public buildings. One of those paintings is a reminder that we should pray and thank God for the food we eat.

In the painting is a grandmother sitting at a table across from a small boy. They are saying the blessing before they eat. At other tables in the restaurant are rugged working men. A few have hard hats on; others look like truck drivers. These men are watching the grandmother and the boy say the blessing. And the men look happy. They are remembering that they, too, had grandmothers who always said the blessing before a meal was eaten. A few of the men have taken off their hats and are sitting quietly until the blessing is said.

Before Jesus had the disciples pass around the loaves and fishes, He thanked God for the food. Remember, there was not enough originally to feed everyone, but God provided more than enough—with baskets of food left over! That is a miracle!

QUESTIONS

1. Why do families say the blessing before meals?

2. What are some things to pray about before a meal is eaten?

3. Why should we say thank you for food? Does everyone in the world, all the children, have food to eat three times a day?

LIFELINE

"Thank You, God, for the flour the miller made, the baker who baked the bread, and the grocer . . . for our daily bread. And thank You, Jesus, Who taught us to pray."

IN HIS IMAGE
(Mark 8:27-29)

A "cool cat" was strutting down a street in Los Angeles with a blasting jam box on his shoulder. At the corner of Hollywood and Vine, a long, shiny, expensive convertible stopped for the red light. The driver was a handsome man, and the "dude" did a doubletake at him. He dashed to the open convertible and yelled, "Hey, man, who do you remind me of? Aren't you a famous actor?" To which the driver kindly and firmly answered, "I remind you of Jesus Christ, in whose image I was made."

After Jesus healed the blind man, He asked His followers, "Who do you say I am?" The followers had been witnessing the miracles Jesus performed. They knew He had to be someone from God. He did remind them of the prophets and heroes of their Holy Scriptures that they had read and heard about in synagogue. But Peter was the only one who answered, "You are the Christ."

QUESTIONS

1. Would you recognize Jesus if you saw Him on a street corner or at your door? How?

2. What would you say to Jesus if He showed up at your door?

3. How do you know that Jesus is truly the Christ, the Son of God?

4. What do you think about when you see Jesus? Do you go to sleep at night with a picture of Jesus in your mind?

LIFELINE

You were made in the image of God. He chose you to be like Him.

ON THE MOUNTAIN
(Mark 9:2)

Have you seen a magician pull a fluffy pink bunny out of a tall black top hat? Or change a pretty lady into fluttering silk scarves? You know that what you are seeing are tricks. But you can't figure out how the magician did them.

When Jesus went up on a high mountain, He took Peter, James, and John with Him. They were all alone there. While those followers watched, Jesus was changed: His clothes became shining white. Then two men appeared, talking with Jesus. The men were Moses and Elijah. Peter, James, and John were convinced that the men were the Old Testament prophets. It was very real to them.

But it was not a trick. Only God the Father and Jesus the Savior can do miraculous things like that.

A few verses later, the Bible says, "Then a cloud appeared and enveloped them, and a voice came from the cloud: This is my Son, whom I love. Listen to him!"

QUESTIONS

1. Why did the voice say, "This is my Son, whom I love"?

2. What do you think Peter, James, and John thought when they saw the change in Jesus? Can you describe how they must have felt?

3. Why do your mom or dad take just one of you children sometimes on a little errand or trip and not take everyone? And why do you think Jesus took just three disciples with Him?

LIFELINE

Don't forget that God has said before in the scriptures you have read, "Listen." Who did Jesus say you must listen to? Now you have heard God say, "Listen to my Son."

FOR ANYONE WHO BELIEVES
(Mark 9:23-24)

A boy named Cooper had brushed his teeth and climbed into his bed. He had made a fortress with extra pillows to keep himself snug, secure, and brave. His mom came into his room to tuck him in and lie down with him. Sometimes Cooper's dad would do it. Tonight was his mom's turn. The two talked quietly about Jesus and the Bible lesson they had had with the rest of the family around the table that night. This time of the day was one of the happiest for Cooper—having Dad or Mom all to himself. Cooper proudly recited a new Bible verse he had memorized. He loved to please his parents and say the scriptures by heart. He couldn't read yet, but he liked repeating the verses just like his big brother and sisters.

After his mom prayed with him, kissed him good night, and turned off the light, a little voice spoke to her through the darkness, "Mommy, I'm lonesome and afraid."

She went back to the bed and said, "Cooper, you are not alone. You believe that Jesus is always with you in your heart, don't you?"

And Cooper answered, "Yes, but I want someone *outside* my heart to lie down with me."

QUESTIONS

1. Why do you think Cooper didn't want his mother to leave?

2. What do you do when you don't want to go to bed at night? Have you ever felt like Cooper?

3. What would you say to Cooper if you were his mom and he told you he didn't want you to leave him alone in his room?

LIFELINE

Keep Jesus in your heart and you will never be alone.

RICH MAN, POOR MAN
(Mark 10:17-22)

On Halloween every year, three boys in a family down the street from our house would go trick-or-treating. The parents had taught the boys how to live by the Golden Rule: "Do unto others as you would have them do unto you." The boys would return home after knocking on the doors of the neighbors, and their sacks would be running over with goodies. The treats would then be spread out on the kitchen table. Each boy kept a jar of his favorites from the generous pile. Then the father would drive the boys to a neighborhood in the small town. There poor children would be waiting for their friends to bring candies just as they did every year. The three boys learned early to help the poor, to know them as friends, and to share with them.

At Christmastime the same boys eagerly selected toys from their rooms for the same children in the poverty-stricken part of town. The toys had to be in good condition and desirable. The parents of these poor children would make up a list of presents each year and the boys' parents would buy them. The neighbors helped out as well, taking pleasure in sending boxes of food along.

Jesus told the rich man that he must sell all he had and give it to the poor. Jesus wants us to share whatever we have with others who do not have our good fortune.

QUESTIONS

1. Why did Jesus tell the rich man to sell all he had and give it to the poor?

2. What can you do to help children less fortunate than you?

3. Why do you suppose some people have more than others?

4. Why should we all be concerned about people who have no food?

LIFELINE

Giving and sharing is good, but there is an even more necessary thing to do: believe in Jesus Christ and ask forgiveness of your sins. And He will be with you always.

WILL YOU SERVE?
(Mark 10:43, 45)

When Dan Marino was eight years old, he went to football practice with his dad, who helped coach the Catholic school's team. Dan was too young to participate, since only fifth graders and up were allowed to play football. But Dan had a burning desire to be a quarterback. On the sidelines, he would pass the football to anyone who would play with him. Sometimes his dad would stay with Dan after the workouts and pass the ball to him. Dan never gave up trying to be a part of the team. On a very hot day when the team took a break in the middle of the field, Dan came running out with a bucket of water. No one had told him to do this. He had decided to do it on his own. From that time on, Dan became the official water boy of the team. When the coaches started noticing Dan's dedication to the team, they presented him with a football jersey. It was slightly tattered and well used and too big for Dan. But Dan didn't care. He was wearing a "number" like the other players!

Later, on a team where the starters were mostly eighth graders, Dan—a fifth grader—made a place for himself. He was so small that on extra points he would take the snap and run behind the bigger linemen until he saw a hole. Then he would head for the end zone. Dan scored a lot of points that way because the other team could not see him behind the linemen.

Dan was a "server" long before he became the all-pro quarterback he is today. He had a goal. He practiced. And he served his teammates.

QUESTIONS

1. How do you think Dan Marino learned how to serve?

2. What is there that you would like to do very much? Are you willing to serve your friends and your family?

3. How can you become the kind of person Jesus spoke of?

4. What does it mean "to serve"—to be a servant to others?

LIFELINE

As you lie in bed tonight, think about ways that you can be a helper and a server. People who serve are following Jesus' example, and they also discover that helping others is a source of great joy.

BE HUMBLE
(Mark 11:1-11)

In a book written over 100 years ago, *A Girl of the Limberlost*, the main character, a girl named Elnora Comstock, lived way in the backwoods. Her family was extremely poor, and they did not understand or support Elnora's desire to get an education at the high school in the town several miles away. Elnora was an intelligent girl who had a dream to learn more than she had learned in the local schoolhouse, where all the grades were taught by one teacher in one room. Elnora collected rare moths, butterflies, and dragonflies. There was a company she could sell them to, so she made enough money to buy herself shoes to walk to school every day.

The walk through the dense woods, over muddy, running creeks, and down dusty roads did not help her appearance when she reported to the principal at the high school. As she entered the classroom, she was greeted by giggling, stares, teasing, and laughter. She had no books, and no one helped her. Her clothes were strange, different from those worn by the other girls. Elnora prayed during that first horrible day: "Hide me, O God, hide me under Thy wings." But Elnora soon displayed uncanny knowledge that surprised everyone. She had suffered humiliation and shame, but she had a goal, and she did not let them deprive her of the education she wanted. Of course, the story ends sweetly. Right will overcome in all things.

Jesus was humble when He requested a donkey to ride upon into festive Jerusalem during the Passover. Jesus was on His way to a week of much humiliation and shame. This He knew because He knows everything. He would be scorned, scourged, and subjected to suffering. But He overcame! He is alive! And He did it for us.

QUESTIONS

1. Why was it important for Elnora Comstock to meet her goal?

2. Why did Jesus have to go to Jerusalem if He knew He would be ridiculed, tortured, and killed? What was His reason for going at that time?

3. How do you feel when you hear about a girl like Elnora? Do you feel compassion for her? Do you feel tender and sad for Jesus?

LIFELINE

Both stories end in triumph! Jesus is King of kings and Lord of lords! He sits on a throne in the beautiful city in heaven. He watches over all who believe in Him. Do you believe in Him?

ANGER
(Mark 11:25)

Johnny is a good father to his three girls and boy, but it's not easy for him to keep house while his wife is away on a trip. Brushing little girls' hair, braiding, making ponytails, tying on ribbons and bows . . . No way! Johnny is all thumbs. He is a good executive in his company, and he is a fine athlete on the courts. But when it comes to cooking meals, washing dishes, and getting kids to school on time, he is a disaster!

Recently, his wife attended a seminar for three days. The weekend was a piece of cake, but when Monday morning rolled around, everything went wild. His little boy was sick most of the night, his three girls were not awakened on time, Johnny burned the bacon, one of the kids spilled hot chocolate on school clothes and had to change, and the oldest girl and Daddy were at odds with each other.

By the time the school bus stopped outside their house, Johnny had worked up a lather. He was raising his voice and was even a little angry at his oldest daughter. As she ran with her sisters toward the bus, Johnny got sentimental and ran after them. He yelled, "Shannon, I love you! I'm sorry I lost my temper! I love you!"

Jesus told His followers, "When you stand praying, if you hold anything against anyone, forgive him."

QUESTIONS

1. What do you do when you're mad or unhappy at someone? Do you say you are sorry, too?

2. What does Jesus want you to do when you're rude or sassy or disrespectful to someone? Does it make you feel down on yourself when you're tacky?

3. Why should you also ask God to forgive you when you've been angry at someone and said things you shouldn't have?

4. How can you learn to control your temper?

LIFELINE

At the end of verse 25, Jesus said that if you ask forgiveness of another person, God will forgive you also. That means God will not forgive you until you ask forgiveness of others.

EYES ARE ALWAYS WATCHING
(Mark 12:17)

One Sunday morning, a minister preached a sermon about honesty and not cheating another man. It was a fine sermon. The people stopped to shake the minister's hand as they went out the front door, and they thanked him for such a good subject. After church, the minister had to catch a bus to get to his home because his car was in a repair shop. He boarded a bus, paid the driver, received change back, and then walked to the back of the bus. As he sat down, the minister noticed that the driver had given him too much change. He thought, *Oh, I am all settled now, and a little tired, too. I'll just wait and give the driver his money when I get off.* When the minister's stop came up, he walked to the front and gave the driver the extra change. "You gave me too much when I got on," he said.

The driver answered, "Sir, I was in your church at the first service this morning. I just wanted to know if you are as honest as you preached we should be. I am glad you didn't disappoint me."

Jesus preached that sermon, didn't He? What belongs to someone else, we should not envy or keep for ourselves. If it doesn't belong to us, we have no right to it.

QUESTIONS

1. Why do you suppose the driver of the bus tested the minister?

2. What do you think it means to give to God the things that are God's?

3. What do you have that is God's?

LIFELINE

Someone is always watching us. We never do things in secret.

"A BUSHEL AND A PECK"
(Mark 12:29-31)

The words of an old song go like this: "I love you a bushel and a peck and a hug around the neck." Jesus wants everyone—and that includes you—to love Him like that. With all your heart and mind and soul—all of you! And to love your neighbor just as much as you do yourself!

When young children are learning to talk, their most-used words are "me," "mine," and "me first." It's natural for people to think of themselves first! Jesus understood this. That's why He said to love your neighbor as you love yourself.

Anyone who is in contact with you—a neighbor, a teacher, a baby-sitter, a housekeeper—anyone you are near and communicate with—is your neighbor! The best neighbor, for example, might be Mr. Rogers on the television. Don't you think Mr. Rogers is a good neighbor to have? He's friendly to everyone. He likes to do kind things for his neighbors. He is unselfish and likes to make everyone happy.

So, love God the Father and Jesus first, then your family and everyone else. Loving God just naturally makes you loving, kind, and good to others, doesn't it?

QUESTIONS

1. How can you love God first?

2. What do you think that means?

3. Who are some of your neighbors (the "others" Jesus talked about)?

4. Why should you love with all your heart and mind and soul?

LIFELINE

Can you name ways in which the world would be a better place to live if everyone loved God first? Talk about it.

BEST GIFT OF ALL
(Mark 12:42)

In the book *The Littlest Angel*, a four-year-old boy is called to heaven. Everyone in the Beautiful City loved the Littlest Angel. But the Littlest Angel was always getting into mischief: dropping his halo and chasing it too lickety-split down the Golden Streets, running into Gabriel, singing too shrilly in the Heavenly Choir. The Littlest Angel just couldn't seem to be where he should be on time! All the angels were in despair about what to do. Finally, the Littlest Angel was called to come before the Great Throne of God. Afraid, the Littlest Angel tried to hide by pulling the robe over his face. But as soon as the Great Voice spoke, all his fear melted away. "Why are you sad sometimes, Littlest Angel?" the Voice asked. "Do you want to go back to your home on earth?"

"Oh, no, Sir! If I had my little box I left under my bed back on earth, I would behave and be very happy."

A messenger, the fastest winged angel in heaven, was summoned to fetch the box from earth. When the Littlest Angel received it, he was never a problem again.

There came a time when word spread through the kingdom that a child of God would be born on earth. All the angels became very busy making the perfect gift for the Christ Child. All, that is, except the Littlest Angel. He was sad because he had nothing to give to the Baby Jesus. The only thing he had was the small, rough, unsightly box—his precious box! Just before the Holy Child was born on earth, the angels took their gifts and laid them in front of the Great Throne. The Littlest Angel timidly laid his box there too, among rare and radiantly fine gifts from the host in heaven.

God chose the Littlest Angel's gift to represent the gift to be sent to earth for His Son. The gift of the Littlest Angel pleased God the most. "The box began to glow with a bright, lustrous flame. It became a radiant brilliance that blinded the eyes of all the angels: The shining star of Bethlehem."[1]

QUESTIONS

1. Why do you think God picked the simplest and dullest-looking gift over all the others?

2. Why was the Littlest Angel's gift more meaningful than the priceless gifts of the other angels?

3. What would you give to the Baby Jesus if you had to choose among all your possessions?

4. How are the widow's mite and the Littlest Angel's box similar?

LIFELINE

God loves a cheerful giver.

TELL THE GOOD NEWS
(Mark 13:16)

Remember how Henny Penny ran to tell the king the sky was falling? Busy Henny Penny stopped long enough to tell everyone she saw along the way, too. And everyone was in a panic because that was bad news! It frightened them.

Good news makes people feel happy. They need hope. When the weather person on the news gives a report for weather conditions each day, the bad weather is emphasized far more than the good. The same is true of bad happenings reported in the news. Wouldn't it be lovely if everyone emphasized the "flip" side of the news? Maybe the weather person would sound like this:

> Ladies and gentlemen, look for 40 percent sunshine today! Great time to fly kites today in the sunshine. Wild, wonderful winds will be kicking up their heels, but those kites will think they are on a roller coaster. Up, up, and away!

Tell the good news! The good news is Jesus is alive! He wants everyone to believe in Him, so let your friends know that Jesus is a good friend and loves everyone very much. Spread joy to the world! We all need to think good news!

QUESTIONS

1. What do you like to hear and see during the day? Does it make you sad if you hear bad news?

2. What can you do to make folks you see and talk to feel better?

3. How did the disciples, Jesus' pupils, respond to this verse? Until it happened, did they understand?

4. Why should you, and all of us, spread the good news?

LIFELINE

You can be God's messenger. That would please Him very much. Being happy, joyful, kind, and helpful encourages people who know and see you to be happy, too. They will see Jesus in you.

SOLDIERS OF THE CROSS
(Mark 13:26-37)

The Armed Forces of the United States of America are trained to protect their homeland, to guard against dangers that destroy the land, to save the people from enemies. The militia are brave and unselfish. They chose to be soldiers! They risk their lives for their country.

During Operation Desert Storm, our army, navy, marines, air force, and other branches of the armed forces served faithfully, ungrudgingly, and courageously. When they are called to do their duty, they are prepared. They are ready! The hours, days, months, and years of marching, flying, shooting, building, and studying make each man and woman in service ready!

Jesus warned the people in His time, and is warning people today, to believe in Him as the Savior and to love and serve Him. Be ready!

QUESTIONS

1. How can you be ready to serve Jesus? Can you name some ways that will show others you are ready?

2. How did Jesus tell His followers that they would know He was coming back?

3. Who are His followers?

4. When will Jesus return to set up His kingdom?

LIFELINE

A "forever and ever" life will be the reward for Jesus' followers.

JESUS KNOWS EVERYTHING
(Mark 14:10, 13)

Have you watched a person talk—communicate—to another using sign language? It's beautiful to see. Did you know that God knows what you think even before you say what you're thinking? Did you know that He knows what you will be doing after a while, tomorrow, the next day . . . from now on? Weird, isn't it? Well, think about this: When you pray, He hears your thoughts, doesn't He?

A camp director was standing in the dining hall giving announcements for the afternoon activities. The meal was about to be served. The director asked a young girl at a table on the other side of the dining hall from where he was standing, "Sally, would you say grace, please? Thank God for the food?"

When Sally's sweet prayer had been lifted on high, the camp director said, "Sally, I couldn't hear you."

Sally answered, "I wasn't praying to you."

God heard Sally's prayer, and He hears our prayers, even when they're whispered or unspoken.

Jesus knew that a man would be carrying a jar of water at the very time the disciples would be at the spot Jesus described. And Jesus knew when Judas would sell information to the leading priests so that they could arrest Jesus.

QUESTIONS

1. How does your mom or dad know when you do something in secret that you don't want your parents to know?

2. Why does Jesus always know something before it happens?

3. What question would you want to ask Jesus when you see Him face to face?

4. Where is Jesus now?

LIFELINE

Jesus was a good teacher. The things He said to the disciples are meant for us today. These things teach us to live as He wants us to live.

BE WILLING
(Mark 14:36)

A story is told about a seven-year-old boy whose younger sister had a disease that would cause her to die if she did not receive blood from a member of her family. The blood type had to be the same as hers. Her brothers, sisters, father, and mother lined up for the doctor to take blood samples from each person. Only one had the right type to match hers. It was her seven-year-old brother. The doctor explained to the brother how the blood would be taken and transferred to his little sister's arm. The boy was courageous and willing to do this for his sister because he loved her very much.

He lay on a hospital bed close to the bed his sister lay on, their hands touching while the blood was drawn and transfused. After a long while, as blood was still being drawn, the brave little boy looked into the doctor's eyes and asked, "Am I nearly dead yet?"

He had not confided this fear to anyone before. He thought all along that when his blood was given to his sister, he would die and his sister would live. Yet he was willing to do it.

Jesus knew the horrible and humiliating death He would go through on the cross. He Who had never sinned would be taking on the sins of the whole world as He hung on the cross. Yet He was willing to do God the Father's will!

QUESTIONS

1. Why was it God's will that Jesus die on the cross?

2. Where did the seven-year-old boy get the courage to give blood to his little sister?

3. Why was Jesus agonizing about the death facing Him?

4. What would you do if you had a situation to choose from like the seven-year-old boy? Would you be willing to lay down your life for someone in your family?

LIFELINE

The little sister lived because her brother loved her. God loves us so much that He gave His only Son so we could live forever.

PIECES OF GOLD
(Mark 14:45)

Once there was a Turkish king. He was a greedy king, and he was a self-ish and foolish king. He was not satisfied with the power and possessions he had. He always wanted more, and so he was miserable. A lot of stories were told about this hated king. The ancient Greek myth of King Midas is about this Turkish king.

King Midas wished that everything he touched would turn to gold. A Greek god allowed King Midas's wish to come true. That night when the king was walking in his garden, he touched a branch of an apple tree. Immediately, it turned to pure, shining gold. Of course, King Midas was excited and pleased. He wanted his court to see his power. He gave a banquet where he sat at the head table by himself. When he touched the bread it became gold. He picked up grapes, and they turned into little gold balls and rolled away on the royal floor. All his food and drink turned to gold. The people were in awe at what they saw.

Yet King Midas got bored. He called for his most cherished possession, something he truly loved besides himself: his young, beautiful daughter. King Midas kissed her when she was given to him, and the little princess turned to gold. A statue of gold! Golden tears rolled down the king's face. He had lost what he loved the most because of his desire for gold.

Judas was greedy and foolish, too. He betrayed Jesus, the only friend he ever had, his prize possession. By being greedy and conniving, Judas lost everything—even his life.

QUESTIONS

1. What moral do you see in the story of King Midas and his golden touch?

2. How could this be a lesson to you?

3. What do you think Judas felt when he saw the guard take Jesus away?

4. How did Jesus know this would happen to Him?

LIFELINE

Jesus said to the guards, "But the Scriptures must be fulfilled" (Mark 14:49).

THE ROYAL CROWN
(Mark 15:17)

Today in countries around the world, visitors can enter museums that contain objects worth millions of dollars, among them that nation's crown jewels. In Russia in the Kremlin, as in other countries, solemn, no-nonsense guards keep keen eyes on the spectators. In Egypt the mummies of pharaohs and the priceless possessions entombed with them are now on display. In China the dazzling displays are unbelievable. In England, too, there are rooms filled with tiaras, jewelry, and gold- and jewel-bedecked robes once worn by Britain's rulers. Each country has scores of precious gems worn by its kings and queens, emperors and empresses, czars and czarinas.

Then there was the crown of thorns that cruel, mocking guards made from a bush. They jammed it on Jesus' head, ripping His forehead. They threw a used purple robe over His beaten body. And they laughed. Yes, a crown of thorns and a tattered robe for our Lord!

QUESTIONS

1. How does the story make you feel?

2. What would you have done had you been there to see them do that to Jesus?

3. What can you do now?

4. Why did the guards make fun of Jesus? What kind of men would do that?

LIFELINE

But after three days Jesus wore the Crown of Heaven!

GOD'S SON
(Mark 15:33, 43)

Jesus was hung on the cross. He died at noon, and for three hours, God caused a curtain of darkness to be drawn over the whole country! It was like nighttime in the middle of the day! All sins ever committed—before and after—were laid on Jesus. That burden caused Jesus more suffering than being beaten, being mocked, and being falsely accused. God could not bear to see His beloved Son carrying such a burden, and He turned away from Him. It broke God's heart to carry out the divine plan to save all people for all times. But God's plans always have good endings. Jesus would be resurrected, and He would reign like the King of kings He is.

After Jesus' death, the Bible tells us a brave man named Joseph went to

Pilate and asked for Jesus' body. Joseph was an important man who was rich enough to own land with a proper burial place for Jesus' body. Joseph was also one of the people who wanted the kingdom of God to come.

There is a similarity here to young David of the Old Testament. David was the only one brave enough to face the giant Goliath. David asked King Saul for the opportunity to kill Goliath when the king's trained men refused to battle him out of fear. David was also the one God asked Samuel, God's prophet, to anoint as the next king. It was God's plan.

QUESTIONS

Discuss the following things that Joseph of Arimathea and David had in common:

- They were both brave enough to go before the men of highest authority.

- Each one asked to do a necessary deed that no one else dared to do.

- Each man was important (Joseph was on the Jewish council and rich; David was the one God wanted to be the next king of Israel).

- Each man was concerned with the future of the kingdom of God to come.

LIFELINE

"It is finished!" Jesus died for mankind. Life everlasting can now be received by those who believe in Him and ask to be saved. Jesus loves you very much. Do you love Jesus for dying for you?

AT LAST! THE GOOD NEWS!
(Mark 16:13-19)

They could kill Jesus because God allowed it to be done, but they could not hold Him in a grave! He did rise again! It was all in God's divine plan. Jesus was alive then and is alive now. Jesus appeared to His disciples and then, only then, did they believe that He was alive as He had told them He would be.

Jesus said to His followers, "Go into all the world and preach the good news to all creation." That is His command to each of us. Tell the good news to everyone you meet.

Have you ever read or had someone read a story that you liked very much? Did that particular story have a happy ending? Think for a minute. What are some of your favorite stories? Do all of them have happy endings?

This story is a true story, and it has a happy ending.

In verse 19, the Bible tells us: "After the Lord Jesus had spoken to them, he was taken up into heaven and he sat at the right hand of God."

QUESTIONS

1. Why does God want believers to tell the good news?

2. What could you tell someone about the good news and why it is good news?

3. How did Jesus get unwrapped from His burial clothes to rise up?

LIFELINE

Jesus did come back to see the disciples. He is alive!

DEVOTIONS FROM THE BOOKS OF JOHN AND JAMES

INTRODUCTION TO JOHN

Perhaps the most valuable and insightful book in the New Testament is the Gospel of John, because the New Testament is all about Jesus, and John knew His heart better than anyone.

Many great leaders in the Bible had one special, loyal friend called by God for a priceless mission. Moses had Joshua. Nebuchadnezzar had Daniel. Of all Jesus' followers, He chose John to reveal Himself to most intimately. John saw Jesus as He really was: Son of God, Lord, Messiah, and great Lover of all sincere believers.

ONE WITH WHOM?
(John 1:1-4)

Keith Chancey is a dy-no-mite friend with a sparkling personality. Once a stellar pass-catching wide receiver, Keith now works with youth and celebrates every minute of it. His home base is Denton, Texas. His "hobby" is the growing church of Katmandu (a third-world basket of poverty at the base of 29,000-foot Mount Everest). Keith recently returned from two weeks of mission work with the nation he "taught to have fun." His packs were full of deflated soccer balls, footballs, and basketballs . . . and a hand pump. People have learned to smile when Keith comes to town. On the 26-hour flight to his mission field via Germany and Saudi Arabia, Keith sat next to a New Age mountain climber who was heading for Mount Everest to become "one with the mountain." Keith chuckled as they talked. "One with the mountain?"

"Yeah," the searching climber said. "The mountain and I will become united, like one and the same."

Keith thought for a while: *How weird! You can become one with your wife and one with God, but one with a pile of rocks?* After a few hours, Keith looked at the climber carefully and said, "How would you like to become one with the God Who made the mountain? It is really possible through a personal relationship with His Son."

The climber smiled. "One with God . . . Hmm . . . I didn't know it was possible. That's the first time anybody explained it to me like that."

QUESTIONS

1. Who is "the Word" in this passage?

2. Where was Jesus when the universe was created?

3. Why did He come to earth?

4. How is it possible to become one with God? (See John 14:20.)

LIFELINE

Jesus is most real in the home where parents and kids show His love in the way they treat each other.

BAPTISM
(John 1:31-33)

John the Baptist announced the coming of Jesus by proclaiming His imminent arrival and immersing sincere believers in the water of the Jordan River. Jesus Himself was baptized in water as a sinless man to set a pattern for all Christians to follow. Believing in Jesus as your Savior and sincerely committing your life to follow Him baptizes a person in the Holy Spirit. A look at *baptism*'s original meaning explains it with wonderful clarity. The word comes from the Greek word *Baptizo*, which means "to place into." It's like taking a white knit shirt and placing it in a vat of pink dye—the shirt takes on the properties of the dye and comes out pink. To be baptized into Christ means you go in looking and acting like you and come out looking and acting like Him. As believers, we get baptized as an important symbol of what happens in our hearts when we become Christians.

QUESTIONS

1. Why did Jesus get baptized?

2. How is baptism in water like being baptized into Christ?

3. What properties or characteristics of Christ are we supposed to take on when we become believers?

LIFELINE

As a family, discuss answers to this question: How can we help each other be more like Christ today?

DISCIPLES
(John 1:40-43)

Are you a disciple of Christ? A disciple is a follower. I have counseled thousands of hurting teenagers and adults in the last 20 years, and I have found that almost all people who got caught up in sin and got badly hurt made a decision not to follow anyone. They rebelled and quit following their parents, and, while often calling themselves Christians, they quit following God as well. The happiest people I know are the real followers of Christ and His teachings, and they have a good, solid role model.

Are you a disciple of Christ? A disciple is a disciplined learner. Twelve men followed Jesus for three years. Although one disciple (Judas Iscariot) had plugged-up ears and no self-control, eleven learned from Him everything He taught. They eventually changed the world.

QUESTIONS

1. What do the words *discipline* and *disciple* have in common?

2. It sounds bad, but in reality it is easier to be a Judas sometimes. Why is that so?

3. What do you think Jesus was looking for when He picked eleven good men?

4. What kind of disciple does God find in you today?

LIFELINE

How can we be more like the eleven good disciples and less like Judas?

OINOS
(John 2:1-10)

When is alcohol bad for you? How much is too much? If Jesus turned water into wine, is today's wine okay to drink? The Bible is very clear that certain things are harmful to the body and a sin to indulge in. Would Jesus make something that God wouldn't like?

The New Testament was written in the very colorful Greek language. The original meaning of each word makes the questions above easy to understand. *Wine* in the English language comes from one of two Greek words. *Oinos* (the kind of wine Jesus made) referred to purified grape juice that was ½ to 1 percent alcohol. It was always diluted with 20 times pure juice or water. *Sikera* referred to strong drink, or 2 to 12 percent alcohol. Getting drunk with strong drink is condemned in the Bible. Modern beer (5%), wine (+12%), and hard liquor (+20-30%) all fall into this category. *Sikera* is the most destructive drug in America. It's responsible for more deaths, abuses, and broken homes than any other substance (see Resource I). Proverbs sounds the warning: "Do not gaze at wine when it is red, when it sparkles in the cup, when it goes down smoothly! In the end it bites like a snake and poisons like a viper" (Prov. 23:31-32).

QUESTIONS

1. Why did Jesus make *oinos* and not *sikera*?

2. Why are people so attracted to strong drink?

3. Why is getting drunk a sin?

LIFELINE

Alcohol leads to a lot of trouble for a lot of people. What should our family policy toward it be?

RIGHTEOUS ANGER
(John 2:13-17)

I'm so mad at Hollywood that I wouldn't even consider going to a movie where they take God's name in vain, something almost all PG-, PG-13-, and R-rated movies do repeatedly. My God has been so good, so faithful, and so giving that I refuse to support an industry that cuts Him down. I'm mad at the television set that repeatedly curses God and portrays Christians as wimps or bigots. (Ted Turner, owner of CNN and TNT, said, "Christianity is for losers.") Because they feel the same, our kids have agreed to watch only one or two carefully selected TV shows a week.

Anger can be a sin—but certainly not when God's reputation is at stake. Today our God is being dishonored at every turn. The money changers of the temple are everywhere. People take His name in vain ("My God!" "Oh, my God!" "Jesus Christ!") repeatedly to sound cool or fit in with the crowd. Some don't care. Some use the church or the TV church to get rich. Anyone who loves God would be angered at such disrespect.

Love your enemies and pray for those who persecute you. Don't reward anger for anger. Loving God means being concerned for His honor and doing what you can to see that He is exalted, not mocked.

QUESTIONS

1. When is it wrong to get mad?

2. Why was Jesus righteously angry?

3. Why is it wrong to take God's name in vain?

4. Practically speaking, how can you oppose those who take advantage of God or put Him down?

LIFELINE

What habits in our home (e.g., TV viewing) might need to be changed in light of our desire to honor God?

GOD'S TIMING
(John 3:1-3)

When my soft-hearted oldest daughter was growing up, we raised geese, rabbits, squirrels, raccoons, dogs, deer, possums (who but Jamie could love a possum?), and any other stray animal that found its way to our door. While incubating some duck eggs one spring, I made a drastic mistake. You see, it takes a baby duck 28 days to hatch. The last two to three days, it is busy pecking its way out of its shell. The pecking time is a great struggle, but it makes the duckling strong enough to survive once it's out in the world.

I felt so sorry for one of the struggling little ducklings that I helped it out of its shell on the second day after it had pecked a hole in the egg. It died that night. God's timing included one more day of struggle for the little duck. The other ducklings struggled on their own and got free of their eggshells in God's time. They all survived.

QUESTIONS

1. What does it mean to be born again?

2. Why did Nicodemus (a very religious man) need to be born again?

3. Why do we need to depend on God's timing for someone to be born again?

4. How do we sometimes "open the shell" too soon?

LIFELINE

Whom can we pray for that they'll be born again?

THE GREATEST BIBLE VERSE
(John 3:16)

For God................................	the greatest lover
So loved	the greatest love
The world.............................	the greatest need
That He gave........................	the greatest gift
His one and only Son...........	the greatest life
That whoever	the greatest offer
Believes in Him....................	the greatest faith
Shall not perish....................	the greatest death
But have eternal life............	the greatest hope

QUESTIONS

1. Why do some people call John 3:16 the greatest verse in the Bible?

2. What does it mean to you?

3. What does the word *whoever* mean in this verse?

4. What does the word *believe* mean in this verse?

LIFELINE

Let's memorize this verse and repeat it to each other tomorrow.

THE AUCTION
(John 3:33-36)

The upstate New York man was rich in almost every way. His estate was worth millions. He owned houses, land, antiques, and cattle. But though on the outside he had it all, he was very unhappy on the inside. His wife was growing old, and the couple was childless. He had always wanted a little boy to carry on the family legacy.

Miraculously, his wife became pregnant in her later years, and she gave birth to a little boy. The boy was severely retarded, but the man loved him with his whole heart. When the boy was five, his mom died. The dad drew closer to his special son. At age 13, the boy's birth defects cost him his life, and the father died soon after from a broken heart.

The estate was auctioned before hundreds of bidders. The first item offered was a painting of the boy. No one bid. They waited like vultures for the riches. Finally, the poor housemaid, who helped raise the boy, offered $5 for the picture and easily took the bid. To everyone's shock, the auctioneer ripped a handwritten will from the back of the picture. This is what it said: "To the person who thinks enough of my son to buy this painting, to this person I give my entire estate."

The auction was over. The greedy crowd walked away in shock and dismay.

QUESTIONS

1. How is this auction like God's offer to us?

2. What exactly is God's offer?

3. Who will be disappointed when the auction is over?

LIFELINE

Will we value each other as much as the rich man valued his son?

LIVING WATER
(John 4:6-10)

Perrier, Coke, Gatorade, Quick Kick, Canadian Coolers, Dr. Pepper. Thirst-quenching drinks have always been big business. Gatorade paid Michael Jordan double-digit millions just to call him "Mike." Pepsi paid him double-digit millions to drink Pepsi in front of a TV camera. In some drought-stricken countries, people will walk over 20 miles for a pitcher of water.

Drinks of all kinds have incredible value for two reasons. One, people get thirsty; and two, drinks don't permanently quench thirst.

Jesus said that He has quenched your thirst for meaning and purpose in life and that you'll never thirst again as you continue to trust in, and live for, Him.

There are as many cults and God-seeking religions as there are soft drinks in America. People flock by the millions to new "thirst-quenching" religions every day. Eighteen hundred mystical cults claim to be a new way to God. The New Age movement has millions of American followers. Atheism has millions more. All of these people are thirsting for God, and they'll try many drinks to quench this thirst. Unfortunately, most will die parched.

QUESTIONS

1. What authority did Jesus have when He told the woman He has living water?

2. Why did Jesus call Himself "living water"?

3. Why does a sincere follower of Christ never thirst for another drink?

4. How can someone get a drink of living water?

LIFELINE

Make your home an oasis: Give each other a "drink" of love and grace today.

MESSIAH
(John 4:21-26)

It's the Super Bowl MVP, the winner of the PGA tournament, the winning driver of the Indy 500, the gold medalist in the Olympics—it's the best of the best!

But the Messiah is even more than that. Much more!

Messiah means "the Christ," "the Son of God," "the Savior of the world."

The Old Testament saints longed for and wrote about this long-awaited Messiah. He would be "the Anointed One of God." He'd be the "wonderful Counselor, mighty God, Prince of Peace." He'd be a Lamb, a sacrifice for man's sins for all time; soft, gentle, kind; a friend. He'd be a Lion, Savior, Leader, Conqueror, everlasting King.

All of this and more—much more—is wrapped up in one man, one name: Jesus. To reject Him is to lose your soul. To accept and follow Him is to gain eternal salvation.

QUESTIONS

1. What does *Messiah* mean to you?

2. Compare *Messiah* to other great names you know. How is Jesus unique?

3. Why is Jesus known as the Lamb and the Lion?

LIFELINE

Let's make our life in this home such that Jesus will be glad He's a part of it.

IT'S TOUGHEST AT HOME
(John 4:41-45)

Young Brett Posten came to camp to become a better soccer player. He learned to dribble, kick, and defend better than ever. But Brett also accepted Jesus into his heart one evening and went home a different person. After becoming a Christian, his prayer was that his mom and dad would see a change and accept Jesus into their hearts, too. His mom was into New Age. His dad went to church but didn't know a personal Savior.

Brett smiled, served, loved, obeyed, and honored his parents like never before. They couldn't resist. One by one, his mom, dad, and sister accepted Christ. Today the family stands united.

It's toughest to live your faith at home! Even Jesus was misunderstood at first.

Brooke was 16 when she and her father lost their friendship. At camp she decided she had been wrong. She made a list of 36 specific ways to serve her dad when she went home, like cleaning his office and packing his lunch. In September she called me to say it was working. In January she called to tell me he was her best friend.

It's toughest at home, but home is where Christian living is at its best!

QUESTIONS

1. Why did Jesus' family misunderstand Him?

2. What did He tell them that threw them for a loop?

3. Why is it hardest to live your faith at home?

4. Why is it essential not to pretend to be a Christian away from home if you're not living it at home?

LIFELINE

Since it's toughest to be a Christian at home, let's make it easier for each other by the way we live, serve, and sacrifice.

DO YOU *WILL* TO GET WELL?
(John 5:2-9)

I was traveling through Texas hiring summer staff for our sports camps, when Beth, a cute sophomore at Texas Tech University, came to me confused and in need of counseling.

"I feel so bad these days," she began with tears in her huge, brown eyes. "My relationship with God is going nowhere right now."

We talked for a while, and she sobbed as she explained her boyfriend problems. It wasn't a good relationship, but she held on to it for the feeling of security it gave her.

"Beth," I said, "you've got to give God your *will*."

She looked up in wonder. "How did you know that was his name? My boyfriend's name is *Will*."

Your *will* is your heart. It's the driver's seat of your life. It's the quarterback around whom your decisions huddle. When you give God your will, you can stop anything that is wrong and do anything that is right. It's a process that may take a while and be difficult, but surrendering your will to God is the all-important first step.

QUESTIONS

1. When you need to do something that's right but also hard, why is saying "I'll try" a cop-out?

2. What's the difference between wanting to do something and deciding to do it?

3. When Jesus owns your will, what does that mean?

LIFELINE

The paralytic *willed* to get well. He took up his pallet and walked. How can we, as a family, help each other walk away from sinful habits?

INSTANT REPLAY
(John 5:22-24)

We were playing a tough national championship college football team in front of 80,000 biased fans and millions more on television. After making an embarrassing mistake during one of the plays, I wanted to hide my number under the pile of players so no one could recognize me. Fortunately, the play went by quickly, and on the sidelines our coach hadn't had a clear view of it. Then he saw the film of the game. He played it over and over again, correcting me staunchly for my error. I really felt small in that film room with my teammates. What I would have given to be able to erase the film before the coach saw it!

God is like a coach in that He sees it all and knows it all. He has "filmed" every sin, every mistake, every failure. He is no fool. When you and I meet Him face to face, the film of our sins will start to play, and an amazing thing will happen. A man named Jesus will step forward on our behalf and say to God, "Their films have been erased. They are My children. I live in their hearts. Their films are perfect. I died for the bad places in them." We will then fall at His feet in praise.

QUESTIONS

1. How is sin a failure?

2. How can Jesus erase our life films?

3. Should we sin freely since He's erasing our errors?

LIFELINE

Let's help each other make good life films with no disappointing "instant replays."

BEARING WITNESS
(John 5:32-34)

The poor blind boy sold pencils in the busy train station to buy food and clothing. The people in the station rushed by him each day paying little attention to his need. Occasionally someone would drop a quarter in the boy's money box and grab a pencil as a good deed for the day.

One morning the crowd in the station was especially large. The rush from train to train was intense. As everyone dashed onto the crowded trains, one careless businessman ran into the blind boy, knocked him out of his chair, and sent his coins and pencils flying across the floor. Desperately the boy crawled around the floor searching for his precious coins and pencils. Then a kind old man gently picked him up, gathered his pencils and coins, and helped the boy get started again. Finally, the man handed the boy a $20 bill and began to walk away.

The blind boy cried out, "Mister, are you Jesus?"

"No, son," the man replied, "I'm just one of His followers."

Tears fell from the boy's wounded eyes as he cried, "I knew you were some kind of kin."

QUESTIONS

1. How do we bear witness for Christ?

2. Name one situation that you were in yesterday where you had a chance to be a witness.

3. Describe one way you can bear witness in the family today.

LIFELINE

Bearing witness starts at home. Let your family members see Christ in you today.

WHAT'S IN YOUR "LUNCH SACK"?
(John 6:5-13)

Laura is a precious high-school junior. She gets kidded by her older friends because she's a junior. She just smiles and never seeks to get back at them. In her lunch sack is forgiveness.

Anne is 16. Several boys have tried, but no one has been "the one" for her first kiss. Boys at school tease her for her prudishness. In her lunch sack is purity.

If it's not G-rated or an extra-clean PG, Jamie doesn't go to a movie. She loves Disney movies. You can find her at the mall at the Disney store. Her friends call her a goodie-goodie cartoon freak. In her lunch sack is a clean heart.

Scott is a professional jeweler. Nine out of 10 jewelers he knows lie about diamond purity to make more money. Last week Scott turned down a $20,000 profit on a diamond deal because it was dishonest. In his lunch sack is honesty.

Trevor is a great doctor. One day while getting ready for surgery with seven other doctors, the conversation turned to faithfulness in marriage. All seven doctors were unfaithful to their wives. Trevor stood alone. He would never consider any other way. In his lunch sack is faithfulness.

Everyone's lunch sack is unique, but imagine what Jesus could do if we gave what we had in ours to Him today!

QUESTIONS

1. What's in your lunch sack today?

2. How does one at your age give his or her lunch to God?

3. How great is it to have a good lunch to give Him?

4. What will He do with your lunch if you give it to Him?

LIFELINE

Let's pack a "lunch sack" today that will be an honor to give to Jesus.

RIGHT ON TIME
(John 6:16-20)

Jesus set it up perfectly. There had been a lot of talk about faith over the past few days. Now it was time to go to the faith lab. He knew there was no better laboratory for faith building than in a boat at night on a giant lake, in a storm. The conditions were ideal. I'd bet my bottom dollar that the moon wasn't even out. This was a place where fear was in full bloom. Winds make the leaves rustle in the trees—strong winds blow roofs off of houses. Dramamine hadn't been invented yet. Those guys were scared sick!

Jesus probably waited for their prayers to come deeply from their hearts. Faith's finest hour is when it is stretched to the breaking point. I can almost hear them calling desperately for their Lord and Master as water begins to fill their boat and childhood stories of sea monsters fill their imaginations. Then Jesus appears, and the boat reaches shore.

A Southern preacher explained, "Jesus may not be there when you want Him to be, but He'll get there right on time."

QUESTIONS

1. When was the last storm in your life? When did Jesus appear?

2. Why do we fret when Jesus doesn't immediately solve our problems?

3. Why did Jesus wait to calm the storm?

4. What should we do when the night is dark and the winds are blowing?

LIFELINE

Remind each other during strong winds and dark nights that Jesus won't be even a second too late.

WAKE-UP CALL
(John 6:35-40)

Kyle Rote, Jr., is a good friend of mine who won the Rookie of the Year award in professional soccer several years ago. Recently he told me how he had received a call from the president of the United States shortly after he'd won. When he picked up the phone and the president introduced himself, Kyle thought it was a prank call from a buddy who often called pretending to be a famous person.

Kyle said, "Sure, the president of the United States! You're a big fake, a fraud, and you're crazy if you think I'm going to believe something as stupid as this joke."

The president paused, cleared his throat, and said, "Kyle, this *is* the president of the United States, and I want to invite you to the White House to congratulate you on your recent honor."

Kyle was embarrassed beyond words.

Imagine going to sleep one night and waking up in the White House or in the home of the most famous person you know of but have never gotten a chance to meet! Death to a follower of Christ will be just like that. Jesus will be there to greet you when you wake up.

QUESTIONS

1. Why are we sometimes scared of death?

2. What do you think it will be like to go to sleep and wake up in Jesus' house?

3. What do you hope to hear Jesus say to you at that time?

LIFELINE

Let's encourage each other with the hope that life ends with a wake-up call from the greatest Man Who ever lived.

WHAT IS GOD'S WILL?
(John 6:65-68)

"This is good, and pleases God our Savior, who wants all men to be saved and to come to a knowledge of the truth" (1 Tim. 2:3-4).

"The Lord is not slow in keeping His promise, as some understand slowness. He is patient with you, not wanting anyone to perish, but everyone to come to repentance" (2 Pet. 3:9).

For decades, countless faithful young American men complied with the pointed finger and scowl of the Uncle Sam posters proclaiming "Uncle Sam Wants You!" But God wants you to fight and win a different sort of war. He wants you to join His eternal army to win the souls of people in your neighborhood and around the world.

God's will is that you give your life to Christ and spend forever in heaven. Men and women have to deliberately walk around the Cross to get to hell, which was created for Satan and his angels. Heaven was created for men, women, and children who followed God's will and trusted Christ for salvation.

QUESTIONS

1. When someone asks you what God's will for your life is, how can you answer?

2. Who did Jesus die for? (See John 3:16, John 1:12, and Rev. 3:20.)

3. How do you know that true Christians go to heaven?

4. What does God's army do?

LIFELINE

Whenever someone in the family leads a person to Christ, celebrate it at the dinner table so all can rejoice.

WHO IS TEACHING?
(John 7:14-18)

Every time you turn on the TV set, someone is teaching you. Every time you put in a cassette or CD, someone is teaching you. Every time you choose a magazine or book, you're being taught by someone. The 10 billion cells in your brain take in every sound you hear and every sight you see. Each sight and sound is stored in the subconscious, to be recalled at a later day.

If someone watches the average amount of TV, he'll see over 10,000 beer commercials showing fun at wild parties. What's he being taught?

The first American schoolteachers taught the Bible. The *New England Primer* was used to teach American kids to read for the first 100 years of this nation's existence. The alphabet was taught with Scripture like this:

A   "A wise son maketh glad a father" (Prov. 10:1).
B   "Better is a little with righteousness" (Prov. 16:8).
C   "Come unto me all ye that labour" (Matt. 11:28).

What place does the Bible have in public schools today? Since the schools and the media are bombarding us with unscriptural teaching, what do we need to do at home?

QUESTIONS

1. Who are your main teachers? Whom do you listen to more than anyone else in the world?

2. According to John 7:18, what is the test for a good teacher?

3. What can you do when you find you're listening to a bad teacher?

LIFELINE

Help each other identify bad teachers in your lives.

"I HAD THE WORLD"
(John 7:33-34)

There are a zillion ways to try to get to God. You can follow Muhammad, Joseph Smith, Shirley MacLaine, or any number of men and women who claim to have a shortcut (and end up cut short).

You can get so many worldly treasures that you don't need God; you can get so famous and successful that you might think you *are* God. (It happens every day.)

One of the richest and most famous athletes who ever lived was a world champion millionaire boxer named Muhammad Ali. No doubt, Ali was a boxing phenomenon. As he said about himself, "I am the greatest! I am the greatest!" *Sports Illustrated* did a cover story on the great boxer 15 years after Ali quit boxing. The reporter visited Ali's farm one cold winter day and candidly traced the champ's rise . . . and fall. The two went out behind the house, to Ali's training barn, which was full of Ali's trophies and life-sized posters of himself with his arms thrust high overhead in defiant victory. The trophies and posters were streaked with droppings from pigeons in the rafters overhead. One by one, Ali turned them toward the wall in shame and disgust. He walked outside and said softly, "I had the world . . . and it wasn't nothin'."[1]

QUESTIONS

1. Jesus said, "What good will it be for a man if he gains the whole world, yet forfeits his soul?" (Matt. 16:26). What does that mean to you?

2. What activity are you involved in now that could get between you and God?

LIFELINE

Home is the place to remind each other that there's no other way to God but Jesus.

A MAN OF PROPHECY
(John 7:40-42)

Josh McDowell is one of the most intelligent men I know. In his book *Evidence That Demands a Verdict*, Josh points out that during the 1,000 years before Jesus' birth, several hundred specific prophecies were given by the Old Testament saints accurately predicting the birth, life, death, and resurrection of the Messiah. The following prophecies give interesting details of Jesus' coming:

	Prophesied	*Fulfilled*
Born of a virgin	Isa. 7:14	Matt. 1:18, 24-25
Family line of Jesus	Isa. 11:1	Luke 3:23, 31
Of the house of David	Jer. 23:5	Luke 3:23, 31
Born in Bethlehem	Micah 5:2	Matt. 2:1
His pre-existence	Micah 5:2	Col. 1:17
He shall be called Immanuel	Isa. 7:14	Matt. 1:23
Preceded by a messenger	Isa. 40:3	Matt. 3:1-2
Ministry begins in Galilee	Isa. 9:1	Matt. 4:12-13, 17
Sold for 30 pieces of silver	Zech. 11:12	Matt. 26:15
Hands and feet pierced	Isa. 53; Ps. 22:16	Luke 23:33

The odds that any other man could have fulfilled these and other prophetic claims about Jesus are as impossible as the odds that you could fill the solar system with golf balls, mark one with a red dot, ask a blind golfer to take a swing, and have him hit the marked ball on the first swing. It's crazy to imagine, but then so is the idea that any other man could have been the true Jesus of the Bible.

QUESTIONS

1. What do Jesus' fulfilled prophecies tell you about your faith?

2. What difference does today's devotional make in your life?

3. How else can we be sure that Jesus is who He claimed to be?

LIFELINE

If you have a difficult task today, know that as a believer, you have the one and only Jesus of prophecy living in your heart and doing His work through you.

GETTING CAUGHT
(John 8:1-11)

When I was growing up, I didn't have extra money to go to the movies or buy soft drinks. But God is good, and I always had what I needed. Unfortunately, as a junior-high kid, I often wanted more.

One Friday night, I wanted to see the high-school football game, but my pockets were empty. So I thought, *No big deal. I'll just crawl over the fence and get in free.* Up I went. The fence led conveniently to the top row of the grandstand, so I would have no problem getting a seat once I climbed safely over . . . no problem, that is, except one. As I got about two-thirds of the way up, I saw Mr. Ozment, our high-school principal, peering down at me. I was caught in the act. I knew I was fast becoming an endangered species. I could feel the sting of the paddle on my bottom when I got to school on Monday. I was miserable the whole weekend.

But a funny thing happened that Monday. I entered Mr. Ozment's office with great hesitation and fear, only to find him standing behind his desk, smiling. I think he knew I was sorry, and he forgave me. I'll always love that man.

QUESTIONS

1. Why is getting caught in the act such a dreadful experience?

2. Think of a time you were caught doing something wrong. What happened?

3. How did Jesus handle the adulteress?

4. What does that say about God's love for us?

LIFELINE

Although there are times when the Bible commands parents to discipline, the home is a great place for family members to give each other the kind of grace Jesus gave the adulteress.

PLEASING GOD
(John 8:28-30)

I love to please my daddy! He's 80, yet I still get the greatest thrill when he notices something I did. He gets so excited! It's amazing! Playing football around the country was worthwhile for one simple reason: Daddy was in the grandstands!

God flooded the whole sinful world but spared Noah's family because "Noah found favor in the eyes of the LORD" (Gen. 6:8). God built the entire Jewish nation on David's strength because God was pleased that David had a heart for the Lord. God built His kingdom for Jesus because He was His Son, in whom He was well pleased. God loves it when we live a life pleasing to Him!

Julie went to the sophomore party after the game Friday night. About 11:30, things got wild. Two football players brought a fifth of Jack Daniels and poured it into the punch. "Everybody" started getting crazy, and let me tell you, it wasn't cool to leave before midnight. Julie ignored what was "cool" and headed for home. She knew whom to please.

Andy was crammed into the backseat of Mike's Bronco with the starting five basketball players. A joint was being passed from player to player. "Everyone" took a drag. When his turn came, Andy said, "No thanks, boys. Not me." God smiled.

It happens every day, in every American town, by everyday people like you and me. God-pleasers are the best people I know.

QUESTIONS

1. How can God find pleasure with people?

2. Why did God give people the freedom to please or displease Him?

3. Think of a way that you can please God this week.

LIFELINE

Being a God-pleaser is a task that takes the encouragement of a caring family.

FREEDOM AND SLAVERY
(John 8:34-36)

Harriet Tubman, "a woman called Moses," was an African-American who lived during the Civil War era. Born into slavery, Harriet was told by her mom at the age of seven that she might as well face the fact that she was a slave, she'd always be a slave, and she'd die a slave.

Harriet didn't buy it. That day, she determined in her heart that she'd either be free or die trying. By age 40, not only had she crossed the dangerous pathway to freedom, but she had also helped others find dignity, hope, and freedom. Before she died, this "woman called Moses" had literally escorted over 300 slaves from slavery to freedom . . . from death to life.

Sin is slavery. Sin is subtle. No one taking a first drink becomes a hopeless alcoholic. No one toking on a first joint becomes a hopeless drug addict. No one kissing too much takes a trip to the abortion clinic. Sin seduces you into taking first one step and then another, until suddenly you realize you have been trapped by it and are now its slave.

QUESTIONS

1. What sins can you name that lead to slavery?

2. How does Satan make sin look so appealing?

3. How can you gain freedom when you find yourself in a sin trap?

4. Why can only Jesus set you truly free?

LIFELINE

If someone in the family is moving toward a trap, let's lovingly lead him or her away from it.

LORD, LIAR, OR LUNATIC
(John 8:54-59)

What if one of you around this table stood up right now and announced to the rest of the table that you were Shaquille O'Neal or Michael Jordan? What would everyone's response be?

"You're crazy! Sit down."

"You're kidding or lying, buddy."

No one would say, "Well, you're close. Maybe you're just a little confused. But you may make it someday."

No. Only a liar or a nut would claim to be the best basketball player in the world when he wasn't.

Folks, Jesus Christ didn't claim to be just another prophet. He didn't claim to be just a good man with some great moral teachings. He claimed to be God in the flesh. To Jews, that was blasphemy, and that's why Jesus was crucified.

Today we all have a chance to ponder: Jesus was God, He was lying, or He was crazy. Easter morning witnesses to the fact that He couldn't have been a liar or a lunatic. That leaves us with only one choice.

QUESTIONS

1. Why do people try to lower Jesus to less than He claimed to be?

2. Why is Jesus in a completely different class than Muhammad, Buddha, or Confucius?

3. If He is Lord, what does that mean to us?

4. Who do you say that Jesus is?

LIFELINE

Let's be sure Jesus is Lord of this home today.

BLIND SPOTS
(John 9:1-7)

It would have been a horrible accident if my mom had not seen the car approaching at breakneck speed just behind my right shoulder on a busy six-lane freeway. Because of the design of my car, the rearview mirror had a blind spot behind the right taillight.

Blind spots. A college student focuses only on sports. A beautiful girl wears clothes that are too tight. A bodybuilder spends his days in the gym. A smart businessman thinks only about work. A mother complains constantly about her hard life. A guy likes his girlfriend more than he loves God. A junior-high girl will do anything to be popular. A little boy won't share his candy. None of them see the blind spots until they get into trouble.

Blind spots are areas in our lives where we can't, or don't want to, see the truth. They are places where Satan gets his way.

QUESTIONS

1. How do we get blinded to the truth that's around us?

2. How can Jesus heal a blind spot?

3. What do we need to do to let Him?

LIFELINE

As a family, we are God's best instruments to help Jesus identify and heal blind spots in each other.

BELIEVING
(John 9:30-39)

My teenage friend was angry with his parents about moving to a new town. Oh, was this boy mad! His anger got him into fights. I confronted him in love: "Tim, why are you striking out at everyone?"

With tears in his eyes, he mumbled, "My dad's moving me from my friends. I'm mad. I don't even like God. I don't believe in anything anymore."

I took off my watch and handed it to him. Tim looked up in surprise.

"Whose watch is it, Tim?" I asked.

"Yours."

"But you are holding it."

"It's still yours."

"Well, I want you to have it. Here, take it. It's a gift."

"It is? For me? Your watch?" He was pleased and puzzled.

"Whose is it now, Tim?"

"Uh, it's mine, I guess. Yeah, it's mine."

"When did it become yours? When I handed it to you or when you accepted the gift into your heart?"

Tim smiled softly. He understood belief. He understood faith. Belief is accepting a gift into your heart. To believe is to receive. To receive is to follow.

QUESTIONS

1. What does it mean to believe in Jesus?

2. What happens when a person puts his or her faith in God?

3. Why did the blind man instantly worship Jesus when he believed in Him?

4. What do we as believers need to do today?

LIFELINE

Unconditional family giving helps us understand God's gift of faith to us.

MORE THAN ENOUGH
(John 10:7-10)

Noah Webster, who compiled the original *Webster's Dictionary*, was a devoted Christian man who, like almost all of America's great early scholars, knew the Bible backward and forward. Webster defined the word *abundant* as "more than enough."

More than enough. Think about it. Jesus came to give abundant life . . . abundant peace . . . abundant joy. Can beer, popularity, sports, money, a car, or a girlfriend do that? How good-looking is more than enough? How much pleasure is more than enough? How much fame and success are more than enough?

When Jesus healed the blind man, the guy didn't need to go out and buy glasses. He saw perfectly!

When Jesus fed the 5,000, they didn't leave the gathering and head for McDonald's. They were full, and there were baskets left over!

When will we stop trying to get high on the stuff of this world? Ten thousand kids come to our Christian camps, and we get high on God! I see kids tapping into Christ's abundance all over this country. Bible studies of two kids, four kids, eight kids, even 10 kids, Christian music on the jam box, quiet times before bed, youth groups with a purpose, parents encouraging their kids to make honest business decisions. Abundant life! Live it!

QUESTIONS

1. What's the difference between living and abundant living?

2. Why do real believers have more fun?

3. Why did God invent fun, happiness, and pleasure, and how did He intend for us to have them?

LIFELINE

How abundant are our lives today? How can we help each other make our lives better?

TWICE MINE
(John 10:5-30)

Mike was only 12 years old, but he was especially handy with a pocketknife and a block of wood. Because he was quite poor, his few precious toys were all handmade.

For three months, he poured his spare time into carving a beautiful little boat—a miniature replica of the *Pinta* that brought Columbus across the Atlantic Ocean. Mike took his boat to a nearby creek after a rain shower to test his prize. As the boat took off in the current, Mike's wonder and admiration quickly turned to panic. The water was carrying away his one-of-a-kind masterpiece. He ran and ran to catch up with it, but to no avail. In tears, he wandered back home.

Two months later, Mike was walking by a hobby shop in his hometown, and there in the window was his boat. Someone had found it! He rubbed his eyes in disbelief. The price tag was $10; it might as well have been $100. He rushed home, emptied his life savings out of his piggy bank, scraped the $10 in change into a paper bag, and hurried back to town.

Mike bought his boat back and walked proudly out of the store. With tears in his eyes, he looked down at the boat and said, "Little boat, I made you and you ran away. But I bought you back. So, little boat, you're twice mine."

QUESTIONS

1. How are we like the little boat?

2. What did God do to buy us back?

3. How does it make you feel to be "twice mine" to God?

LIFELINE

Let's help each other see how thankful we can be today as we remember our God, Who gave His all so we could be twice His!

MY FATHER IN ME
(John 10:32-38)

Yesterday had to be one of the most "sheer fun" days of my life: flying across a Tennessee pasture on a red-hot four-wheeler behind Paul Overstreet, one of country music's greatest songwriters and recording artists. We were as wild as two young mustangs sprinting through the mountains. Paul sincerely loves Jesus Christ and writes and sings to draw families closer to God's plan of loving His Son and serving each other. Paul has a song I like a lot that says,

> I'm seeing my father in me
> And that's how we both agree
> . . . more like him each day.
> I notice I walk the way he walks.
> I'm seeing I talk the way he talks.
> I'm startin' to see my father in me.[2]

People knew that Jesus was of God (all the fullness of deity dwelt in Him) because He consistently behaved like God. He never wavered in producing a lifestyle that was godly.

Even today, a dad's number-one responsibility is to follow God in his lifestyle at home, at work, and at church. As the apostle Paul said, "Imitate me as I imitate Christ."

The older a son or daughter gets, the more he or she desires to imitate a godly father. My father once said: "Imitation is the greatest compliment." When I was a teenager, I didn't imitate Dad enough, but shortly thereafter he became the smartest man on earth.

QUESTIONS

1. What did Jesus do that let people know He was, indeed, God in the flesh?

2. The only thing harder than being a teenager is being the parent of one. Nevertheless, how can a son or daughter pay the highest compliment to a godly parent? Can you give examples?

LIFELINE

People can best see God when they see us doing the works of God.

THE HUMAN MAZE
(John 11:9-10)

Last week my son Brady drew a maze on a sheet of paper for me to try to solve. There were so many detours and dead-end streets that I never could get to the finish line.

In our tourist town, there is a maze that people can run through. Before you enter the maze, you're handed a card upon which the four letters M-A-Z-E must be placed. The letters are given out at four separate stations within the maze. You have five minutes to find these stations and get the letters put on your card. If you make it in time, you get a free T-shirt. What a trip!

After losing this race to my son, I climbed the stairs to an observation deck where I could see the maze spread out clearly before me. The path to victory was so simple to memorize. Anyone could win after a careful view from the top.

As I counsel countless teenagers, college students, and adults, I see so many "bruised foreheads" from bumping into the walls of our sin-riddled society. How much easier would be the race through our daily mazes if we started each day with a view from above!

QUESTIONS

1. How is life like a maze?

2. What are the "walls" and "dead ends" of growing up?

3. How do we get God's view from above?

4. What does it mean to walk in the light?

LIFELINE

Let's help each other keep the view from above today.

JESUS WEPT
(John 11:32-36)

Have you ever wondered where tears come from? Have you cried so long that you wondered if your tear ducts would dry up? Physical pain from life's bumps and bruises can bring tears to your eyes. But tears from heart pain—such as when a friend says good-bye or when you lose someone dear to you—seem to come from deeper within.

In the original Greek in which the New Testament was written, the apostle John said that Jesus sobbed, that He actually groaned with pain, when Lazarus died. Why? Didn't He know that He'd bring Lazarus back to life?

I think He cried because He loves His people so much that even though everyone will eventually be over all pain forever, He feels every pain you do. He cares deeply and knows your pain—when your boyfriend says good-bye, when someone calls you names or spreads rumors about you, when you lose your job or your dog. Only a deeply caring, loving, sensitive God would weep for a friend. The source of heart-pain tears is love.

QUESTIONS

1. What do Jesus' tears say about God's love for you?

2. When was the last time you cried over someone else's pain? What were those tears saying?

LIFELINE

Empathy means feeling someone else's pain and caring deeply for the person. Home is the "Empathy Capital" of your life.

SECURITY
(John 11:47-52)

Yesterday a proud mother came and told me about her daughter, Janis, who was running for junior-class president. Janis was well liked in her public high school and prepared an excellent campaign. At the completion of her "make it or break it" 20-minute campaign speech in front of the entire student body, the panel of judges asked her the leading question, "Janis, who is your hero?" Janis, knowing that her truthful response would alienate many students and lose her precious votes, responded in a heartbeat, "My hero is undoubtedly Jesus Christ, Who died for my sins."

Last week at a youth-group party, Jill, a seventh grader and a close friend of mine, told me how tough junior-high social life was. She was amazed, when she went to her first junior-high party, that a boy had brought some things that were against her morals. Almost everyone told him how cool that was, but Jill knew it was wrong. Risking her popularity and being called a freak, she called her mom to come get her.

QUESTIONS

1. What security were the Jewish leaders afraid of losing with Jesus in town?

2. How did Jesus shake their security?

3. How does being a Christian put your temporary security at risk?

4. What would cause you to hide your Christianity?

LIFELINE

Let's encourage each other to build our security in Christ.

PARADES
(John 12:12-16)

Kids of all ages wait in line for days to buy tickets to a Garth Brooks concert. Sixteen people are smothered almost to death as 50,000 young people press toward the stage at a Guns 'N Roses concert. Tens of thousands scream until they're breathless when Amy Grant, Michael W. Smith, or D.C. Talk play a show. What would we do if Jesus came to town?

Rock stars travel in personal jets. Jesus came on a donkey.

Rock stars make thousands of dollars a day. They could drive to their concerts on streets of gold. Jesus rode into Jerusalem on streets covered with palm leaves.

Rock stars are raised up on stages arrayed with hundreds of lights. Jesus was raised up on a Roman cross.

Rock stars will be forgotten almost before they play their last chorus. Jesus' song of love will be a number-one hit forever.

QUESTIONS

1. What would people do if Jesus came to your town?

2. What star would you go across town to see?

3. Why did the crowd say on Palm Sunday, "Blessed is He Who comes in the name of the Lord"?

LIFELINE

Give Jesus the welcome He deserves in your home today.

THE PACK
(John 12:23-28)

Jim Ryun is a great fellow with a terrific heart. He wanted to run track but was too slow his ninth-grade year, so he got cut from the team. The setback increased his determination, and he trained even harder. He ran for hours every day. When asked if he was in pain, he would say, "Yes, but I've learned to run with the pain." Jim was the first high-school runner to run a four-minute mile. He held the world record in the mile for 15 years. He never won a gold medal in the Olympics, however.

I was at the Olympics in Munich, Germany, watching Jim run for the U.S.A. track team when a tragic event occurred. As Jim rounded the curve on the last lap of the race, he got caught in a pack of runners and was tripped. He fell in sheer pain, and although he was the best in the world, he finished last. His champion's spirit never dimmed, however. He continues to be one of the greatest men I've ever known.

The pack in your life are the peers who surround you. The influence they exert over you to try to get you to do what they want is called *peer pressure*. Peer pressure kills more dreams than any other agent in teens' lives.

QUESTIONS

1. How did Jesus stay out of the pack?

2. What "finish line" kept Him in focus?

3. What is the pack that's trying to pressure you right now?

4. How can you avoid getting trapped?

LIFELINE

Let's help keep each other aware of the pack and focused on the finish line.

APPROVAL OF MEN
(John 12:37-43)

Eric, Joey, Brian B., Craig, Bryan G., Jason, Brandon, and Ryan met at my home every Friday before school from ninth grade until they graduated from high school. They studied the Bible and learned to be Christian leaders in their school. We had a blast together. If anyone missed, they got a donut in their locker (in their shoe, in a book, in their sports bag). "The Guys" made some strong commitments to each other and to God. Although they went to public school, where drinking was cool and sex was rampant, they made a pact not to drink and to treat girls with respect.

They weren't invited to the "fun" parties at the lake, and people often called them names behind their backs. But during their senior year, four of them were elected captains of the football team, three led the basket-ball team, two led the golf team, one received the school spirit award, and one was chosen "Most Outstanding Senior." The school won the all-sports trophy for its conference because they pulled the school together like glue.

The approval of men was not their worry. The approval of God was far more important. That school will never be the same.

QUESTIONS

1. Why is the approval of men often more valued than the approval of God?

2. How do grown-ups struggle with wanting man's approval over God's?

3. Why is God's approval more important?

4. What can you do today to go after God's approval?

LIFELINE

Let's commit this family to seek first *God's* approval.

WASHING FEET
(John 13:3-5)

The dishes get dirty three times a day. Who's going to wash them? The front porch is filled with leaves every time the wind blows. Who's going to sweep it? The dog wets the rug. The baby needs a bottle. The lights are on in the back room. Dad had a hard day at the office. Mom's back is killing her. Larry just got cut from the basketball team. Angie missed becoming a cheerleader by one vote.

Opportunities for "foot washing" are all around the house. Golden, wonderful opportunities to demonstrate the God Who lives in your heart are readily available.

Look at the verses again: Jesus, even though He knew He was God, did the job of the meanest servant. Wow! How easy it is to let a parent serve, to let a wife serve, to let the youngest kid serve, and to hold a position of authority over others.

How exciting, fun, and fulfilling it is to "wash feet" and seize the opportunities God gives us each day to express our care to those we love. Washing feet is the mortar that holds the bricks of a house together. Washing feet is the heart in the Valentine card and the Christ in the Christmas card. When Dorothy said in *The Wizard of Oz*, "There's no place like home," she was speaking of a house full of foot washers of all ages.

QUESTIONS

1. Why is it hard to be a foot washer?

2. What are some practical ways to wash feet in a home?

3. What did Jesus' foot-washing episode say about God's love for you and me?

LIFELINE

Get creative! Wash someone's feet today!

THE BROKEN FINGER
(John 13:21-26)

A joke is told about the man in great pain who went to the doctor. The doctor said to the man, "Where do you hurt?"

The man replied, "Doctor, I hurt *everywhere*."

"Show me where."

The man placed his right forefinger on his knee and said, "Doctor, every time I touch my knee, I hurt bad." Then he touched his forehead. "Every time I touch my head, I hurt bad." Then he pressed his finger to his chest. "Every time I touch my chest, I hurt bad." Then he touched his nose. "Every time I touch my nose, I hurt bad."

The doctor took the man's hand and said, "Buddy, let me examine your finger." One close look was all it took, and the doctor exclaimed, "You crazy man! You've got a broken finger."

So much for jokes, but isn't sin exactly like a broken finger? Everything you touch hurts! If you make money, you become greedy. If you make a friendship or go on a date, the relationship turns sour. If you succeed or get a compliment, you get a big head. The surface problem worries you, and you can't figure it out until someone points out your "broken finger": the sin in your heart.

QUESTIONS

1. What are some ways we betray Jesus?

2. How is betrayal a sin?

3. What was the root of Judas's sin?

4. Why is sin a direct assault on God?

LIFELINE

Let's purpose in our hearts to be loyal to Jesus every day, in every way.

WHOSE WAY?
(World Religions)
(John 14:1-7)

America has over 1,800 active religious cults; each one has a leader who claims to be the way to God. These cults all lower Jesus to less than He truly is and elevate their own leaders to more than they were intended to be. They all claim to have a special word from God, and each commits a drastic sin when they add to or replace scripture with their own beliefs, supposedly obtained from "divine revelation." (See Resource H for more detailed information.)

Joseph Smith, founder of the Mormon Church, said, "All Christian denominations are wrong and their creeds are an abomination in God's sight." Church father Joseph Fielding Smith said, "There is no salvation without accepting Joseph Smith."

Shirley MacLaine, spokesperson for the New Age movement, said, "I know that I exist, therefore I AM. I know that the God-source exists, therefore It IS. Since I am part of that force, then I Am that I AM."

Mary Baker Eddy, founder of the Church of Christian Science, said in her "Bible," *Science and Health*, "The material blood of Jesus was no more efficacious to cleanse from sin when it was shed upon 'the accursed tree,' than it was when it was flowing in His veins as He went daily about His Father's business."

The Watchtower Bible of the Jehovah's Witnesses teaches that Jesus was not God incarnate and the doctrine of the Trinity is false doctrine. (Jesus said, "I and My Father are one," and "If you have seen Me, you have seen the Father.")

These religions are all tragically mistaken, because Jesus stated simply and firmly about Himself, "I am the (only) Way, the (only) Truth, the (only) Life. No one gets to the Father except by Me." The first commandment also warns, "Thou shalt have no other gods before Me."

QUESTIONS

1. Why is Jesus the only way for sinful man to spend eternity with a holy God?

2. Why do people follow cult leaders?

3. What is wrong with cults and other world religions?

LIFELINE

Many people who join cults are better followers of their faith than Christians are of theirs. How can we change that in our home?

IN GOD WE TRUST
(John 14:18-31)

I guess I'm sort of a second dad to Shannon Marketic, who's even prettier on the inside than she is on the outside. Her outside is beautiful enough to have recently brought her the Miss U.S.A. title. But what I like best is her passion to put God first in her life!

While traveling the country as Miss U.S.A., Shannon had lots of chances to sign autographs for youthful admirers. Beneath her name, she'd always put her favorite Bible verse or say something clever to let a fan know that her first love was her Lord and Savior.

The Miss U.S.A. Committee didn't approve of her declaring her first love; it wasn't "politically correct" to talk about Jesus anymore. So Shannon tried something new. When a teenager asked for an autograph, Shannon would get out a dollar bill, sign it, and circle the words "In God We Trust." I asked Shannon if her idea worked. She laughed and said, "Yes, it works, but it gets expensive after a while."

After her Miss U.S.A. reign ended, Shannon moved to Hollywood, where the new wave of sleazy movies beckoned her talents and beauty. Though completely broke, Shannon turned down her first million-plus-dollar movie offer confidently because, though it was only a PG or PG-13, it had one bedroom scene and a four-letter word that would cause her to compromise her Christian convictions.

QUESTIONS

1. Jesus knew we'd be put to the test as Christians, so He gave us the Holy Spirit to live in our hearts as believers. How does the Holy Spirit help us stand for what we believe in?

2. What opportunities to witness for Christ is God giving you these days?

3. There's only one Shannon, but each of us faces equal temptations to compromise each day. What are those for you?

LIFELINE

When you accepted Christ, the Holy Spirit came into your heart. Give Him an even better home today.

FRIENDS WITH GOD
(John 15:9-15)

It's an awesome thought to ponder: We are friends with God. Hmm . . .

Have you ever had a truly best friend? One who would never let you down? One who was always there when you needed him? One who always brought the best out in you? One who'd never talk behind your back?

A soldier I know was in a bloody battle in Vietnam. He and three other guys were in a foxhole, and the enemy threw in a hand grenade. In an instant, one of the soldiers dove on the grenade and absorbed the explosion so his friends could live. The unselfish soldier died instantly, but his commitment to friendship will live forever.

It's easy to see that God is big and powerful and mighty and a keeper of the rules, but why is it so hard to see Him as a friend . . . a best friend?

Jesus died to give you and me one central message: "I'm the best friend you'll ever have."

Friend is a word that's explained best in the Bible. It's a relationship that calls for "lovingkindness," which means that the amount of love you have for someone is based not on what they've done for you but on what *you* have done for *them!*

QUESTIONS

1. How much has Jesus done for you? How much does He love you?

2. Can you honestly call Jesus a "best friend"? Why or why not?

3. What kind of friend are you to Him?

LIFELINE

The best way to demonstrate Jesus' level of friendship is to give that kind of friendship to each other.

THE COUNSELORS
(John 15:26)

She had been abused as a small child, and her sadness and depression still lingered across her precious 19-year-old face. I picked up on her sadness one day as she diligently served meals in our camp dining hall. We talked for a long while, and amid many tears she let me in on her seemingly unsolvable problems.

With much assurance of God's amazing unconditional love, I told her that His Word and His Spirit were her constant companions. She literally had a problem solver living in her heart. She began to memorize God's Word to feed her mind her Counselor's thoughts. She prayed to God constantly to fill her heart with her Counselor's love. She trusted God continuously to fill her soul with her Counselor's assurance.

A week went by and I saw a smile. A month went by and I saw a happy heart. A year went by and I saw her dance like a little kid at Christmas.

The Holy Spirit comes into you the moment you accept Christ as Savior. He is a humble person and always lifts up Jesus. His ministry is to make you like Christ.

QUESTIONS

1. What are other names for the Holy Spirit?

2. How is He tied into the Trinity?

3. Why did God give us His Spirit?

4. How can His ability as a counselor help you today?

LIFELINE

When you think about the Holy Spirit, you can agree with the apostle Paul when he said, "Thanks be to God for the indescribable gift."

THE HOLY SPIRIT—GOD'S VOICE INSIDE
(John 16:7-14)

The Christian psychologist specialized in helping people break their bad habits, relieve the stress they were experiencing, and get their lives back on track. A young lady entered his office one day with eyes that told a story of a life of misery and sin. As she sat down, the counselor asked what was wrong. She told him of her godless lifestyle, her guilty conscience, and how miserable she was because of it all.

The psychologist asked her if she wanted some help to change her ways, and she quickly replied, "No, I don't want to change. I just want you to weaken my conscience."

Little did she know that a conscience is like the nerves in the hand that make one pull away from a hot flame before it sears the skin. And a Christian's conscience is aided by the Spirit of God, Who guides a believer into the things that are right and leads him or her away from mistakes caused by sin. When your conscience speaks, you'd better listen!

QUESTIONS

1. How does the Holy Spirit speak to us?

2. What part does God's Word play in our consciences?

3. What happens when we ignore the voice inside?

4. How does the Holy Spirit glorify Jesus?

LIFELINE

As we keep God's Word alive in the home, we'll keep our consciences sharp.

EVERY DAY
(John 16:23-24)

Every day—well, almost every day—America bakes 2,739,726 Dunkin' Donuts and makes 17,600,000 Tootsie Rolls AND 100,000,000 M&M's. Each day, 79,250,000 Americans read the comics, while 86,202,000 read the sports page.[3] I don't know how many families do what you're doing right now every day, but I'm afraid you may be in the happy minority. It's a good bet that the satisfaction you'll receive will outlast any bag of M&M's you'll ever eat, even if you're a slow eater.

You can be sure of one thing, though: Jesus prayed every day He was on earth. Taking time to pray daily is without a doubt the most important thing you'll ever do. Donuts don't make happy families; prayer does. Tootsie Rolls don't buy love; prayer does. M&M's don't make dreams come true; prayer does.

Jesus said prayers are best when they're honest, from the heart, simple, and not done for show. Best of all, He promised that God hears and answers all of them . . . in His way, in His time. Prayers are hindered only when they are selfish or not based on faith in our Savior.

QUESTIONS

1. If God could accomplish everything He wanted to anyway, why did He give us the gift of prayer?

2. Why did Jesus (being God the Son) pray to God the Father?

3. Why is prayer such an important part of our lives?

4. What do you pray for the most? Why?

LIFELINE

Let's pray together as a family as often as we're together.

ONE NATION UNDER GOD
(John 17:1-6)

The phrase "One nation under God" is being thrown out of the pledge of allegiance in many public places. The Boy Scouts are under legal fire for saying "I will do my duty to God and my country." The United Way is refusing to give them money because they won't allow avowed homosexuals into their leadership. The Girl Scouts have taken God out of their pledge.

Today it is illegal in some cities to put up a nativity scene on government grounds because courts say it is a violation of the First Amendment. But it is also illegal to deny government funding, according to the same First Amendment, to a national art fund that paints pornographic pictures of Jesus and makes fun of His work on the cross.

The laws that govern our land are being twisted from their original God-fearing meaning to an anti-God bias that makes it difficult for Christians to live and worship God with their daily lives.

Jesus showed deep reverence and awe in His devotion to God. Our Founding Fathers knew that reverence. This nation was not founded by religionists but by Christians, on the gospel of Jesus Christ. Benjamin Franklin said, "He who introduces into public affairs the principles of primitive Christianity will change the face of the world." Thomas Jefferson said, "Of all the systems of morality, ancient or modern, which have come under my observation, none appear to men to be so pure as that of Jesus. No power over the freedom of religion is delegated to the United States government." (See Resource I.)

Even though it is more difficult today, we can still give God the honest respect He deserves.

QUESTIONS

1. How is America turning its back on God?

2. In today's scripture, what did Jesus say that tells us how to reverence God?

3. What did He mean when He said that "eternal life is knowing God"?

LIFELINE

Home is a place where God is highly respected and put in a position of greatest honor.

FAMILY UNITY
(John 17:17-23)

During the height of the Vietnam War, a father and a son (both in the military) watched the battlefield reports carefully from their safe base in the States. Tens of thousands of American soldiers were losing their lives in the fierce battles across the Pacific Ocean. Then the father was called to do a 12-month tour of duty on that very battlefront. He miraculously returned home without injury. A few months later, when his son was called to Vietnam to fight, the father asked the commanding officer if he could take his son's place so his son could stay home. The substitution was approved, and the dad returned to battle, risking his life every day, to demonstrate his love to his boy.

Today Johnny is packing up his home and his family and leaving his wonderful job to move 400 miles so that he can be close to his mom, who is fighting for her life in her final days on earth.

Andy's brother is a paraplegic. Each day Andy feeds him, clothes him, and returns home every second possible to meet his many daily needs.

The world sees Jesus in our homes when our families stick together and sacrificially love each other in ways that amaze the unbeliever.

QUESTIONS

1. How does our love for each other bear witness of Christ?

2. How can we demonstrate our devotion to each other?

3. What part does God play in family unity?

LIFELINE

They'll know we're His disciples if we really love each other.

HOLY
(John 18:1-6)

During a wonderful era of early Jewish tradition (long before copy machines), a scribe would make copies of the Holy Scriptures by taking his feather pen (quill) and carefully, accurately, and perfectly hand copying God's Word from one scroll to another. When the scribe would get to the word *God*, he would stop, pray, undress, take a bath, put on clean clothes, get a new quill, and then go back to his work and write the word.

In contrast, today we defy God's third commandment by throwing His name around as if it were dirt. We take His name in vain in our conversations, on TV, in movies, and in books. "Oh, my God!" "My God!" "Jesus Christ!" people exclaim when they're mad, upset, or just want words to fill in the blanks of day-to-day conversation.

You don't need to bathe and change clothes to say "God," but Jesus made it clear that God is holy and awesome and should be placed in a position of reverence and highest respect.

QUESTIONS

1. Who is speaking through us when we say "Oh, my God!" or "God!" as a trivial exclamation?

2. What did God mean when He said, "Thou shall not take my name in vain"?

3. What does "holy God" mean?

4. When Jesus said, "I am he," what was He saying?

LIFELINE

Let's make this home a temple of the holy God.

GOING IN THE WRONG DIRECTION
(John 18:25-27)

Our sixth-grade basketball team was good because we had Bill Gilliam. He was taller than everyone, faster than everyone, and stronger than everyone. His only difficulty was that he'd get confused sometimes when he became excited during a game!

It has been decades since I was in sixth grade, but I'll never forget one particular night. We were playing Hearne, Texas, in a tournament, and boy, did we want to win! Bill tipped the opening jump ball so hard that it hit Jerry Davis's knee and bounced back to Bill. In the thrill of the moment, Bill dribbled the ball in the wrong direction all the way to the wrong basket (needless to say, no one on Hearne's team tried to stop him), where he made an easy layup. His up-stretched arms of self-praise fell over his head in self-pity when he saw everyone pointing and laughing at the hilarious mistake he had made.

QUESTIONS

1. How is sin like taking the ball to the wrong basket?

2. Hebrews 11:25 says that sin satisfies for "a short time." Why does it look good at first?

3. How can you actually turn back when you're going in the wrong direction?

4. Denying Jesus is going in the wrong direction. How do we deny Jesus today?

LIFELINE

Let's work hard together to keep this home going in the right direction.

DON'T FORGET THE CROSS
(John 18:28-32)

An older friend worked closely over the years with evangelist Billy Graham. This friend told me that one evening during one of Dr. Graham's earlier crusades, Dr. Graham left the crusade disheartened over his own perception that it was weak and ineffective.

An old German man happened to encounter Dr. Graham at that timely moment and firmly, but lovingly, confronted the young evangelist with this exhortation: "Dr. Graham, you forgot the Cross tonight. Don't forget the Cross, Billy! Don't forget the Cross!"

Those words became a guide for Billy Graham, and many years later he (who has personally led more people into a saving faith in Jesus Christ than any man who ever lived) said that his crusades always have their greatest success in reaching the lost when he talks about the Cross. He never lost sight of those simple words: "Don't forget the Cross, Billy! Don't forget the Cross!"

QUESTIONS

1. Why is it that the simple shape of the crossed pieces of wood is the most respected symbol in the world?

2. What does the Cross mean to you?

3. What happens to you when you forget the Cross in your daily life?

LIFELINE

Just as Jesus loved us to the death, let's sacrificially love each other today.

TAKE IT THERE, PUT IT THERE, AND LEAVE IT THERE
(John 19:4-6)

At our summer camp for forgotten kids, 300 teenagers from the inner city listened with question marks in their eyes as I attempted to explain the miracle of the Man Who died on the cross. With a large ax, I hacked a 15-foot elm tree into a cross. Huge wood chips flew through the air into the silent crowd of precious kids. As I completed the life-size cross, all of us were challenged to write our sins on a piece of paper and, one by one, nail those sins to the cross. The atmosphere had grown somber and pensive as each kid made his way with hammer and nail to the cross.

The paper display of unknown burdens filled the cross when a teenage boy stopped at my feet . . . troubled . . . scared . . . confused. His paper was covered with hurts and sins that only a Savior could bear.

A dear-hearted street worker put his arm around the teen's shoulder and said, "What's wrong?"

The boy mumbled, "I dunno."

The man pointed to the sin-filled paper, pointed to the hammer and nail, and then motioned carefully to the cross. He said, "Just take it there, put it there, and leave it there."

"That's it?" the boy queried.

"That's all there is to it. Take it there, put it there, and leave it there."

QUESTIONS

1. Why do we try to complicate the simple message of salvation?

2. How could Jesus carry all those sins at once?

3. What happened to those sins that were nailed to the cross?

4. What can you do with your sins today?

LIFELINE

As a family, secretly write down your sins and have a family praise time as you throw them into the fireplace and give them to Jesus.

FINISHING THE RACE
(John 19:17-19)

During George Bush's term as president of the United States, I toured the White House with his receptionist, Kathy Wills. Kathy took me to the historic Oval Office, where the president did his daily work. On top of his desk, in a pencil holder, stood a simple two-by-four-inch American flag glued to a small stick (the kind you buy at Wal-Mart for 49 cents). I asked Kathy why it was there in such a position of prominence. She said it was the president's favorite flag because when he was visiting some wounded soldiers in a military hospital, a severely wounded paratrooper called him over to his bedside. The president greeted the man, and the man gave Mr. Bush the small flag. The president thanked him, and the soldier shook his hand, looked him in the eye, and said from the bottom of his dedicated heart, "Mr. President, my only regret is that I cannot fight again."

Kathy said that of all the famous and invaluable historical relics in the Oval Office, that flag meant more to the president than anything else.

QUESTIONS

1. How did Jesus live so that He could die with no regrets?

2. Why do you suppose that flag meant so much to the president?

3. How can we be as dedicated to God as the soldier was to his country?

LIFELINE

What kind of "flag" could we give God when our battle is over? What will we tell Him when He takes it?

MUCH LOVE, LONG WALK
(John 19:30-37)

The story is told of a kind missionary lady who gave her life to teach African kids how to read, write, and understand a Man named Jesus. In a secluded country along the African coast, the missionary spent an unusually large amount of time with a nine-year-old orphan boy, walking him down the road from illiteracy to the wonderful world of knowledge. As the boy grew in his skills, he grew in his appreciation and love for the teacher who had given him such a gift.

One Christmas, the boy worried and pondered over his desire to give his beloved teacher a special gift to express his heart. Without any money, what could he do? Then a smile swept across his face as he remembered a rare seashell he had read about that could be found on a secluded beach three days' walk from his beach hut. A week before Christmas, he set out on his long walk of love.

Early on Christmas morning, the teacher heard a knock on her door. She opened the door and saw the boy, who had a giant beaming smile of success across his face. He opened his hand to present his valuable, unusual gift.

"Here, teacher. It is for you."

"Oh, this is so beautiful. For me? Wow, where did you get it?"

"Three days' walk down beach."

"Why? Why did you go get it for me?"

"Much love."

"I know, but you walked so far!" the teacher exclaimed in amazement. To which the boy humbly replied, "Much love . . . long walk."

QUESTIONS

1. Why does much love mean a long walk?

2. How much was Jesus' love for us? How long was His walk?

3. How can we, like the little boy, make a long walk to thank Jesus for what He's done for us?

LIFELINE

How can we make long walks regularly to show our appreciation for family members?

NOT FINISHED YET
(John 20:1-8)

Abraham Lincoln lost at least six elections before he became one of the most famous presidents in U.S. history.

Willie Mays struck out his first 29 times at bat before he became one of the greatest major league batters of all time.

Jim Abbott was born with only one hand, but he pitched the victorious Gold Medal game for the United States Olympic team and pitched a rare no-hitter for the New York Yankees.

Michael Jordan was cut from his ninth-grade basketball team because he wasn't good enough.

Warren Moon's junior-high coach said he "stunk" as a quarterback.

Joe Montana was knocked out of the game "permanently" before he led the 49ers to a Super Bowl championship.

Jesus was buried as a dead man before He rose from the dead on Easter morning.

Your greatest dreams will die before their most glorious moment. You'll be knocked down every time you dream big. But down is not out. Great success comes after great failure. That's when God gets all the glory.

QUESTIONS

1. Describe a time when you thought your dream had died.

2. Why does God let visions die before they are completely successful?

3. What's the difference between being down and being out?

LIFELINE

When someone you know is in "the tomb," remember Easter.

WINGS
(John 20:27-29)

When an airplane races down a runway, the wind rushing over the top of the wings creates a vacuum under the wings. The air that rushes up to fill the vacuum under the wings pushes the wings upward and gives the plane the lift it needs to get off the ground.

As a Christian, God gives you wings to fly, and even though you don't have to run to activate those wings, the more you swiftly activate the wings, the higher you will go. Faith flies when you trust God with your needs, your worries, and your plans. Scripture flies when you read it carefully and do what it says. Prayer flies when you talk to God with a sincerely believing heart. Witnessing flies when you live a life that others can see is unique and not like the crowd. Fellowship flies when you keep the right friends and spend time with other believers.

QUESTIONS

1. Why did Thomas need to touch Jesus to believe?

2. How can you put faith in Jesus if you've never seen Him?

3. What's your favorite lift God gives you? Why?

4. Why do you have to put your wings in motion before you can fly?

LIFELINE

What can we do to put lift under each other's wings?

JUST DO IT—JESUS' WAY
(John 21:1-6)

My best friends are fishermen! Aren't yours?

Brady is a fisherman. He "fishes" for basketball goals every Monday and Thursday night during basketball season. Courtney is a fisherman. She "fishes" for good crowd support as she cheerleads at her school. Ryan is a fisherman. He "fishes" for good art projects as he uses his artistic talents to their fullest. Michael is a fisherman. He "fishes" for songs to entertain kids across the country. Scott is a fisherman. He "fishes" for fair, honest ways to help his business grow. Debbie is a fisherman. She "fishes" for ways to make her home a home that's full of love and pleasing to God.

In a way, we all fish for a living. Every day we decide from which side of the boat to cast our nets. The left side of the boat is man's way of fishing. It says that successful fishing happens when you join the crowd in gossip, cheating, telling lies, drinking, going to questionable movies, and taking advantage of other people to "catch fish." Almost everybody has fished on the left side of the boat. Sometimes it feels good over there, but the net always comes up empty in the long run.

Jesus still manifests Himself today through His Word in our minds, in our consciences. He still calls to us to throw our nets on the right side of the boat. It seems awkward with everyone else fishing on the left side, but (just as the disciples learned) the catch is so abundant there, you can hardly get it to shore.

QUESTIONS

1. What is everybody fishing for?

2. What is a "great catch" of fish to you?

3. Why is fishing so much better on the right side of the boat?

4. Why do most people fish on the left?

LIFELINE

Every fisherman needs someone to remind him or her where the good fishing is located.

DESIRE
(John 21:15-17)

A poor boy in India sought out a great Indian sage (wise man) to ask him a very pressing question. When the boy found the sage, he said to him, "Sir, how might I find the kingdom of God?"

The sage looked carefully into the boy's eyes and said, "You don't want it bad enough."

The boy departed with great disappointment. But he returned the next day and again asked, "Sir, how might I find the kingdom of God?"

Again the sage said, "Boy, you don't want it bad enough."

The boy came back the third day and repeated his question.

The sage replied, "Meet me at the river tomorrow."

The next day the boy was at the river, ready for his answer. The sage walked into the water with the boy until they were waist deep. The sage abruptly dunked the boy under the water and held him until he ran out of breath. The boy jerked his head up, gasping for air.

The old sage said to him, "Boy, when you were under the water, what did you want more than anything?"

"Oxygen, sir, oxygen. I wanted air!"

"Well, boy, when you desire the kingdom of God as much as you desired that breath, you'll find it!"

QUESTIONS

1. It's easy to say "I love God," but to show it by loving others takes great desire. Why?

2. What did Jesus mean when He said to Peter, "Tend my lambs"?

3. Why does loving Jesus mean loving others?

LIFELINE

Love begins at home. If it doesn't happen there, it can't truly happen anywhere.

INTRODUCTION TO JAMES

Although there are four men named James in the New Testament, careful study leads us to believe that the author of this wonderful letter was James, son of Mary and Joseph, the half-brother of Jesus.[4]

Many scholars believe James wrote this book between a.d. 45-50, only 10 to 15 years after his dramatic conversion upon his brother Jesus' miraculous resurrection.

This letter is what I call "grace on wheels," because it's all about what a person does (by grace) after he has been saved (by grace). James rightfully teaches that faith works! God's grace doesn't sit still. Grace delivers grace to others. A family study of this book will bring tremendous joy to your home as each member serves the other "until college do us part."

JOY IN THE MORNING
(James 1:2-5)

My mom and dad had dreamed and prayed that they would have three children someday. The first baby was a precious boy named Frank. Because of complications during childbirth, Frank lived for only one hour. Mom was terribly sad, but she knew that she and Frank belonged to God and that her heavenly Father had a plan for the seemingly tragic death. Mom and Dad knew the truth of Psalm 16:11: "You will fill me with joy in your presence." Frank awaits our ultimate family reunion with God.

As the years went by, my mom had three more boys, and her dream came true. The third son was me. If Frank would have lived, I probably wouldn't be here today.

Our family has had many bumps and bruises. We've shed countless tears and clung to God in prayer, but Mom and Dad find joy in all circumstances because with one baby in heaven and three boys on earth, God has shown them that He is sovereign in the most difficult times.

QUESTIONS

1. What is one trial that you are experiencing right now?

2. How have you seen God turn a trial into a joyful experience?

3. When trials come, your reaction to them will make you either bitter or better. What kind of reaction makes you bitter? What kind of reaction makes you better?

4. How do trials produce endurance, and why is endurance such an essential quality to possess?

LIFELINE

As a family, how can we help each other become better and not bitter in times of trial?

TACKLING TEMPTATION
(James 1:12-16)

Two and a half months ago, our TV set broke. Boy, did that make me mad! (Ha!) I'm so mad, I can't seem to find the phone number for the TV repairman. I'm so mad, I keep forgetting to get it fixed! I'm so mad, I think it's the greatest thing that's happened in our home since we started this family!

TV (Temptation Vision) . . . In the average American home, television pipes over 180,000 rapes, murders, and acts of violence, beer commercials, sexual innuendoes, and so on, into the minds of every man, woman, and child who lives there every year. Then we wonder why we're tempted to argue, lust, fight, and such. William James, the father of modern psychology, said, "Truth is something that happens to an idea. . . . [I]t becomes true when it is verified (by repetition)."[5] The polluting influence of television is perhaps one reason that 12 million Americans are infected with a sexually transmitted disease each year and teenage AIDS cases double every 14 months, and why more college students die of alcohol-related deaths than the number who will go on to graduate school.[6]

QUESTIONS

1. When we pray to God to "lead us not into temptation," what are we asking for?

2. If God doesn't tempt you, how does temptation come to us, and what are the results?

3. Besides TV, what other sources of temptation do we expose ourselves to?

4. What is the difference between trials and temptations?

LIFELINE

As a family, how can we help each other fight temptation in this home and in our private lives?

JUST DO IT!
(James 1:22-25)

One evening, five-year-old Cooper asked to memorize Ephesians 6:1. But when he found out it said, "Children, obey your parents in the Lord, for this is right," he smiled and said, "That verse isn't there. You just made that up."

The Nike slogan "Just Do It" sells in excess of $3.6 billion worth of shoes and sports accessories annually.[7] Slogans sell shoes; slogans don't save souls.

Although James didn't wear Nikes, this "Just Do It" passage is the heartbeat of his epistle. Nike says, "Don't talk about jogging. Go out and jog this morning!" James says, "Don't just read about giving. Put some money in a piggy bank for the less fortunate today!" Don't talk about a better prayer life. Pray often today! Don't talk about that overstuffed closet. Thin it out and give some things away!

Thanks, Cooper, for the joke; but thanks, James, for the idea. Thanks, God, for the example. Thanks, Nike, for reminding us every day.

QUESTIONS

1. Why is it not enough to be a "hearer of the Word only"?

2. What is an example of something you've been reading in God's Word that you're ready to "just do it"?

3. Can anyone think of someone in need whom we could help as a family project? How could we help him or her?

LIFELINE

Does anyone in the family need an "accountability partner" in some area of life to help them follow through with "be doers of the Word, not just hearers"?

UP WITH THE UNDERDOG
(James 2:1-4)

I've learned so much from my daddy that an encyclopedia couldn't contain it all. Ninety-nine percent of what I learned from him was what he did. (Like most kids, I didn't appreciate all I learned from him until I had my own kids. My, how I wish I had listened more!) He's 80 years old now, and he's still my hero. I'm still learning from him!

My daddy never told me to love the underdog or the less fortunate, but I will never forget watching Daddy meet the garbage collectors at the back door of our house every Monday and Friday morning and give them each a cup of hot coffee and a sweet roll, along with a huge smile and words of encouragement. Sometimes he'd come home from work without his coat or shoes or without any money because he'd met a janitor or someone less fortunate who needed what he had. In church or at social gatherings, he automatically finds his way to the "lowest man on the totem pole." Those humble poor people are always Daddy's best friends. Funny thing about it all . . . Daddy is the happiest man I know.

QUESTIONS

1. Why do we tend to push aside the less fortunate?

2. Why is it a sin to show partiality?

3. What is our responsibility as representatives of Christ toward the less fortunate?

4. Specifically, what are ways to show our love and care for the less fortunate around us?

LIFELINE

Can each of us name someone less fortunate we come into contact with and how we can show him or her Christ's love?

FAITH THAT WORKS
(James 2:14-18)

An old friend (a true "relic" of a man) ran a sawmill where I used to buy my lumber for building projects. Mr. Plummer, in his mid-80s, was living out the final days of his life in the beautiful Ozark Mountains. I spent hours visiting with this savvy old character, and once I asked him where he went to church. He scowled and told me he would never go to a church because the people of one church bought some lumber from him 30 years ago and cheated him on money they were supposed to pay. Mr. Plummer died not knowing Christ.

What use are beautiful prayers and hymns if they're not matched by godly living? What good are Bibles in a home if they're not read? What good is a huge savings account if it's not used for those in need? What good is a smile that's not shared? What use is a hug or an "I love you" that's not given today? What use is faith that doesn't work?

QUESTIONS

1. What is faith that works? Why is this kind of faith a true faith, a sincere faith, a saving faith?

2. Why is faith dead if it doesn't have arms and legs?

3. Bread and butter, peanut butter and jelly, faith and works—why do they come in pairs?

LIFELINE

Yesterday we talked about the less fortunate. Can someone tell how he or she put faith into action in this area?

TERRIFIC OR TERRIBLE TONGUE
(James 3:2-8)

Gossip, cursing, negative comments, sarcasm . . . or encouragement, enthusiasm, compliments, praise.

I have a friend named Snake who actually trains rattlesnakes. He doesn't turn them into play toys, but he subdues them and makes a type of pet out of them. When I was a kid, the most fun part of going to the circus was seeing the tamed lions, elephants, and bears. My kids and I love to ride horses together and run those big, beautiful animals across the pasture and through the woods. At our sports camps, wind surfing has become quite a popular sport, as we catch the wind and skip quickly across the water.

Harnessing the wind, guiding a horse, training a wild beast, subduing a rattlesnake—all are possible with time, patience, and a few tools. But our tongues continue to hurt others with poorly chosen words.

On the other side of the coin, what a great encouragement it is to get a love letter, a pat on the back, or an "I'm proud of you" or "Good job!" from someone I care about! An encouraging word brings sunshine to a cloudy day!

QUESTIONS

1. Why is taming the tongue more difficult than taming a lion?

2. Why is the tongue like a match to a forest fire?

3. How can God help you use the rudder of your personality, the tongue, wisely?

4. How can we each keep our tongues on the good, happy side in our home?

LIFELINE

Each person contribute one positive idea and one negative idea of how the tongue can be used for good or evil.

WISE AS AN OWL
(James 3:13-17)

As recorded in 1 Kings 3, two women came to Israel's King Solomon and asked him to decide a matter. It seems the two women, who lived in the same house, had given birth within three days of each other.

Unfortunately, one night shortly thereafter, one of the women rolled over on her baby in her sleep and smothered him to death. She awoke and realized what had happened while the other woman was still sleeping, and then she quietly switched the babies. In the morning, that second woman figured out what her housemate had done, and she demanded the return of her living child.

Now the two women were standing in front of Solomon, asking for his judgment since neither of them could prove the living newborn was hers. But how was Solomon going to ascertain the truth?

In a display of great, God-given wisdom, Solomon came up with a test. He ordered that a sword be brought and the baby be cut in two. That way, he said, each woman could have half.

As Solomon expected, the true mother of the living child wanted him to live more than she wanted to keep him, so she begged the king to spare the boy's life. The other, hard-hearted woman said, "Neither I nor you shall have him. Cut him in two!"

Then the king commanded, "Give the living baby to the first woman. Do not kill him; she is his mother" (1 Kings 3:26-27).

Proverbs 2 reveals four great things about wisdom. The Lord gives wisdom. If you seek wisdom from God's Word, you will find it. Wisdom is a treasure to be sought like gold. And the person who finds wisdom will be greatly blessed.

QUESTIONS

1. What is godly wisdom, and how can we get it?

2. What is the difference between being smart and being wise?

3. Why do selfishness and greed let you know you're not being wise?

LIFELINE

If wisdom comes from God's truths, let's work together today to speak wisely to each other.

FRIEND OR FOE
(James 4:4-8)

Shaquille O'Neal and Michael Jordan basketball cards are getting more valuable every year. At the peak of Jordan's success, he was the most popular man in America to kids. Some Mickey Mantle baseball cards are worth hundreds of dollars today. Football fans will pay a lot for autographs from Roger Staubach, Terry Bradshaw, or Joe Montana. Everybody loves a winner. People want to be on the winning side in a game or war.

God is a winner. He always coaches the winning team. He never loses. Satan is a loser. He is, and will be, ultimately defeated.

Satan gains your everlasting destruction by giving you temporary highs through such things as partying, sex, and money. But God gives you everlasting joy through helping you to reject Satan's bribes and to recognize as counterfeit the happiness he offers you.

You can choose God's team, and stay on His team, by refusing to accept Satan's alluring temptations.

QUESTIONS

1. Why does everybody love a winner?

2. Specifically, how do you draw nearer to God? How do you resist the devil?

3. What is God like as the coach of a winning team?

4. What is Satan like as the coach of a losing team?

LIFELINE

As parents and children, let's lovingly point out to each other today things that surround us that are of God and things that are of Satan.

THE MYSTERIOUS LADY
(James 4:11-12)

She always wore a bright red dress and dark sunglasses. Each Wednesday she could be seen at exactly 9:30 A.M. meeting a stocky, bearded man in front of the drugstore, where he would quietly exchange a bottle of pills for a package of dollar bills. As soon as she paid for the pills, the mysterious lady would slip into her BMW and drive quickly away to her tiny house in the country.

No one was ever seen going in or out of the lady's home except a tall, handsome, young man every Friday from 6:30 to 7:30 P.M.

What do you think the lady was up to?

Before you answer, let me explain that this lady's name was Ruth, and she had an eye disorder that made it difficult for her to see in broad daylight. Her father had died the year before, and her best memory of his smile was when she wore red, because it complimented her blonde hair so beautifully. Her mom was bedridden and needed her prescription and weekly doctor's visit to stay alive.

QUESTIONS

1. What did you first think the mysterious lady was up to?

2. Why are we so quick to jump to conclusions and judge others?

3. The boy in school who calls you names is probably missing something at home. What might it be?

4. What is the dangerous side of judging others?

LIFELINE

How can we help each other to refrain from judging others and speaking negatively about them?

ROTTING RICHES
(James 5:1-3)

My friend Norm owns a very large corporation. He has lots and lots of money. Anyone would say that Ol' Norm is a rich man.

Norm gives to 1,600 different ministries, and he pays his employees well. He uses his spare time to do mission work in impoverished countries around the world, and he prays diligently for everyone. He loves his wife, loves his kids and grandkids, loves to pray, and loves to laugh.

Another man I know inherited over $100 million when his father died. He is very tight with his money and spends most of it on himself and his businesses. He has lost over 90 percent of his inheritance in the last 20 years and may end up losing it all. He smiles very little, and he rarely shares the joy of helping other ministries and people in need.

I know a teenager quite well who started a clothing company and now makes about $100,000 a year. Since the beginning, she has given, and continues to give, every cent of what she earns to the needy kids of the world. Even as a child, she would give 25 to 50 percent of her small allowance to her church and to relief ministries.

A dear 10-year-old friend in humble circumstances makes 25 cents a day by memorizing Bible verses. Each quarter goes into a piggy bank for poor inner-city kids.

I know God appreciates the great gifts and the humble gifts equally.

QUESTIONS

1. Jesus warns about the misuse of money more than almost any other single subject. Why?

2. How do you know when you're giving enough?

3. Is it better in God's eyes for a man with a million dollars to give $250,000 or for a young boy with a dollar to give 25 cents? Why?

LIFELINE

As a family, how can we work together to give all that God wants us to give and to use our resources wisely?

PRAYER POWER
(James 5:13-18)

Eight thousand kids shivered like wet puppies as the early spring rain turned the outdoor youth rally into an event that only Noah would have enjoyed. As we tried to make a final "go/no go" decision on holding the music concert in the open-air arena, I stood in the sound and light booth with a group of unbelieving technicians huddled around their cups of coffee.

"Should we call 'er off, Joe?" they teased.

I quoted this passage from James: "Elijah was a man just like us. He prayed earnestly that it would not rain, and it did not rain on the land for three and a half years" (5:17).

"Fellows," I said, "God says that 'the effective prayer of a righteous man accomplishes much!' I'm going to pray that the rain stops."

They laughed. "Yeah, but that was Elijah!"

Elijah's God is my God, I thought. I walked to the sound stage and asked God to let us do the concert. Within 60 seconds, the rain had stopped. We had the rally.

Our youth rally hasn't been rained out once in 17 years. (Rained on, but not out!)

Does it rain or stop raining every time I pray? No. Does everyone get instantly healed every time I pray for people? No. But I've seen God answer every prayer faithfully. Sometimes His answer is "yes," sometimes "no," sometimes "now," sometimes "later."

QUESTIONS

1. Why do you think God invented prayer?

2. What prayer have you seen God answer?

3. What are you praying about today?

4. Why is it good to pray as a group or family?

LIFELINE

Pray together for any suffering and any rejoicing in the family. Commit yourselves to praying for each other often.

CREATION SCIENCE

The Study of the Intelligent Design
of the Universe

Harvard's Nobel prize–winning biologist Dr. George Wald opened a picture window of understanding into the great creation-evolution debate when he said:

> There are only two possible explanations as to how life arose: Spontaneous generation arising to evolution or a supernatural creative act of God. . . . [T]here is no other possibility. Spontaneous generation [a now discarded theory that living organisms can arise from nonlife matter] was scientifically disproved 120 years ago by Louis Pasteur and others, but that just leaves us with only one other possibility . . . that life came as a supernatural act of creation by God, but I can't accept that philosophy because I do not want to believe in God. Therefore I choose to believe in that which I know is scientifically impossible, spontaneous generation leading to evolution.[1]

Did God create the universe according to the Genesis account, or did the cosmos and all therein evolve through naturalistic processes over billions of years without a divine Creator? One thing is certain: Scientists are divided on the issue, and those who try to explain our origin without God do so not because of the evidence, but because, like other humanists, they simply don't want to acknowledge our existence before an all-powerful God.

THE THEORY OF EVOLUTION

The theory of evolution, or Darwinism, was postulated in 1859 by a wayfaring preacher's son, Charles Darwin, who didn't have one scientific degree to his name. Though there was no evidence to support his theory, it was jumped on by atheistic science and continues to have many advocates today.

Evolution teaches various hypotheses, including the Big Bang theory, which surmises that the universe began with a nuclear explosion approximately 20 billion years ago. Then, over the next several billion years, our solar system mysteriously developed.

According to evolutionists, planet earth began its transition from nonlife to life about 4.5 billion years ago, when a pool of lifeless chemicals (pre biotic soup) underwent biogenesis, or spontaneous generation, and a living cell "miraculously" formed. This single cell, over billions of years, somehow reproduced many others, which mutated into higher, more-complex forms of life. Through a process of natural selection, the strongest survived, and the amoeba eventually gave rise to the jellyfish, the jellyfish to the vertebrate fish, the fish to the frog, the frog to the lizard, the lizard to the bird, the cow to the whale, and the ape to modern man.

SCIENTISTS VOICE CONCERNS ABOUT DARWIN'S THEORY

Many of the world's most respected and honored scientists, though for the most part non-Christians, totally disagree with Darwin's theory of the origin and development of life on earth. Unfortunately, their reservations are carefully eliminated from public-school textbooks by humanistic authors, thereby contributing to the growth of a godless society. It is impossible, however, to turn a deaf ear to the observations of these scientific leaders concerning the gross flaws in the theory of evolution, several of which have surfaced since Darwin's death.

The Big Bang Theory

Evolutionist and astrologer Dr. Robert Jastrow, director of the Goddard Institute (NASA) for Space Research, said:

> Most remarkable of all is the fact that in science, as in the Bible, the world begins with an act of creation. That view has not always been held by scientists. Only as a result of the most recent discoveries can we say with a fair degree of confidence that the world has not existed forever; that it began abruptly, without apparent cause, in a blinding event that defies scientific explanation. . . . Now we see how the astronomical evidence leads to a Biblical view of the origin of the world. All the details differ, but the essential elements in the astronomical evidence and the Biblical account of Genesis are the same. The chain of events leading to man commenced suddenly and sharply, at a definite moment in time—in a flash of light and energy.[2]

He concluded:

> For the scientist who has lived by his faith in the power of reason, the story ends like a bad dream. He has scaled the mountain of ignorance, he is about to conquer the highest peak; as he pulls himself over the final rock he is greeted by a band of theologians who have been sitting there for centuries.[3]

Physicist and mathematician Dr. Wolfgang Smith agreed with Jastrow's assessment:

> A growing number of respectable scientists are defecting from the evolutionist camp. . . . [M]oreover, for the most part, these "experts" have abandoned Darwinism, not on the basis of religious faith or biblical persuasions, but on strictly scientific grounds, and in some instances, regretfully.[4]

Prebiotic Soup

Drs. Charles B. Thaxton (chemist, Iola State University and Harvard University), Walter L. Bradley (University of Texas), and Roger L. Olsen (geochemist, Colorado School of Mines) pointed out: "[N]o geological evidence indicates an organic soup ever existed on this planet. We may therefore with fairness call this scenario 'the myth of the prebiotic soup.'"[5]

Evolutionist-turned-creationist Dr. Arthur Ernest Wilder-Smith said, "It is emphatically the case that life could not arise spontaneously in a primeval soup."[6]

Mutations

Dr. Pierre-Paul Grosse, former president of the French Academie des Sciences and the scientist who held the Chair of Evolution at the Sorbonne in Paris for 20 years, stated:

> No matter how numerous they may be, *mutations do not produce any kind of Evolution*. The opportune appearance of mutations permitting animals and plants to meet their needs *seems hard to believe*. Yet the Darwinian theory is even more demanding. A single plant or a single animal would require thousands and thousands of lucky, appropriate events. *Thus, miracles would become the rule*: events with infinitesimal probability could no longer fail to occur. . . . *There is no law against daydreaming, but science must not indulge in it.*[7]

Dr. C.P. Martin, in *American Scientist*, reported that "the mass [of] evidence shows that all, or almost all, known mutations are unmistakably pathological and the few remaining ones are highly suspect."[8] In other words, mutations are destructive to life, not the building blocks of higher life forms.

Natural Selection

Charles Darwin refuted his own theory when he said,

> To suppose that the eye, with all its inimitable contrivances for adjusting the focus to different distances, for admitting different amounts of light, and for the correction of spherical and chromatic aberration, could have been formed by natural selection, seems, I freely confess, absurd in the highest degree.[9]

Transitional Forms in the Fossil Record

According to Darwin's theory of origins, there should be countless millions of fossils of transitional types of organisms between lower forms (e.g., lizards) and higher forms (e.g., birds) of species. As Darwin said:

> But just in proportion as this process of extermination has acted on an enormous scale, so must the numbers of intermediate varieties, which have formerly existed on the earth, be truly enormous. Why then is not every geological formation and every stratum full of such intermediate links? Geology assuredly does not reveal any such finely graduated organic chain; and this, perhaps, is the most obvious and gravest objection which can be urged against my theory [of evolution].[10]

This lack of transitional forms in the fossil record continues to be the major stumbling block to universal acceptance of Darwin's theory within the scientific community.

Dr. Colin Patterson, chief paleontologist and senior principal scientific officer of the Paleontology Department at the British Museum of Natural History, has long been recognized as one of the world's leading fossil scientists. In response to a query, he admitted there was no evidence to support evolutionary theory:

> I fully agree with your comments on the lack of direct illustration of evolutionary transitions in my book. If I knew of any [transitional form], fossil or living, I would certainly have included them. . . . Yet Gould and the American Museum people are hard to contradict when they say there are no transitional forms. . . . You say that I should at least "show a photo of the fossil from which each type of organism was derived." I will lay it on the line—there is not one such fossil for which one could make a watertight argument.[11]

Fraud and the "Missing Links"

A tremendous amount of fraud has been used to try to convince the general public that the universe is a godless entity. Human beings have such a strong desire to "be their own bosses" and to get God out of their world that they have stretched the truth to the breaking point in attempting to advance Darwin's theory. Such is the case with the supposed missing links in the horse family and in the human family.

Biologist and paleontologist Dr. Gary Parker said this about the "evolution" of the horse:

> More detailed information has now forced us to abandon the idea that horses have truly evolved. We find that the size difference between the fossil horse [and the modern horse] is not crucial. It is now possible to breed extremely small horses.
>
> What about the so-called "dawn horse"? We now know that it was not a horse at all. Instead, it was a rock badger or a coney—what scientists call a hyrax. It was the ancestor NOT of the horses, but of the conies that still live on Earth today.
>
> What about the "in-between forms" that show how the toe number was gradually reduced? Some living Shire horses have been known to have more than one toe per foot. Also, all of the supposed "in-between forms" are found buried in the same geological formations, which indicates they lived at the same time and could not have been the ancestors of one another.
>
> Instead, it's more like a scene we might see around an African water hole, where animals of many sizes and shapes— animals with a few toes or with many toes—all lived together at the same time.[12]

Paleontologist and evolutionist Dr. Niles Eldredge from the American Museum of Natural History admitted the same problem:

> An awful lot of that [fantasy] has gotten into the textbooks as though it were true. For instance, the most famous example still on exhibit downstairs [in the American Museum of Natural History] is the exhibit on horse evolution prepared perhaps fifty years ago. That has been presented as literal truth in textbook after textbook. Now, I think that that is lamentable, particularly because the people who propose these kinds of stories themselves may be aware of the speculative nature of some of the stuff. But by the time it filters down to the textbooks, we've got science as truth and we've got a problem.[13]

Several missing links have been put forward to explain the evolution of human beings from apes.

- *Peking Man*. The plaster of paris skull fragments of this fraud proved to be from apes hunted and killed by men.[14]
- *Java Man*. Eugene Dubois combined a human leg bone, a human tooth, two orangutan teeth, and the skullcap of a large ape to produce this fraud. Although Dubois found two human skulls in similar rock strata near his "discovery," he concealed the fact for 30 years.[15]
- *Neanderthal Man*. When scientists learned that this fully human man had conducted religious ceremonies and buried his dead, the myth of the great human missing link disappeared forever.[16]

Scientists entertain no delusions about these frauds. Evolutionist Dr. R. Martin, senior research fellow at the Zoological Society of London, said, "In recent years several authors have written popular books on human origins which are based more on fantasy and subjectivity than on fact and objectivity."[17] Evolutionist William Fix said:

> The fossil record pertaining to man is still so sparsely known that those who insist on positive declarations can do nothing more than jump from one hazardous surmise to another and hope that the next dramatic discovery does not make them utter fools. . . . Clearly, some people refuse to learn from this. As we have seen, there are numerous scientists and populariz- ers today who have the temerity to tell us that there is "no doubt" how man originated. If only they had the evidence.[18]

According to paleontologist Alan Mann:

> Human evolution is a big deal these days. Leakey [is] world known; Johanson is like a movie star, women swoon over him and ask for his autograph. Lecture circuit, National Science Foundation: big bucks. Everything is debatable, especially where money is involved. *Sometimes people deliberately manipu- late data to suit what they're saying.*[19]

Trees have been trees since day 3 of creation. Fish have been fish and birds have been birds since day 5 of creation. And man has been man since day 6 of creation.

> At the present stage of geological research, we have to admit that there is nothing in the geological records that runs contrary to the view of conservative creationists, that God created each species [creationists would say "baramin," not "species] separately, presumably from the dust of the earth.[20]

Evolutionist Stephen Jay Gould has admitted "we're not just evolving slowly. For all practical purposes we're not evolving. There's no reason to think we're going to get bigger or smaller toes or whatever—we are what we are."[21]

Dr. S. Lovtrup summed up the grave concern that modern science feels when it looks honestly at the Darwinian theory of origins:

> I suppose that nobody will deny that it is a great misfortune that an entire branch of science becomes *addicted to a false theory*. But this is what happened in biology: . . . I believe that *one day the Darwinian myth will be ranked the greatest deceit in the history of science*. When that happens, many people will pose the question: "How did this ever happen?"[22]

It would be fun to write volumes covering other aspects of the evolution hoax, but I'll leave it to your personal study. Some particularly insightful books are *The Illustrated Origins Answer Book*, by Paul S. Taylor (Films Christ, 1991), *Why Not Creation?* edited by Walter E. Lammerts (Creation Research, 1970), *Speak to the Earth*, edited by George F. Howe (Creation Research, 1990), *Scientific Creationism*, by Henry M. Morris (Master Books, 1986), and *Scientific Case for Creation*, by Bert Thompson (Apologetics Press, 1985).

FURTHER READING

For a more detailed study of this topic, I recommend the following resources:

Bind, Wendall R. *The Origin of Species Revisited.* 2 vols. New York: Philosophical Library, 1989.

Davis, Percival, and Dean H. Kenyon. *Of Pandas and People.* Dallas: Houghton Publishing Company, 1989.

Johnson, Phillip E. *Darwin on Trial.* Washington, D.C.: Regnery Gateway, 1991.

Ham, Ken. *The Lie: Evolution.* El Cajon, Calif.: Master Books, 1987.

Morris, Henry M., and Gary E. Parker. *What Is Creation Science?* Rev. ed. El Cajon, Calif.: Master Books, 1982, 1987.

THE AUTHENTICITY
OF SCRIPTURE

U.S. News & World Report (not famous for its appreciation of biblical Christians) dedicated an October 1991 issue to biblical answers afforded in the discovery of the Dead Sea Scrolls.

> They were the archaeological discovery of the century—a price-less trove of sacred writings whose ancient secrets lay hidden in the Judean desert for nearly 2,000 years. . . . They have excited the imagination of biblical scholars and historians, offered new insights into the nature of the Bible and provided tantalizing glimpses into the turbulent times that gave birth to Christianity and modern Judaism.[1]

The article underscored the laborious accuracy of biblical scribes in reporting:

> "We have here the veritable remains of a library dating back to John the Baptist and Jesus. It illuminates a crucial period for Jews and sheds important new light on early Christianity," says Magen Broshi, curator of the scrolls at the Shrine of the Book in Jerusalem. "In 66 chapters of the Isaiah Scroll—one of the few

almost entirely intact scrolls found in the Qumran library—only 13 minor variations from the modern text were discovered."[2]

Those 13 minor variations were insignificant spelling changes (like "honor" versus "honour") and the presence of a conjunction, none of which changed the meaning of the text in the least. Imagine a work so committed and accurate that 2,000 years has not changed the text to any measurable degree.

The *U.S. News* article also pointed to some early New Testament writings that show the Gospel of John and the Gospel of Luke were written very close to the time Jesus lived, not decades later, as some liberal theologians asserted.[3] The Bible is surely the most accurate book in all of antiquity.

THE BIBLE ON THE BIBLE

The Bible is very clear when it speaks of its own writings, its source, its purpose, and its accuracy. Some liberal theologians and non-Christian historians would lead us to believe that the Book is full of inconsistencies, errors, man-made ideas, fictitious "stories," and good moral teachings thought up by man. Nothing could be further from biblical truth.

The Bible says that it is literally "God's Word"—that is, God speaks *His* thoughts through the minds of the 40 writers in the 66 books. In the original Hebrew, He says Scripture is "God-breathed."

2 Timothy 3:16: "All Scripture is God-breathed and is useful for teaching, rebuking, correcting and training in righteousness."

2 Peter 1:21: "For prophecy never had its origin in the will of man, but men spoke from God as they were carried along by the Holy Spirit."

2 Samuel 23:2: "'The Spirit of the LORD spoke through me; his word was on my tongue.'"

Jeremiah 1:9: "Then the LORD reached out his hand and touched my mouth and said to me . . ."

Acts 4:24-25: "When they heard this, they raised their voices together in prayer to God. 'Sovereign Lord,' they said, 'you made the heaven and the earth and the sea, and everything in them. You spoke by the Holy Spirit through the mouth of your servant, our father David:

"Why do the nations rage and the peoples plot in vain? The kings of the earth take their stand and the rulers gather together against the Lord and against his Anointed One.'"' (This refers to God speaking through David in Psalm 2.)

These passages show an absolute identification of Scripture with the speaking of God. The Bible speaks of divine inspiration over and over again!

JESUS' VIEW OF SCRIPTURE

Jesus Christ also believed that Scripture is the Word of God.

Matthew 5:18: "I tell you the truth, until heaven and earth disappear, not the smallest letter, not the least stroke of a pen, will by any means disappear from the Law until everything is accomplished."

John 10:35: "If he called them 'gods,' to whom the word of God came—and the Scripture cannot be broken— . . . "

If Jesus is accepted as Savior and Lord, it would be a polar opposite if we did not accept Scripture as the Word of God.

In many places Jesus refers to the Old Testament (beginning with Genesis) as the accurately recorded Word of God. "He quoted from many parts of the Bible, including passages that have been ridiculed by modern skeptics. Thus, He accepted as true the account of man's creation, quoting from Genesis 1 and . . . 2 in Matthew 19:4. He referred to the great flood, accepting it as worldwide (see Matt. 24:37-39). He cited the destruction of Sodom (see Luke 17:28-32) and the miracles of Elijah (see Luke 4:25-26). He believed in the Mosaic authorship of the Pentateuch (see John 5:46-47; Luke 20:37-38) and also that Isaiah wrote both parts of the book of Isaiah (see Matt. 4:14-16; 12:17-21), seemingly unimpressed [with] the fact that twentieth-century critics would later deny these claims. He accepted the writings of Daniel as true prophecies (Matt. 24:15)."[4]

FULFILLED PROPHECIES
AND THE RELIABILITY OF SCRIPTURE

Literally thousands of very specific prophetic details are recorded in

Scripture where God's prophets predicted an event and, at a later date, the prophecy was accurately fulfilled. God used prophecies to demonstrate His supernatural involvement in Scripture. Unlike "futurists," who make generic predictions, the Bible's prophecies are very specific, often involve entire nations, and sometimes are fulfilled hundreds of years after the prophecy is given. No futurist has ever even approached such dimensions of amazement. For example:

In Daniel 9:25, God gave Daniel a prophecy that predicted the year Jesus would make His triumphant entry into Jerusalem some *560 years* after the prophecy was given.

In A.D. 70, the Romans banished the Jews from their land, but Ezekiel and Isaiah prophesied that they would return as a nation in the latter days. Then in 1948, almost 2,000 years later, the Jewish nation was reborn in Palestine. No other nation in history ever accomplished such a feat.

Jesus Himself fulfilled over 300 prophecies in intricate detail, prophecies such as His bloodline, His exact birthplace, the amount of money for which He would be betrayed, and the way He would die. Several hundred years before crucifixion was introduced as a means of execution, Isaiah prophesied Christ's death on a cross.

The so-called prophecies of Jeane Dixon, Nostradamus, the Koran, and the Confucian Analects can't hold a candle to the Bible's prophetic accuracy.

WHAT ABOUT ALL THE CONTRADICTIONS IN SCRIPTURE?

Critics are eager to pounce on any event in Scripture that is not completely explained or that is difficult to understand. In their overzealousness to support their nonbiblical faith, they jump to conclusions too quickly to demonstrate wisdom.

For example, critics have continually picked on Genesis 4:17, saying, "If all people started with Adam and Eve, where did Cain get his wife?"

Any time Scripture appears difficult to explain, read further and reason. If Adam lived 930 years and his call by God was to populate the earth, think how many offspring, grand-offspring, and great-grand-offspring he would have had with Eve. They had sons and daughters, and with a gene pool young and void of mutant genes, no harm would have been caused by brothers, sisters, cousins, and other relatives marrying in the earliest days.

It was only later that laws were enacted prohibiting family members from intermarrying.

Other supposed Bible "contradictions" have very plausible, sound defenses when carefully examined. If you have other questions about difficult passages or if a skeptic tells you that Scripture is contradictory, consult well-documented books such as *Answers*, by Josh McDowell and Don Stewart (Tyndale, 1986), and *The Encyclopedia of Bible Difficulties*, by Gleason L. Archer (Zondervan, 1982).

SCIENTIFIC DATA WERE GIVEN IN SCRIPTURE LONG BEFORE "SCIENCE" DISCOVERED THEM

The Bible is not a book of science, but every time science and the Bible cross paths, the Bible gives more evidence of what later proved to be true. Here are just a few examples:

Isaiah 40:22 speaks of a round earth. Columbus was laughed at over 2,000 years later when he said it was round, because at that time "science" believed it was flat.

2 Peter 3:7 speaks of the law of conservation of mass and energy.

Ecclesiastes 1:7 speaks of the hydrologic cycle.

Psalm 102:25-27 speaks of the second law of thermodynamics.

Job 26:7 speaks of gravitational forces.

It wasn't until the mid-twentieth century that scientists realized that all matter is not made of building blocks (atoms) but, in fact, is made from an electrical attraction of invisible neutrons, protons, and electrons. The writer of Hebrews 1,900 years earlier stated this fact: " . . . we understand that the universe was formed at God's command, so that what is seen was not made out of what was visible" (Heb. 11:3).

THE AMAZING UNITY AND CONSISTENCY OF THE BIBLE

The Bible is a collection of 66 books written by 40 authors over a period of 2,000 years. The writers came from many nations on three continents. They were carpenters, fishermen, shepherds, kings, soldiers, nomads, prisoners, doctors, historians, philosophers, and prophets. Each wrote not knowing his work would someday be placed with the others. Some wrote in palaces, some wrote in dungeons, some wrote at universities, and some wrote in the mountains. Yet when the 66 pieces of the puzzle were placed together, it was clearly one book with one continuous story: God's great work in the creation and redemption of humanity through His only Son, Jesus Christ.

THE UNPARALLELED CIRCULATION OF THE BIBLE

The Bible has always been the world's best-seller. It is translated into nearly 2,000 different languages and dialects, with more every year. There have been more Bibles, and more books about individuals in the Bible, printed and sold than the total number of the next best-sellers combined. Literally billions of Bibles have circulated on every continent from the first manuscript until today.[5]

THE HISTORICAL RELIABILITY OF SCRIPTURE

The *Handbook of Classical Literature* points out that the Bible is the single most historically reliable book in the entire world.[6] The classic measurement of such reliability is to determine how many extant manuscripts (handwritten copies) there are that agree identically with the earliest surviving versions of the text and how many years elapsed between the writing of the original text and that of the oldest existing manuscript. Here are some statistics:[7]

- Caesar's *Gallic Wars* ......10 manuscripts
  Closest manuscript - 1,000 years
- Plato ....seven manuscripts
  Closest manuscript - 1,200 years
- Herodotus ....eight manuscripts
  Closest manuscript - 1,300 years
- Aristotle ....five manuscripts
  Closest manuscript - 1,400 years
- New Testament ....5,300 Greek manuscripts
  ....8,000 Latin manuscripts
  ....9,300 other early versions
  The first manuscripts and the original text are only 100 years apart. Museums hold exact manuscripts from as early as A.D. 130.

When it comes to the time sequence, there is more reliability in the New Testament than the next ten pieces of classical literature combined!

THE ARCHAEOLOGICAL ACCURACY OF SCRIPTURE

The Bible, though aggressively criticized for centuries by skeptics, has proved to be extremely sound archaeologically. Every year archaeologists dig up new relics that verify the writings of Scripture and silence the skeptics.

The most renowned expert on Palestinian archaeology is Dr. Nelson Glueck. As president of the Hebrew Union College, he states conclusively "that no archeological discovery has ever controverted a Bible reference. Scores of archeological findings have been made which confirm in clear outline or exact detail historical statements in the Bible."[8]

THE EYEWITNESS ACCOUNTS OF SCRIPTURE

Scripture is not stories haphazardly handed down from generation to generation, as we are taught in the secular classroom. Rather, they are *eyewitness* accounts of biblical events.

2 Peter 1:16 says, "We did not follow cleverly invented stories when we told you about the power and coming of our Lord Jesus Christ, but we were *eyewitnesses* of his majesty" [emphasis added].

1 John 1:1 says, "That which was from the beginning, which we have heard, which we have *seen with our eyes*, which we have looked at and our hands *have touched*—this we proclaim concerning the Word of life" [emphasis added].

Luke 1:1-3 says, "Many have undertaken to draw up an account of the things that have been fulfilled among us, just as they were handed down to us by those who from the first were *eyewitnesses* and servants of the word. Therefore, since I myself have carefully investigated everything from the beginning, it seemed good also to me to write an orderly account for you . . . " [emphasis added].

No writings of antiquity have been as dedicated to accuracy as has Scripture. Though the Bible has been scrutinized and criticized by skeptics for centuries, its writers had documented everything, often recording it on the spot. Centuries before the New Testament was written, Jewish scribes were famous for their accurate, often eyewitness presentation of events. These Jewish historians did not tolerate heresy, legends, or stories handed down casually through the generations.

Sir Walter Scott summarized the uniqueness of Scripture with these timely words of praise:

> Within that awful volume lies
> The mystery of mysteries.
> Happiest they of human race
> To whom God has granted grace
> To read, to fear, to hope, to pray
> To lift the latch, and force the way;
> And better had they ne'er been born,
> Who read to doubt, or read to scorn.[9]

FURTHER READING

For a more detailed study of this topic, I recommend the following resources:

Archer, Gleason L. *A Survey of Old Testament Introduction.* Rev. ed. Chicago: Moody Press, 1994.

Blomberg, Craig. *The Reliability of the Gospels.* Downers Grove, Ill.: InterVarsity Press, 1987.

Bruce, F.F. *Are the New Testament Documents Reliable?* 5th ed. Downers Grove, Ill.: InterVarsity Press, 1960.

Comfort, Philip Wesley, ed. *The Origin of the Bible.* Wheaton, Ill.: Tyndale House, 1992.

Free, Joseph P. *Archaeology and Bible History.* Rev. ed. Grand Rapids, Mich.: Zondervan, 1992.

Geisler, Norman L., and William E. Nix. *A General Introduction to the Bible.* Rev. ed. Chicago: Moody Press, 1968, 1986.

Guthrie, Donald. *New Testament Introduction.* Rev. ed. Downers Grove, Ill.: InterVarsity Press, 1990.

McDowell, Josh. *Evidence That Demands a Verdict.* 2 vols. San Bernardino, Calif.: Here's Life, 1981.

THE UNIQUENESS OF JESUS IN HISTORY

I. Jesus' Claims About His Own Divinity
 A. "I and the Father are one" (John 10:30).*
 B. "He who has seen Me has seen the Father" (John 14:9).
 C. "Truly, truly, I say to you, before Abraham was born, I AM" (John 8:58).
 D. "I am the way and the truth and the life; no one comes to the Father, but through Me" (John 14:6).

II. Biblical Claims About Jesus' Divinity
 A. Paul: "For in Him all the fulness of Deity dwells in bodily form" (Col. 2:9).
 B. John: "In the beginning was the Word [Jesus], and the Word was with God, and the Word was God" (John 1:1).
 C. The Roman centurion who nailed Jesus to the cross: "Truly this man was the Son of God" (Mark 15:39).
 D. Thomas the doubter: "My Lord and my God!" (John 20:28).
 E. Stephen the Martyr: "Lord Jesus, receive my spirit!" (Acts 7:59).

*All Scripture quotations in this section are from the NASB.

F. Peter: "Thou art the Christ, the Son of the living God" (Matt.
16:16).

III. Even the Jews Recognized Jesus' Claims to Deity
A. "And Jesus said, 'I am [the Christ].' . . . The high priest said,
' . . . You have heard the blasphemy. . . .' And they all condemned
Him to be deserving of death" (Mark 14:61-64).
B. Jesus answered them,"' . . . I and the Father are one.' The Jews
took up stones again to stone Him. Jesus answered them, 'I
showed you many good works from the Father; for which of them
are you stoning Me?' The Jews answered Him, 'For a good work
we do not stone You, but for blasphemy; and because You, being
a man, makeYourself out *to be* God'" (John 10:30-33).

IV. Modern Claims About Christ's Uniqueness
A. Philip Schaff, a Christian historian and author: "A character so original, so complete, so uniformly consistent, so perfect, so human
and yet so high above all human greatness, can be neither a fraud
nor a fiction. The poet, as has been well said, would in this case be
greater than the hero. It would take more than a Jesus to invent a
Jesus."[1]
B. Napoleon, French general and emperor, said: "I know men; and I
tell you that Jesus Christ is not a man. . . . There is between
Christianity and whatever other religions the distance of infinity.
. . . Everything in Christ astonishes me. His spirit overawes me,
and His will confounds me. Between Him and whoever else in the
world, there is no possible term of comparison. He is truly a being
by Himself."[2]
C. Kenneth Scott Latourette, historian of Christianity at Yale University: "It is not His teachings which make Jesus so remarkable,
although these would be enough to give Him distinction. It is a
combination of the teaching with the man Himself."[3]
D. Thomas Schultz, Dallas Theological Seminary student: "Christ is
the only religious leader who has *ever* claimed to be deity and the
only individual *ever* who has convinced a great portion of the world
that He is God."[4]
E. Ralph Waldo Emerson, nineteenth-century essayist and poet:
"Jesus is the most perfect of all men that have yet appeared."[5]

F. *Encyclopaedia Britannica* uses over 20,000 words to describe the person of Jesus Christ, more than any other historical figure: "These independent accounts prove that in ancient times even the opponents of Christianity never doubted the historicity of Jesus."[6]

G. The Roman historian Cornelius Tacitus, in A.D. 112: "Christus, the founder of the name [Christians] was put to death by Pontius Pilate, procurator of Judea in the reign of Tiberius."[7]

H. Flavius Josephus, Jewish historian, in A.D. 66: "Now there was about this time Jesus, a wise man . . . a doer of wonderful works. . . . He was the Christ . . . was condemned by Pilate to the cross . . . appeared to them (His followers) alive on the third day. . . . "[8]

I. *U.S. News & World Report*: "The death of Jesus of Nazareth should have put a quick and quiet end to what had been a minor religious disturbance in the smoldering tinderbox of Roman-occupied Palestine. There was no public outcry when the enigmatic Jewish preacher was executed after he challenged the religious authorities by declaring 'the kingdom of God' at hand. His demoralized disciples had simply given up and gone home. Whatever it might have become, this tiny dissident sect of Galilean Jews had been decapitated and seemed destined to be quickly forgotten."[9]

V. Old Testament Prophecies Fulfilled in Jesus' Lifetime

Most amazing of all is the fact that numerous details of Jesus' life were specifically prophesied or predicted in the Old Testament 500 to 2,000 years before Jesus was born.

	Prophesied	*Fulfilled*
That He would be born of a virgin	Isa. 7:14	Matt. 1:18, 24-25
That He would be the Son of God	Ps. 2:7	Matt. 3:17
That He would be of the seed of Abraham	Gen. 22:18	Gal. 3:16
That He would be the Son of Isaac	Gen. 21:12	Luke 3:23, 34
That He would be the Son of Jacob	Num. 24:17	Luke 3:23, 34
That He would be from the tribe of Judah	Gen. 49:10	Luke 3:23, 33

That He would be a descendant of Jesse	Isa. 11:1	Luke 3:23, 32
That He would be of the house of David	Jer. 23:5	Luke 3:23, 31
That He would be born in Bethlehem	Mic. 5:2	Matt. 2:1
That He existed before the world was created	Mic. 5:2	Col. 1:17
That He shall be called Lord	Ps. 110:1	Luke 2:11
That He shall be called Immanuel	Isa. 7:14	Matt. 1:23
That He shall be called a prophet	Deut. 18:18	Matt. 21:11
That He would be preceded by a messenger	Isa. 40:3	Matt. 3:1-2
That His ministry would begin in Galilee	Isa. 9:1	Matt. 4:12-13, 17
That He would enter Jerusalem on a donkey	Zech. 9:9	Luke 19:33-35
That He would be a light to the Gentiles	Isa. 60:3	Acts 13:47-48
That He would be resurrected from the dead	Ps. 16:10	Acts 2:31
That He would be seated at the right hand of God	Ps. 10:1	Heb. 1:3
That He would be sold for 30 pieces of silver	Zech. 11:12	Matt. 26:15
That His hands and feet would be pierced	Isa. 53; Ps. 22:16	Luke 23:33
That none of His bones would be broken	Ps. 34:20	John 19:33
That He would be buried in a rich man's tomb	Isa. 53:9	Matt. 27:57-60

Canon Liddon is the authority for the statement that there are, in the Old Testament, 332 distinct predictions that were fulfilled in Christ.[10]

The odds that any other man in history could have fulfilled these prophecies in one lifetime are 1 in 10^{157}—that's 1 with 157 zeros after it. There are only 10^{80} electrons in the entire universe.[11]

Dr. Emil Borel, who discovered the law of probability, stated that any event with the odds greater than 1 in 10^{50} power could never happen in history, no matter how many opportunities were allotted for the event to take place.[12]

Almost every literate person worldwide believes that Jesus of Nazareth was a historical person. The Bible says that even Satan "believes and trembles." But to believe in Jesus as a true disciple is to believe with one's whole mind, heart, soul, and body.

Jesus never asked His followers to have blind faith; that's why He lived, died, and came back to life—to substantiate our faith. Jesus is, without a doubt, the only religious figure in history who can make the awesome claim that He was the Messiah and then pass the test of history without a flaw.

FURTHER READING

For a more detailed study of this topic, I recommend the following resources:

Anderson, Norman. *Jesus Christ: The Witness of History*. Downers Grove, Ill.: InterVarsity Press, 1985.

France, R.T. *The Evidence for Jesus*. Downers Grove, Ill.: InterVarsity Press, 1986.

Habermas, Gary R. *The Verdict of History: Conclusive Evidence for the Life of Jesus*. Nashville, Tenn.: Thomas Nelson, 1988.

McDowell, Josh, and Bill Wilson. *He Walked Among Us*. San Bernardino, Calif.: Here's Life, 1988.

Resource H

WORLD RELIGIONS, CULTS, AND THE CHRISTIAN FAITH

History is loaded with men who claimed to be God, but there's only one God who claimed to be man.

John 1:14 proclaims boldly, "And the Word [Jesus] became flesh, and dwelt among us"(NASB). Colossians 1:15 says, "He [Jesus] is the image of the invisible God."

There are millions of roads that lead to Jesus Christ; but, according to the Bible, there's only one road that leads to God.

Jesus said on the night before His crucifixion, "I am the way and the truth and the life. No one comes to the Father except through me" (John 14:6).

There are literally thousands of "religions," cults, self-proclaimed prophets and messiahs, and interpretations of God. Other world religions differ from Christianity in five significant ways.

1. Other world religions don't believe Jesus was who He said He was.

- God's only Son (John 3:16).
- The fullness of God: "For in Christ all the fullness of the Deity lives in bodily form" (Col. 2:9).

- One with the Father: "I and the Father are one" (John 10:30).
- The only way to heaven: "I tell you the truth, no one can see the king-dom of God unless he is born again" (John 3:3).

Brigham Young, Mormon church leader, said, "Jesus was not begotten by the Holy Ghost. . . . [H]is birth was as natural as the births of our chil-dren. . . . [H]e was begotten of his father as we are begotten by our fathers."[1]

Mary Baker Eddy, founder of the Church of Christian Science, said, "Jesus Christ is not God."[2]

The Jehovah's Witnesses craftily altered Scripture to back their false doctrine that Jesus isn't God. For example, John 1:1 says, "The Word [Jesus] was God." The Jehovah's Witnesses' Scripture, the New World Translation, says, "The word was a god."[3]

2. While lowering Jesus to *less* than He is supposed to be, other world religions usually elevate some other man to a higher spiritual position than he deserves.

Joseph Smith, founder of the Mormon church, said, "All other denom-inations are wrong, all their creeds are abominations and all the professors of those creeds are corrupt."[4]

Joseph Fielding Smith, a father of the Mormon church and an author of its doctrines, said, "There is no salvation without accepting Joseph Smith."[5]

As Paul warned Timothy, so I warn all Christian parents. We had better quit ignoring the many cults that are luring kids away from their roots. As I noted in chapter 12, there are 700 to 5,000 religious cults in America today, with 20 million followers, *60 percent of whom have Protestant backgrounds*. This includes 100,000 pagan worshipers.[6] Almost all of these cults have a false Christ or charismatic leader who claims to be God or a prophet of God.

The Bible warns against making claims of deity, and according to Jewish law, a person blaspheming God deserves the death penalty (see Lev. 23:16; John 10:33).

3. Other world religions always add a "new revelation" or other religious works to the Bible.

This is a blasphemous and dangerous thing. 2 Timothy 3:16 says, "All Scripture [Gen. 1 to Rev. 22] is God-breathed." No more, no less. Revelation 22:18-19 says, "I warn everyone who hears the words of the prophecy of this book: If anyone adds anything to them, God will add to him the plagues described in this book. And if anyone takes words away from this book of prophecy, God will take away from him his share in the tree of life and in the holy city, which are described in this book."

Islam has the Koran, which was revealed to Muhammad in various visions in A.D. 610. At first Muhammad thought he was possessed by demons (or jinn), but he later dismissed the idea.

Buddhism has the Tripitaka, which was revealed to Buddha after he sat for seven days under a fig tree about 500 B.C. in India.

Confucianism has the Analects, written by Confucius and his followers in Lu China about 500 B.C.

Hinduism has the Vedas, revealed to a number of people from 1400 B.C. to 400 B.C.

Mormonism has the *Book of Mormon,* an account of the supposed original inhabitants of America to whom Christ appeared after His resurrection, as told by God to Joseph Smith in 1820 in Palmyra, New York: "The Bible is not the word of God but the word of inspired translators."[7]

The Jehovah's Witnesses have *The Watchtower*, which claims to be "the sole collective channel for the flow of Biblical truth."[8]

4. Only orthodox Christianity believes in the pure Trinity, the perfect unity of God the Father, God the Son, and God the Holy Spirit.

This truth is usually attacked by cults as being pagan or satanic in origin. For example, the Jehovah's Witnesses say, "There is no authority in the Word of God for the doctrine of the trinity of the Godhead."[9] They also believe that "the plain truth is that this is another of Satan's attempts to keep the God-fearing person from learning the truth of Jehovah and His Son Christ Jesus."[10]

5. Only true biblical Christianity believes that we are totally saved by grace.

"For it is by grace you have been saved, through faith—and this not from yourselves, it is the gift of God—not by works, so that no one can boast" (Eph. 2:8-9).

We believe that Christ's death on the cross totally paid for our sins and that acceptance of this grace gift buys eternal salvation for the believer. Other religions, in various ways, deny this truth.

Hinduism teaches that salvation comes by way of knowledge, by way of devotion, or by way of ceremonial ritual.

Mormonism teaches that "in the kingdom of God there are numerous levels provided for those who are worthy of them"[11] and that "the blood of Christ will never wipe that [your sin debt] out; your own blood must atone for it."[12]

CONCLUSION

If Jesus is who He claimed to be, and if the Bible is the completed Word of God, then all other religions are in vain. "Watch out for false prophets. They come to you in sheep's clothing, but inwardly they are ferocious wolves. By their fruit you will recognize them. Do people pick grapes from thornbushes, or figs from thistles? Likewise every good tree bears good fruit, but a bad tree bears bad fruit. A good tree cannot bear bad fruit, and a bad tree cannot bear good fruit. Every tree that does not bear good fruit is cut down and thrown into the fire" (Matt. 7:15-19).

Don't be deceived! "Do not let anyone who delights in false humility and the worship of angels disqualify you for the prize. Such a person goes into great detail about what he has seen, and his unspiritual mind puffs him up with idle notions" (Col. 2:18). No one's personal experience in conflict with the Bible can be trusted, or you'll be forever confused with the question, Who is right? Whose "experience" is valid? Whose is not? You cannot be too cautious in your choice of spiritual leadership. Your physical and eternal lives are at stake.

While giving sober warnings about any other leader but Jesus Christ, the Bible also warns against judging and condemning those who do follow such leaders. We are called to love those who are being misled and to show them the biblical truth by our godly behavior toward them.

BUDDHISM

Buddhism, an offshoot of Hinduism, began in India about 500 years before the birth of Christ. The people had become disillusioned with certain beliefs of Hinduism, particularly the caste system, which had grown extremely complex. Moreover, the Hindu doctrine that life is an endless cycle of births, deaths, and rebirths was viewed with dread. Consequently, the people turned to a variety of other beliefs, including the worship of animals, to fill the spiritual vacuum. Many different sects of Hinduism arose, the most successful being Buddhism.

The founder of Buddhism, Siddhartha Gautama, was born about 560 B.C. in northeastern India. He supposedly meditated under a fig tree for seven days and reached the highest degree of God-consciousness, or nirvana. (After that, the fig tree was called the bodhi or bo tree, the tree of wisdom.) Siddhartha, now Buddha (or "enlightened one"), began to impart the truths he had learned to the Indian people, who listened intently to the new doctrines. By the time of Buddha's death at age 80, his teachings had become a strong force in India.

Like all other self-proclaimed religious leaders (except the One), Buddha's burial was his personal end. His remains are still in his tomb.

Buddhists believe that the universe was not created but evolved. They deny the existence of a personal God. And they believe that man is worthless and that his body is a hindrance to his striving toward nirvana.

CONFUCIANISM

Confucius, the founder of Confucianism, was born in Lu China 500 years before Christ. A main feature of this religion is the prayerful nurturing of ancestors. Adherents believe that their ancestors can control the fortunes of their families.

Confucian ethical philosophy espouses self-effort, leaving no room or need for God. Confucius taught that man can be spiritually self-sufficient if he only follows the way of the ancients, while Christianity teaches that man does not have the capacity to save himself but is in desperate need of the Savior.

ISLAM

Today there are an estimated 450 million Muslims, or members of Islam, dominating more than three dozen countries on three continents. The word *Islam* is a noun formed from the Arabic verb meaning "to submit, surrender, or commit oneself."[13]

The early history of Islam revolves around one central figure, Muhammad, who was born around A.D. 570 in the city of Mecca in Arabia. Muhammad's father died before his birth, and his mother died when he was six.

Muhammad believed in only one God, Allah. At the age of 40, Muhammad had his first vision. At first he thought he was possessed by demons, but later he dismissed the idea and believed his vision was a call from Allah to prophesy. Muhammad continued to experience visions for the next 22 years, until his death in A.D. 632.

Muhammad's visions (or revelations) were recorded in the Koran (*Qur'an*). "For the Muslims, the *Koran* is the Word of God, confirming and consummating earlier revealed books and thereby replacing them; its instrument or agent of revelation is the Prophet Muhammad, the last and most perfect of a series of messengers of God to mankind—from Adam through Abraham to Moses and Jesus, the Christian claims for whose divinity are strongly rejected."[14] As the scriptural authority, the Koran is the main guide for all matters of faith and practice. Muslims would not consider our New Testament to be the words of Jesus. Rather, it is others' words about Jesus. Muslims believe that only the Koran is infallible. Muhammad and the Koran are the core of Islam.

ISLAM'S FIVE ARTICLES OF FAITH

1. *God*. Allah is not a personal God, for He is so far above humans in every way that He is not personally knowable. The emphasis of the God of Islam is on judgment, not grace. To Muslims, it is blasphemous to call God "Father."

2. *Angels*. The existence of angels is fundamental to Islamic teaching. Gabriel, the leading angel, appeared to Muhammad and was instrumental in delivering the revelations in the Koran to him. In addition, every man and woman has two recording angels, one to record good deeds and one to record bad deeds.

3. *Scripture.* There are four inspired books in the Islamic faith. They are the Torah of Moses, the Psalms of David, the gospel of Jesus Christ, and the Koran. Muslims believe the first three books have been corrupted by Jews and Christians. Also, since the Koran is God's most recent and final word to man, it supersedes all the other books.

4. *The Prophets.* In Islam, God has spoken through numerous prophets down through the centuries. The six greatest are Adam, Noah, Abraham, Moses, Jesus, and Muhammad. Muhammad is the last and greatest of Allah's messengers.

5. *The Last Days.* The last days will be a time of resurrection and judgment. Those who followed and obeyed Allah and Muhammad will go to Islamic heaven, called Paradise, a place of pleasure. Those who opposed them will be tormented in hell.

OTHER ISLAMIC BELIEFS

The Family
Muhammad commanded men to marry and propagate the race. Men may not have more than four wives, yet many cohabit with as many concubines as they desire.

Christ and Redemption
Muslims do not believe Jesus was crucified; rather, many believe Judas was crucified in His place. Some, however, believe it was Christ on the cross but that He did not die.

Muslims do not believe that Jesus has any part of the Trinity or that His death atoned for humanity's sins. There is no need for a Savior in Islam because it makes no real provision for sin. One's salvation is based on a works system and on complete surrender ("islam") to the will of Allah. Therefore, it is never certain.[15]

MORMONISM

"But even though we, or an angel from heaven, should preach to you a gospel contrary to that which we have preached to you, let him be accursed" (Gal. 1:8, NASB).

HISTORY

Joseph Smith, Jr., the founder of Mormonism, or the Church of Jesus Christ of Latter-Day Saints, was born on December 23, 1805, in Sharon, Vermont. Smith was the fourth of ten children of Joseph and Lucy Mack Smith. In 1817 the family moved to Palmyra, New York (near present-day Rochester).

Most of the members of the Smith family joined the Presbyterian church, but young Joseph remained undecided. His argument was that all the strife and tension among the various denominations made him question which one was right. This conflict set the stage for Joseph's first vision.

THE FIRST VISION

In 1820 Joseph allegedly received a vision that became the basis for the founding of the Mormon church. According to Mormon history, the background of Joseph's first vision was a revival that broke out in the spring of 1820 in Palmyra, New York. This led to Joseph's inquiry of the Lord about which denomination was right. Smith reported the incident as follows:

> My object in going to inquire of the Lord was to know which of all the sects was right, that I might know which to join. No sooner, therefore, did I get possession of myself, so as to be able to speak, than I asked the personages who stood above me in the light, which of all the sects was right—and which I should join. I was answered that I must join none of them, for they were all wrong; and the personage who addressed me said that all their creeds were an abomination in His sight; that those professors were all corrupt; that "they draw near to me with their lips, but their hearts are far from me, they teach for doctrines the commandments of men, having a form of godliness, but they deny the power thereof."[16]

MORMONISM: "THE ONLY TRUE CHRISTIAN FAITH"

After Joseph Smith's death in 1844, leadership of the church went to Brigham Young, the president of the Twelve Apostles (the coucil that leads the Mormon church), who convinced the majority of Mormons that he was Smith's rightful successor.

The Mormons claim they are the restoration of the only true church established by Jesus Christ. "If it had not been for Joseph Smith and the restoration, there would be no salvation."[17] There is "no salvation without accepting Joseph Smith. . . . If Joseph Smith was verily a prophet, and if he told the truth . . . then this knowledge is of the most vital importance to the entire world. No man can reject that testimony without incurring the most dreadful consequences, for he can not enter the Kingdom of God."[18]

THE *BOOK OF MORMON* VERSUS THE BIBLE

The Mormon *Articles of Faith* read, "We believe the Bible to be the Word of God in so far as it is translated correctly."[19] Orson Pratt, an early apostle of the Mormon church, put it this way: "Who knows that even one verse of the Bible has escaped pollution, so as to convey the same sense now that it did in the original?"[20]

The Mormons believe the *Book of Mormon* was inspired by God just like the Bible: "We also believe the *Book of Mormon* to be the Word of God."[21] But the Mormon doctrine of God contradicts what the Bible teaches. The Mormons believe in many gods and teach that God Himself was once a man and that He "progressed to godhead."[22] One Mormon authority recently published a widely received book in which he declared that God could "cease to be God" if He lost the support of the other gods.[23] Moreover, Mormon males have the possibility of attaining godhood. Joseph Smith claimed that "man is co-equal with God himself."[24] He made this clear in *The King Follett Discourse*:

> God was once as we are now, and is an exalted man, and sits enthroned in yonder heavens. . . . I say, if you were to see him today, you would see him like a man in a form like yourselves in all the person, image, and very form of a man. He was once a man like us; yea, that God himself, the father of us all, dwelt on an earth, the same as Jesus Christ did. And you have got to learn how to be Gods yourselves, and to be kings and priests to God, the same as all Gods have done before you.[25]

This brings to mind the account of the fall of Satan, as he, too, desired equality with God.

The Bible clearly states that our Lord is the one and only God. Isaiah 43:10-11: "'You are my witnesses,' declares the LORD, 'and my servant whom I have chosen, so that you may know and believe me and understand that I am he. Before me no god was formed, nor will there be one after me. I, even I, am the LORD, and apart from me there is no savior.'" Isaiah 44:6-7: "This is what the LORD says—Israel's King and Redeemer, the LORD Almighty: I am the first and I am the last; apart from me there is no God. Who then is like me? Let him proclaim it."

THE HISTORICAL RELIABILITY OF THE *BOOK OF MORMON*

According to Joseph Smith, Jr., the *Book of Mormon* is "the most correct book on earth."[26] However, unlike the Bible, this most correct book has, from the original edition in 1830 to the modern edition, undergone 3,913 changes.[27] Here are some examples:

Original Edition	*Modern Version*
. . . King Benjamin had a gift from God, whereby he could interpret such engravings . . . (p. 200).	. . . King Mosiah had a gift from God, whereby he could interpret such engravings . . . (p. 176, v. 28).
. . . Behold the virgin which thou seest is the Mother of God . . . (p. 25).	. . . Behold the virgin whom thou seest is the mother of the Son of God . . . (1 Nephi 11:18).
. . . that the Lamb of God is the eternal Father and the Savior of the world . . . (p. 32).	. . . that the lamb of God is the Son of the Eternal Father . . . (1 Nephi 13:40).

Also unlike the Bible, the *Book of Mormon* is not supported by archaeological remains. No cities mentioned in the *Book of Mormon* have been located. No persons, nations, or places mentioned in the *Book of Mormon* have been found in other New World literature or inscriptions. As a matter of fact, no artifact of any kind that would demonstrate that the *Book of Mormon* is true has been found. (By way of comparison, see Resources F and G.)

OTHER MORMON CLAIMS

Joseph Smith claimed that the Lord told him the Latter-Day Saints would build a temple in Zion (Jackson County, Missouri) during his generation.

"Zion would never be removed from its place. . . . This generation shall not all pass away until an house shall be built unto the Lord . . . upon the consecrated spot as I have appointed."[28]

The Mormons believe that Jesus Christ is the "spirit brother" of Satan.[29] They also believe Jesus was conceived as the result of physical sex between God the Father and the Virgin Mary; He was *not* conceived by the Holy Ghost.[30]

The wedding in Cana was the wedding of none other than Jesus Himself, who wed three women: Mary, her sister Martha, and "the other Mary." Furthermore, He had children by them.[31]

The doctrines of the holy Trinity and salvation by grace are, in the words of Mormon apostle Bruce R. McConkie, "the two Great Heresies of Christendom."[32] In a speech at Brigham Young University, McConkie warned students that striving for "a special personal relationship with Christ is both improper and perilous."[33]

Brigham Young University professor James E. Ford sums up Mormon theology this way: "Mormon doctrine means that ultimately we are not dependent upon God for our existence. And since we can make ourselves as godly as the Father, we don't feel any jealousy toward him."[34]

CHRISTIAN SCIENCE

The Church of Christian Science was founded by Mary Ann Morse Baker Glover Patterson Eddy in 1879 in Charleston, Massachusetts. Mary Baker Eddy "discovered" her ideas while convalescing from a near-fatal fall. She called her work *Science and Health* and claimed it was divinely written: "I was only a scribe echoing the harmonies of Heaven in divine metaphysics."[35]

Although Eddy claimed that the Bible was her final authority, she contradicted Scripture repeatedly by saying her writings were the "higher" authority if discrepancies between the two books arose. She said, "The Bible is no more important to our well-being than the history of Europe and America."[36]

Like Hinduism and the New Age movement, Christian Science believes in a pantheistic god:. "God is a divine whole . . . an infinite principle."[37] The God of the Bible is infinite but personal: "I know *whom* I have believed" (2 Tim. 1:12, emphasis added).

Christian Science teaches a duality of Jesus Christ. Eddy said, "Jesus is the human man and Christ is the divine idea. . . . Christ is God . . . Jesus Christ is not God."[38] The Bible teaches diligently that the Trinity is one God in three persons (see Matt. 28:19). Jesus Christ is all man and all God (God incarnate).

Christian Science testifies that sin is an illusion; therefore, Christ did not need to die for us. "The material blood of Jesus was no more efficacious to cleanse from sin when it was shed upon 'the accursed tree' than when it was flowing in His veins as He went daily about His Father's business."[39]

Biblically, we understand that everyone sins and is in dire need of a Savior (Rom. 3:23). Furthermore, because of our sin we'll die forever without that Savior (Rom. 6:23). But by God's amazing grace, through Christ alone, we are saved from judgment and eternal condemnation (John 5:24) and are blessed with eternal life in Christ (John 14:1-6).

(The greatest portion of this section and all documentation are derived from ongoing research by Don Stewart and Josh McDowell in *Handbook of Today's Religions* [Here's Life, 1991].)

THE JEHOVAH'S WITNESSES

Officially known as the Watchtower Bible and Tract Society, the Jehovah's Witnesses are a product of the lifework of Charles Taze Russell, who was born February 16, 1852, near Pittsburgh, Pennsylvania. In 1870, while still in his teens and without formal theological education, Russell organized a Bible class whose members eventually made him "pastor."

By the time of his death in 1916, Pastor Russell, according to the Watchtower, had traveled more than a million miles, had given more than 30,000 sermons, and had written books totaling over 50,000 pages.[40]

Today, worldwide, the Jehovah's Witnesses number over 2 million. The members are zealous and sincere and claim to accept the Bible as their only authority. However, their theology denies every cardinal belief of traditional Christianity, including the Trinity, the divinity of Jesus Christ and His bodily resurrection, salvation by grace through faith, and eternal punishment of the wicked.

The Watchtower believes that it speaks for God in today's world. But it constantly misuses the Scriptures to establish its own peculiar beliefs. This is accomplished chiefly by quoting texts out of context while omitting other passages relevant to the subject. For all practical purposes, the Watchtower's publications take precedence over the Scriptures, as evidenced by such erroneous statements as, "The trinity doctrine was not conceived by Jesus or the early Christians."[41]

In Watchtower theology, neither Jesus Christ nor the Holy Spirit is God: "Jesus, the Christ, a created individual, is the second greatest personage of the Universe"; "He was a god, but not the Almighty God, who is Jehovah"; "The truth of the matter is that the word is Christ Jesus, who did have a beginning."[42]

One favorite passage used by the Jehovah's Witnesses to prove Christ is less than God is John 14:28: "The Father is greater than I." This verse refers to the voluntary subordination of Jesus during His earthly life when He willingly placed Himself in submission to the Father. It says nothing about His nature, only His temporary rank on earth. Thus, the "greater than" refers to His position rather than His person.

The idea that the second coming of Christ took place in 1914 is important to Watchtower theology. "The times of the Gentiles extend to 1914. And the Heavenly Kingdom will not have full sway till then, but as a 'stone' the Kingdom of God is set up 'in the days of these Kings' and by consummating them it becomes a universal Kingdom—a 'great mountain and fills the whole earth.'"[43]

The Watchtower is guilty of false prophecy (see Deut. 18:21-22) in predicting that Christ would return in 1914. It is also wrong in asserting His coming is secret and invisible, because the Scriptures teach completely to the contrary (see Rev. 1:7).

THE NEW AGE MOVEMENT

The New Age movement is the fastest-growing cult religion in America. Its influences (often unrecognized) infiltrate almost every aspect of American life. Psychic counseling services appear regularly in newspapers and shopping malls and on network television. Over 40 million Americans consult their horoscopes daily for advice and counsel. Millions of books, box-office-smash movies, and network TV programs are dedicated to New Age beliefs and practices, such as channeling (basically, spirit possession), out-of-body experiences, Eastern cultic meditation, and seances.

Public-school systems, teachers' associations, large corporations (such as AT&T and GM), and the army, navy, and air force have adopted "growth" and team-building services that are devoted to New Age philosophy (always leaving a divine, supernatural Creator God out of the equation).

The New Age movement insists that the maps of our lives are in the wrinkles in the palms of our hands, our daily plans are in the stars, and God is in everything . . . good and evil. As Shirley MacLaine proclaimed, "I know that I exist, therefore I AM. I know that the God-source exists, therefore It IS. Since I am part of that force, then I Am that I AM. . . . We are 'in reality' multidimensional beings who each reflect the totality of the whole."[44]

Elvis Presley is thought by New Agers to be a reincarnated man of many previous lives. *USA Today* reported that, according to New Age thinkers, Elvis was once a gladiator, a crown emperor, a Renaissance bard, and an actor, poet, and singer in a Greek theater. Also, he was inspired by Saturn and Aquarius and other astrological influences.

The Bible sums up its timely disdain for all such New Age philosophy: "But the Spirit explicitly says that in later times some will fall away from the faith, paying attention to deceitful spirits and doctrines of demons" (1 Tim. 4:1, NASB); "And no wonder, for even Satan disguises himself as an angel of light" (2 Cor. 11:14, NASB).

New Age Beliefs Versus Biblical Christianity

New Age Movement	*The Bible*
Pantheism: Everything, including evil, is a part of God; God is all, and all is good.	God is one. He is separate and distinct over all creation. "I am the LORD your God. . . . You shall have no other gods before me" (Exod. 20:2-3, NASB).
God is impersonal. He should be referred to as an "it," like "the force" in the Star Wars movies. God cannot love, cannot think, cannot be merciful, cannot be known. "It" just is.	God is personal, knowable, and lovable. He became flesh in His Son, Jesus Christ, Who personally died for the sins of men and women who by faith acknowledge

Him as Savior. He adopts His followers as sons and daughters.

Monism: All is one. There is no difference between God, a person, a head of lettuce, and a rock. There are no ultimate divisions.

Creation is a diversity of objects, events, and persons. God is sovereign over everything, and mankind was created in His image to rule over the animals and plants of the earth.

Humanity is God. We as people are perfect. We are, in fact, gods. We are God in disguise.

We are created in God's image. But we are not infinite, omnipotent, omniscient, or omnipresent. We are creatures, not the Creator. We are born in sin and in dire need of a divine Savior. The Bible condemns human pretenders to the divine throne (see Isa. 14:13-15; Ezek. 28:1-2).

All religions are one. All world-religion leaders are equally enlightened, including Jesus, Buddha, Krishna, and Confucius.

Jesus summed up His stance in John 14:6: "I am the way and the truth and the life. No one comes to the Father except through me."

Reincarnation: When a person dies, he or she is reborn in a new body and lives a new life as a different person.

There is one life on this planet, one death, one resurrection (see Heb. 9:27).

Spiritism: (1) Evil is an illusion. All is good, including any type of sexual perversion, pornography, etc. Good and evil are one and the same. (2) By

The Bible classifies spiritism as "unclean spirits" or demons: "Let no one be found among you . . . who practices divination or sorcery, interprets omens, holding crystals, a person can feel and use the energy of God. Crystals release the power of the universe. (3) Magic charms, divining rods, Ouija boards, tarot cards, etc., are useful for gaining supernatural power and insight.

engages in witchcraft, or casts spells, or who is a medium or spiritist or who consults the dead. Anyone who does these things is detestable to the LORD" (Deut. 18:10-12); "He sacrificed his sons in the fire in the Valley of Ben Hinnom, practiced sorcery, divination, and witchcraft, and consulted mediums and spiritists. He did much evil in the eyes of the LORD, provoking him to anger" (2 Chron. 33:6).

SATANISM

Recently, a scared, suicidal 25-year-old woman called me for help. She said she had sacrificed her baby and her dog, and she was now going to sacrifice herself, to Satan. She had given herself to him, and now "they" were controlling her and inflicting physical and mental pain upon her.

Today thousands of America's young and old are attracted to satanic music, cartoons, toys, and rituals. The worship of Satan, or Satanism, is expressed through black magic, the black mass, facets of the drug culture, "sex clubs," perversions of Christ, the mocking of Scripture, blood sacrifices, and so on.

Satanism has deep historical roots. The Church of Satan in modern America was founded in San Francisco in 1966 by Anton Szandor La Vey. As well as being anti-Christian, the satanic church is strongly materialistic and hedonistic. Pleasure-seeking could well describe its philosophy of life. What the world has to offer through the devil is taken full advantage of in the Church of Satan. Even La Vey concedes that it is a blatantly selfish, brutal religion. It is based on the belief that man is inherently selfish and violent, that life is a Darwinian struggle for survival of the fittest, and that the earth will be ruled by those who fight to win.[45] The satanic church espouses any type of sexual activity that satisfies one's needs, be it hetero-sexuality, homosexuality, adultery, bestiality, you name it.[46]

"There are nine satanic statements to which all members must agree: that Satan represents indulgence, vital existence, undefiled wisdom, kindness only to those who deserve it, vengeance, responsibility only to those who are responsible, the animal nature of man, all the so-called sins, and the best friend the church has ever had, as he has kept it in business all these years."[47]

Scripture has many titles for Satan.

1. *Devil* (John 8:44) means "the accuser and slanderer." He makes false accusations against others, he aims to harm God and man, and he will tell lies of any kind to achieve his end.

2. *Satan* (Matt. 12:26) means "the resister or adversary." He reigns over a kingdom of darkness that is opposed to God.

3. *Tempter* (Matt. 4:3) denotes that he seeks to lead people into sin because he himself is a sinner. He tempts them by promising sensual delights or earthly power as a reward for disobeying God.

4. *Father of Lies* (John 8:44) indicates that he is not just a liar, he is the father of lies; that he hates what God loves and loves what God hates.

5. *Lord of Death* (Heb. 2:14) means he seeks to annihilate anyone he can.

6. *Beelzebub* (Mark 3:22-23) means "lord of the dunghill" or "lord of the flies."

7. *Belial* (2 Cor. 6:15) means "worthlessness, wickedness, and enemy."

8. *Evil One* (1 John 2:13) indicates that he is the supreme evildoer.

9. *Ruler of This World* (John 14:30) gives us some idea of the tremendous scope of Satan's power and activity on this earth.

FURTHER READING

For a more detailed study of these topics, I recommend the following resources.

WORLD RELIGIONS AND CULTS

Anderson, Sir Norman. *Christianity and World Religions.* Downers Grove, Ill.: InterVarsity Press, 1984.

Ankerberg, John, and John Weldon. *Everything You Ever Wanted to Know About Mormonism.* Eugene, Ore.: Harvest House Publishers, 1992.

Baron, Will. *Deceived by the New Age.* Boise: Pacific Press Publishing, 1991.

Chandler, Russell. *Understanding the New Age.* Grand Rapids, Mich.: Zondervan, 1993.

Enroth, Ronald, ed. *Evangelizing the Cults: How to Share Jesus with Children, Parents, Neighbors, and Friends Who Are Involved in a Cult.* Ann Arbor, Mich.: Vine Books, 1990.

Groothuis, Douglas. *Confronting the New Age: How to Resist a Growing Religious Movement.* Downers Grove, Ill.: InterVarsity Press, 1988.

_____. *Revealing the New Age Jesus: Challenges to Orthodox Views of Christ.* Downers Grove, Ill.: InterVarsity Press, 1990.

_____. *Unmasking the New Age: Is There a New Religious Movement Trying to Transform Society?* Downers Grove, Ill.: InterVarsity Press, 1986.

Kjos, Berit. *Your Child and the New Age.* Wheaton, Ill.: Scripture Press, 1990.

Larsen, Dale, and Sandy Larsen. *Blinded by the Lies: Discerning Truth in Distorted Times.* Wheaton, Ill.: Scripture Press, 1989.

Lewis, James F., and William G. Travis. *Religious Traditions of the World.* Grand Rapids, Mich.: Zondervan, 1991.

Martin, Paul R., Jr. *Cult Proofing Your Kids.* Grand Rapids, Mich.: Zondervan, 1993.

Martin, Walter. *The Kingdom of the Cults.* Minneapolis: Bethany House Publishers, 1965, 1977, 1985.

_____. *The New Cults.* Ventura, Calif.: Regal Books, 1980.

Mather, George A., and Larry A. Nichols. *Dictionary of Cults, Sects,*

Religions, and the Occult. Grand Rapids, Mich.: Zondervan, 1993.

McGuire, Paul. *Evangelizing the New Age: The Power of the Gospel Invades the New Age Movement.* Ann Arbor, Mich.: Servant, 1989.

Miller, William M. *A Christian's Response to Islam.* Phillipsburg, N.J.: Presbyterian & Reformed, 1976.

Neill, Stephen. *Christian Faith and Other Faiths.* Downers Grove, Ill.: InterVarsity Press, 1984.

Reed, David A. *Jehovah's Witnesses Answered Verse by Verse.* Grand Rapids, Mich.: Baker Book House, 1991.

Rhodes, Ron. *The Culting of America: The Shocking Implications for Every Concerned Christian.* Eugene, Ore.: Harvest House Publishers, 1994.

——————. *Reasoning from the Scriptures with the Jehovah's Witnesses.* Eugene, Ore.: Harvest House Publishers, 1993.

Sire, James. *Scripture Twisting: 20 Ways the Cults Misread the Bible.* Downers Grove, Ill.: InterVarsity Press, 1980.

White, James R. *Letters to a Mormon Elder.* Minneapolis: Bethany House Publishers, 1993.

APOLOGETICS

Frame, John. *Apologetics to the Glory of God.* Phillipsburg, N.J.: Presbyterian & Reformed, 1994.

Lewis, C.S. *Mere Christianity.* New York: Macmillan, 1952.

McDowell, Josh. *A Ready Defense.* San Bernardino, Calif.: Here's Life, 1990.

Nash, Ronald H. *Faith and Reason: Searching for a Rational Faith.* Grand Rapids, Mich.: Zondervan, 1988.

Pratt, Richard L. *Every Thought Captive.* Phillipsburg, N.J.: Presbyterian & Reformed, 1979.

Schaeffer, Francis A. *The God Who Is There, Vol. 1,* in *The Complete Works of Francis Schaeffer.* 2d ed. Westchester, Ill.: Crossway Books, 1982.

Resource I

CURRENT ISSUES
AND THE BIBLE

―――――

ALCOHOL AND OTHER DRUGS

"Don't you know that you yourselves are God's temple and that God's Spirit lives in you?" (1 Cor. 3:16). You are a temple of the Holy Spirit; anything harmful that you put into your mind or your body is a sin.

THE HARMFUL EFFECTS OF ALCOHOL

The devastating effects of alcohol abuse on our society are well documented.

> The damage caused by alcohol-impaired drivers is the same as if a Boeing 747 with more than 500 passengers crashed every eight days killing everyone.[1]

> Alcohol costs us yearly: 97,500 lives lost because of alcohol-related diseases, accidents, murders, and suicides; $100 billion-plus in economic losses; family problems in 1 out of every 4 U.S. homes.[2]

> [A]lcoholic families had a higher incidence of physical child

abuse (31 percent vs. 9 percent) [and] sexual child abuse (19 percent vs. 5 percent).[3]

Alcohol is involved in one out of every three cases of child molestation, and in between 25 percent and 50 percent of all cases of domestic violence.[4]

American children see an estimated 90,000 incidents of drinking in TV programs by the age of 21.[5]

Three out of ten adolescents have a drinking problem—nearly 5 million![6]

Heavy drinking is involved in 60 percent of violent crimes, 30 percent of all suicides and 80 percent of fire and drowning accidents. The suicide rate of alcoholics is 30 times that of the general population.[7]

It is time to ban the advertising of alcohol from broadcasting.[8]

Alcohol is still the USA's most widely used drug. 10.5 million adults show symptoms of alcoholism and 7.2 million more are alcohol abusers. Nearly half of traffic deaths are alcohol related. Drunken drivers are eight times as likely as sober drivers to have a fatal crash per mile driven. Alcohol abuse and dependence will cost the country $136.3 billion this year. Fetal exposure to alcohol is a leading cause of mental retardation.[9]

WHAT THE BIBLE SAYS ABOUT ALCOHOL

"Wine is a mocker and beer a brawler; whoever is led astray by them is not wise" (Prov. 20:1).

"Woe to those who rise early in the morning to run after their drinks, who stay up late at night till they are inflamed with wine" (Isa. 5:11).

The Bible specifically condemns not only getting high or drunk but also partaking of "strong drink." In biblical times, "strong drink" (*sikera* in Greek) referred to any unmixed or undiluted wine. When Jesus turned water into wine in John 2, He didn't make *sikera*, He made *oinos*, wine diluted with water. When Paul told Timothy, in 1 Timothy 5:23, that he should drink wine, he told him to do it for medicinal purposes (e.g., for a stomach problem). Again, it was *oinos*, not *sikera*. (Today we have sophisticated medicines for those medical needs.) According to researcher Robert Stein, in biblical times, people used wine to purify unsafe water, not as a way to get high.[10]

Strong drink in biblical times was from 3 percent to 11 percent alcohol. The least ratio of water to wine mixture was 3 parts water to 1 part wine. That produced a subalcoholic drink that was a maximum of 2.5 percent to 2.75 percent alcohol. Normally, the ratio was even higher, up to 20 to 1.[11]

By contrast, modern wines have 9 percent to 11 percent alcohol; one brand has 20 percent alcohol. Brandy contains 15 percent to 20 percent alcohol; hard liquor has 40 percent to 50 percent alcohol. According to biblical standards, these beverages would all be considered strong drink.

THE BIBLE AND CIVIL LAWS

"Everyone must submit himself to the governing authorities, for there is no authority except that which God has established. The authorities that exist have been established by God. Consequently, he who rebels against the authority is rebelling against what God has instituted, and those who do so will bring judgment on themselves" (Rom. 13:1-2).

The current law in the United States says that drinking is illegal under the age of 21. Since the Bible instructs us to obey our governmental leaders (except if they ask us to do something that goes against God's laws), underage people who drink not only commit a crime against their government, but they also commit a sin against God.

THE HARMFUL EFFECTS OF ILLEGAL DRUGS

Much has been written about the harmful effects of smoking marijuana. Here are a few facts:[12]

- The average marijuana user shifts from a self-activating, interesting, and involved person to one who is withdrawn and given to disordered thinking.
- The user's thought formation tends to be less powerful than before he or she began using marijuana.

- The user's attention span and ability to concentrate are reduced, and his or her memory is shortened.

- The user's facial circulation reflexes are impaired, and the focusing of the eyes is less precise.

- The user's concern for consequences is reduced, and his or her concern for the rights and well-being of others may be largely absent.

- Because marijuana is a hypnotic drug, the user is likely to be talked into many situations that he or she would otherwise avoid.

- The young user tends to remain thin and underdeveloped for his or her age.

- The male user is deficient in the male hormone.

- The user is likely to have a tendency toward paranoia or schizophrenia.

- The user's white blood cell immune response is lowered.

- The user's sleeping and waking cycle is largely inverted.

There are also many harmful effects resulting from the use of cocaine and crack.[13] For example,

- *CBS Nightly News* reported that more than 1,000 babies a day are born drug-damaged. More than 100,000 a year are "crack babies."

- $60 billion a year is spent on cocaine in the United States.

- "According to a study done by Dr. David Hills of Texas Southwestern Medical Center, . . . even small amounts of cocaine can decrease blood flow to the heart, leading to heart attacks."

- Cocaine abuse may lead to serious cardiac complications.

- Individuals who use cocaine on a regular basis may engage in risky behavior that could threaten their lives.

- Research is showing a correlation between crack use and respiratory symptoms and lung dysfunction.

- Doctors at Detroit Medical Center claim that cocaine users may develop brain hemorrhages 20 years earlier than nonusers.

- Symptoms of cocaine abuse include "sleeping problems, headaches, [a] runny nose, nasal sores, lowered appetite, decreased sexual drive, problems at home, school, work, [and] with relationships, financial difficulties, depress[ion], irritab[ility], fatigue, tremors, nausea."

PORNOGRAPHY

Webster's Dictionary defines *pornography* as "the depiction of erotic behavior (as in pictures or in writing) intended to cause sexual excitement." Extensive research has been done on the effects of pornography.[14] Here are some statistics:

- Adult bookstores outnumber McDonald's restaurants in the United States by a margin of at least three to one.

- The pornography industry grosses nearly $8 billion annually.

- Research studies show a relationship between viewing pornography and the desire by some men to commit sex crimes.

- A company in Great Britain is delivering hard-core pornography to homes by satellite television, even though pornography is against the law in that country.

- The FBI has been investigating certain users of the America Online service for transmitting child pornography.

The *CQ Researcher* provided some statistics of its own in its December 20, 1991, issue:

- "A whopping 400 million adult tapes were rented from mainstream video outlets in 1990, according to the Adult Video Association, compared with only 54 million in 1980" (p. 973).

- "The bulk of the 1,960-page *Final Report* of the 1986 Commission on Pornography led by Attorney General Edwin Meese III asserts that pornography harms both the individual and society" (p. 973).

- "Victor Cline, a University of Utah psychologist who has treated sex offenders, says pornography becomes addictive, requiring the user to seek rougher and more sexually shocking material to achieve the same effect. Eventually, the user is prompted to act out what he has seen, often forcing wives to submit to degrading or dangerous sex acts" (p. 974).

- "The Meese Commission added the charge that pornography perpetuates the 'rape myth', the notion that every woman secretly desires to be sexually taken by force" (p. 974).

In addition, CNN reported on April 23, 1992, that 700,000 American women are raped annually. Twenty-nine percent of these are under 11 years of age; 60 percent are under 18.

THE CONNECTION BETWEEN PORNOGRAPHY AND SEX CRIMES AND ABNORMAL SEXUAL BEHAVIOR

In 1986, the U.S. Congress Permanent Subcommittee on Investigations on Child Pornography and Pedophilia gave a report on child pornography stating that the most pervasive characteristic of pedophilia is the obsession with child pornography. The fascination of pedophiles with child pornography and child abuse is well documented and has been established by a multitude of sexually explicit materials involving children.

The report quoted Detective William Dworin of the Los Angeles Police Department, who estimated that, of the hundreds of child molesters he helped arrest during the past few years, more than half had either adult or child pornography in their possession. All the child molesters interviewed by the subcommittee collected or produced child pornography, or did both. Most admitted they had used the obscene material not only to stimulate themselves, but also to lower their victims' inhibitions and to teach them how to pose for photographs or how to behave in sexual encounters with adults.

Drs. Dolf Zillmann and Jennings Bryant, in their 1988 study on pornography and its effect on couples, obtained these results:[16]

- Pornography consumption affects men and women equally on all measured aspects of happiness and satisfaction.
- Exposure to hard-core pornography diminishes satisfaction with the physical appearance of the respondents' sexual partners.

- Pornography consumption reduces men's and women's satisfaction with their partners' attempts at affection.

- Pornography consumption reduces men's and women's satisfaction with their partners' sexual behavior as such.

- Pornography consumption reduces the importance of fidelity in relationships.

- Pornography consumption reduces the importance of "good family relations."

- Pornography consumption increases the importance of having sexual relations with someone with whom one is not emotionally involved.

There is much controversy over whether or not pornography should be legalized. In July 1986, the Attorney General's Commission on Pornography issued a report that described illegal pornography (unprotected by the First Amendment) as "that material which is predominantly sexually explicit and intended primarily for the purpose of arousal."[17] Four basic categories covered by the ruling are obscenity, indecency, child pornography, and constitutionally protected materials. Obviously, our legal system is filled with loopholes and flaws and depicts a degenerate, immoral, and crime-ridden society.

Are there higher, more dependable laws than the laws of men that we can rely on?

God's laws always stand above the laws of men. God's desire is for a man and woman to have pure hearts, to allow for a fulfilling relationship between God and His children. God's plan is for a man and woman to have a pure (fulfilling, lasting, incredible) marriage. Hebrews 13:4 says, "Marriage should be honored by all, and the marriage bed kept pure." God warns us repeatedly, and commands us to heed the warnings, to avoid, at all costs, anything that produces impurity in our lives. "Flee the evil desires of youth, and pursue righteousness, faith, love and peace, along with those who call on the Lord out of a pure heart" (2 Tim. 2:22).

SOME MORE FACTS ABOUT PORNOGRAPHY

- Pornography (as seen in many PG, most PG-13, and almost all R, NC-17, X, etc., movies) is addictive.

- Pornography is anti-Christian.

- Pornography attacks women and children.
- Pornography leads to idolatry.
- Pornography destroys marriages, intimate sex between couples, and families.

SUMMARY

As Christians, we should not ask, "How much viewing of sexual scenes on movies and TV can I get by with?" or "How much can I listen to secular music and not be harmed mentally?" Rather, we should ask, "How much do I want to love God?" and "How much do I want to love my spouse and children?"

THE MYTH OF "SAFE SEX"

ARE CONDOMS SAFE PHYSIOLOGICALLY?

1. Concerning Unwanted Pregnancies

   18.4 percent of single women under 18 years of age have an unplanned pregnancy within the first year of regular contraceptive condom use.[18]

2. Concerning AIDS Prevention

   With a failure rate of 10 to 15 percent, latex condoms aren't a perfect form of birth control. And to keep AIDS from spreading, a condom must work 10 times better. A woman is fertile roughly 36 days a year, but someone with AIDS can transmit it 365 days a year.[19]

   It is clear that the use of condoms will not eliminate the risk of transmission [of HIV] and must be viewed as a secondary strategy. On the basis of current data, only celibacy . . . can be considered truly safe. Reducing risky sex, rather than eliminating it, is like incompletely immunizing a population—there is little benefit to the individual or the community.[20]

   Condoms are unreliable barriers to HIV. A recent scientific study conducted by a University of Miami team concerned heterosexual couples with one person having AIDS antibodies. The study showed that AIDS antibody exposure occurred in at least three out of ten couples who always used condoms. Couples using condoms less than at every intercourse were classified as "never-users."[21]

Scanning skin condoms under an electron microscope, the membranes reveal layers of fibers crisscrossing in various patterns. That latticework endows the skins with strength but also makes for an occasional pore, sometimes up to 1.5 micron wide. That's smaller than a sperm, a white blood cell, or even some gonorrhea bacteria. But it's more than 10 times the size of the AIDS virus, and more than 25 times the size of the hepatitis-B virus.[22]

3. Concerning Other Sexually Transmitted Diseases

Any increase in the more than 50 diseases and syndromes classified as a sexually transmitted disease, or STD, is of concern because these conditions, even excluding AIDS, already account for more than 13 million cases and 7,000 deaths annually, according to the United States Public Health Service.[23]

Sexual intercourse may pass along all kinds of organisms—bacteria, viruses, fungi, and parasites—from person to person. Diseases that may be transmitted sexually [include] AIDS, bacterial vaginosis, chancroid, chlamydial infections, cytomegalovirus infections, enteric infections (hepatitis A & amebiasis), genital herpes, genital warts, gonorrhea, granuloma inguinale, group B streptococcal infections, leukemia-lymphoma/myelopathy, lymphogranuloma venereum, molluscum contagiosum, pubic lice, scabies, syphillis, trichomoniasis, vaginal yeast infections, viral hepatitis.[24]

In some instances, the time from infection to the development of neurosyphilis may be up to 20 years.[25]

Each year in the United States, an estimated 12 million cases of sexually transmitted diseases occur, including four million cases of chlamydia, 1.5 million cases of gonorrhea, 0.5 million cases of genital herpes, and 110,000 cases of syphilis.[26]

The annual comprehensive cost of STDs in the United States is estimated to be well in excess of $5 billion.[27]

Some STDs can spread into the uterus and fallopian tubes to cause pelvic inflammatory disease, which in turn is a major cause of both infertility and tubal pregnancy. The latter can be fatal.[28]

STDs in women may also be associated with cervical cancer.[29]

STDs can be passed from a mother to her baby before or during birth; some of these infections of the newborn can be cured easily, but others may cause a baby to be permanently disabled or even die.[30]

[A] 16-year-old girl was responsible for 218 cases of syphilis and 440 cases of gonorrhea. Here's what happened. The girl had sex with 16 men. Those men had sex with other people who had sex with other people. The number of contacts finally added up to 1,660. "It was an unusual case. . . . It was the biggest pyramid. What if the girl had AIDS, instead of gonorrhea and syphilis? You probably would have had 1,000 dead people by now."[31]

To summarize, since condoms have an average failure rate of one-in-six to one-in-eight, spreading the myth that condoms will prevent the spread of STDs and AIDS can be compared to the idea of giving kids a handgun with six chambers—five empty and one loaded—and saying, "Kids will use guns, so let's supply them with these 'safe guns' and give them our endorsement."

ARE CONDOMS SAFE PSYCHOLOGICALLY?

In personal letters over the years, young people have reported to me their feelings after having sex:

"Since I started dating, I have always promised myself that I would stay a virgin until I was married. I have lived up to that promise until the past year. He said that he loved me and, like all of the others, that we would get married. I really believed he loved me. After our first time, I started taking the pill to keep from getting pregnant. Two months later, he dropped me for his old girlfriend (who was once pregnant by him). I felt as if I had 200 knives go through me. I was crushed."

"The thing I regret most in my life would have to be losing my virginity. I was so young, and most people don't think twelve-year-olds (7th grade) even know about sex. But I did and he did. We really didn't think it was all that wrong. I got my first kiss and lost my virginity all the same day."

"Since my defenses were low and morals were shifting in the wrong direction, I submitted to the desire. It really made me feel like I was important (however, it was only pointing me in the wrong direction). Since we didn't have Christ in the center of our relationship, and I listened to my friend's advice, I made the worst decision of my life. Why was I so stupid?"

"I shouldn't have rushed myself. I regret my entire relationship with that boy. It will always be on my mind. It is still hard for me to believe how just one night could affect my life so greatly."

"Of all the mistakes that I have made, the hardest ones to forget and forgive myself for are those that involved a few of the girls that I dated in my high-school and college years. After my first love and I broke up, I fell in love with another girl, and we flew through the first stages of kissing and petting, taking up right where I'd left off with my first love. Though this girl was a virgin, she had been through a fairly physical relationship with a previous boyfriend. The only thing left for us to make our relationship unique was having sexual intercourse—and it wasn't long until we started doing just that. . . . I never felt good about it. I had gotten myself into a trap and wasn't strong enough to get out. Sex is like that. It is something to be respected. . . . It is really hard to forgive myself for taking away that terrific girl's virginity. I'd be lying if I didn't say that it hurts me to this day."

A condom is not safe psychologically. It can never protect a boy's conscience. It can never protect a girl's fragile self-image. It can never block guilt or prevent hurt in a relationship.

THE NEW TESTAMENT AND "SAFE SEX"

God never says, "Safe sex is okay," or "Safe sex will make you feel better." He says simply, "Your marriage should be undefiled. Keep your marriage bed unspoiled . . . pure . . . honorable . . . trustworthy" (Heb.

13:4; Eph. 5:25-31; Prov. 5:18-21; 1 Cor. 7:1-5). To the unmarried, He says, "Wait for your wife. Wait for your husband. Your body belongs to Christ first and your spouse second. Sex outside of marriage is a sin against me and against your body. When you go against my law, you will reap negative consequences within yourself" (1 Thess. 4:3-8; 1 Cor. 6:15-20; 2 Cor. 6:14).

Christ is the preventative answer. Self-control comes with Spirit-control. "But the fruit of the Spirit is love, joy, peace, patience, kindness, goodness, faithfulness, gentleness and self-control. Against such things there is no law" (Gal. 5:22-23). Christ can and will forgive you for your past mistakes; He will get you on your feet with the confidence to say no to sex until you are married. "If we confess our sins, he is faithful and just and will forgive us our sins and purify us from all unrighteousness" (1 John 1:9).

THE SANCTITY OF LIFE

ABORTION

Our nation's total losses from all the wars we've been in is over 1 million soldiers killed.[32] During World War II, Adolf Hitler murdered over 6 million Jews and others.[33] Since 1973, when *Roe v. Wade* was decided by the Supreme Court, American doctors have taken the lives of almost 30 million babies.[34]

After reading this last sentence, what word best describes your emotions? Numbed? Surprised? Angry? Upset? Disbelieving? Grieved? Sickened? Sad? Confused? Indifferent?

Which term would you use to describe abortion? Medical procedure? Fetal interruption? Pregnancy termination? Murder? Genocide?

If you were asleep in your house at midnight and an armed burglar broke in through your bedroom window, and before you could wake up to defend yourself he shot and killed you, which term would you use to describe the event? Home-entering procedure? Dream interruption? Sleep termination? Murder? Genocide?

In America today, a citizen can be imprisoned (and, in fact, some are currently behind bars) and fined severely for tampering with the egg of an unborn eagle or hawk. But doctors can perform abortions with no legal (at least on earth) consequences.

When is murder wrong? In all circumstances, at any age? When the victim is between the ages of six and 60? During burglaries only? When the victim has a chance to fight back?

The Bible specifically condemns murder, the unjustified killing of a human being. Exodus 20:13 says, "You shall not murder."

In your opinion, when does life begin? At conception? When a baby can live outside the womb? At birth?

Biblically, when does life begin? In Genesis 4:1, God specifically connected the birth of Eve's son Cain to his conception: "Adam lay with his wife Eve, and she became pregnant and gave birth to Cain. She said, 'With the help of the LORD I have brought forth a man.'"

In Job 3:3, that great man of God also connected his birth directly to the night of his conception: "'May the day of my birth perish, and the night it was said, "A boy is born!"'" (The Hebrew word for *boy* used in this text specifically applies to the preborn human.)

In Luke 1, the "fetus" of John the Baptist was graphically described as fully human: "When Elizabeth heard Mary's greeting, the baby leaped in her womb, and Elizabeth was filled with the Holy Spirit" (1:41); "'As soon as the sound of your greeting reached my ears, the baby in my womb leaped for joy'" (1:44). (The word for *baby* in the original Greek is the same word used for "Baby Jesus" in Luke 2:12, when He lay in the manger on the night of His birth.)

God also gave you personal life from the moment of your conception. "For you created my inmost being; you knit me together in my mother's womb. I praise you because I am fearfully and wonderfully made; your works are wonderful, I know that full well. My frame was not hidden from you when I was made in the secret place. When I was woven together in the depths of the earth, your eyes saw my unformed body. All the days ordained for me were written in your book before one of them came to be" (Ps. 139:13-16).

Prayerfully consider the following biblical passages as well:

> "Listen to me, you islands; hear this, you distant nations: Before I was born the LORD called me; from my birth he has made mention of my name" (Isa. 49:1).

> "Before I formed you in the womb I knew you, before you were born I set you apart; I appointed you as a prophet to the nations" (Jer. 1:5).

"But he said to me, 'You will conceive and give birth to a son. Now then, drink no wine or other fermented drink and do not eat anything unclean, because the boy will be a Nazirite of God from birth [from the womb] until the day of his death'" (Judg. 13:7).

A word of caution: The pro-abortion (pro-choice) people have taken many of these Bible passages far out of context and stretched and twisted their message regarding the sanctity of life. For example, some pro-choice people argue that the Scripture that says God calls us by name (Isa. 43:1) means we are nonhuman until we have a name.

That argument is absurd! A child is named by the parents at birth because the sex of a child is not known by most parents until birth. A tiny fetus has a heartbeat, ten fingers and ten toes, and a developing nervous system that feels comfort and pain; the fetus sucks his or her thumb and, yes, depends on Mom for life! In Isaiah 49:1 (see also Gen. 4:1 and Job 3:3), God states that He calls to, names, and knows babies (including you) while they're still in the womb. God will not be mocked; He is grieved and angered by any twisting of Scripture to try to prove an unbiblical point of view.

A letter I received from a scared 19-year-old girl expresses candidly the feelings of a mom who was talked into the abortion procedure by her boyfriend:

"Bobby had stuck by his guns about not marrying me and said if I kept the child, we were through. Bobby stuck by me long enough to make sure I had the operation. He called me every day or wrote and made me feel like he still cared. I went in that day by myself to do the one thing I was most against. I talked to Bobby that night and then he took off. He stuck around long enough to make sure I got rid of the evidence, then left me on my own. I can't explain the feelings I have inside me now. I've never thought less of myself or felt more like trash. How could I have been so naive? I loved him, but he never knew the meaning of the word. I still have nightmares, and at times I hate myself. Abortion is much, much deeper than the scraping of that uterus lining. It involves the destruction of one's whole being, the loss of any self-respect, and, saddest of all, a guilt-ridden experience."

Dr. Ann Speckhard, of the University of Minnesota, published a study on the long-term (5-10 years) manifestations of stress from abortion.[35] Although the women she studied came from diverse backgrounds, their reactions were amazingly similar:

- 81 percent reported preoccupation with the aborted child.
- 73 percent reported flashbacks of the abortion experience.
- 69 percent reported feelings of "craziness" after the abortion.
- 54 percent recalled nightmares related to the abortion.
- 35 percent had perceived visitations from the aborted child.
- 96 percent in retrospect regarded abortion as the taking of life or as murder.

EUTHANASIA

The term *euthanasia* derives from the Greek for "happy death." For many people, it means simply bringing relief to terminally ill patients by keeping them free from pain. It also means refraining from extraordinary measures that keep someone alive after he or she has been declared brain dead. Increasingly today, however, euthanasia means either hastening the death of someone who is considered a nuisance or unproductive or committing suicide with the help of a physician.[36]

As Christians, we should be concerned about the growing acceptance of euthanasia as a means of legally killing "useless" people or killing oneself. Physicians in The Netherlands have been euthanizing patients with the courts' permission since the 1970s. One Dutch cardiologist estimated that half of the doctors in Holland who offer aid in dying have killed conscious patients without their consent.[37] In the States, Dr. Jack Kevorkian (a.k.a. "Dr. Death") has made headlines for his role in helping terminally ill people commit suicide. Several states have considered changing the charge of first degree murder (homicide) in physician-assisted suicides to "aid in dying" (legalized murder). Former U.S. surgeon general Dr. C. Everett Koop believes the eventual death toll from euthanasia will dwarf abortion deaths.[38]

The moral and ethical questions surrounding euthanasia are complex, and it is difficult to state an absolute Christian position on the issue. Our view of euthanasia should be similar to our view of abortion, however. Life is holy, a gift from God. He decides when it will begin, and He decides when it will end. Deliberately taking an innocent life, whether it's someone else's or our own, is an affront to the Creator of that life.

Dr. Koop has offered these insights on the problems inherent in the legalization of euthanasia.[39]

On attitudes toward elderly people:

[Pro-euthanasia forces] have gotten across to a whole segment of the elderly population that somehow because they are living, they are depriving someone else of a prior right to resources. That is a most reprehensible thing.

When I was doing research for [the book and film] *Whatever Happened to the Human Race?* I went to nursing homes and talked to people who felt that pressure. Old people were apologizing to me for using a bed, for being alive, for taking medication, because they "knew" somebody else deserved it more. I think that's pitiful.

On problems with the Living Will (a document in which the signer requests to die rather than be kept alive by artificial means):

The problems are in two categories. There is the very commonplace changing of the mind of individuals who thought the Living Will was great before they were in a situation where it could be used.

The other is that, if you have a Living Will, it sends a signal that you don't want anything done. What the patient might have had in mind . . . [was] pumping on his chest 15 times so he'll be brought back to life only to die the next day, or a respirator to keep him going for six hours in great discomfort when he might have died by himself earlier. But medical personnel may interpret the Living Will so as to assume the patient doesn't want his life prolonged by any means.

On the practice of killing elderly people by denying food and water:

Nothing surprises me anymore. My great concern is that there will be 10,000 Grandma Does for every Baby Doe.

On the church's responsibility:

If you go back over history, it was always the Church's responsibility to care for the sick. Then, when entitlements came along, government became the distributor of all kinds of largesse. The churches kind of figured the government is going to do it, so they don't have to. That was a mistake.

There are alternatives to abortion. There are alternatives to infanticide. Now we have to find *many* alternatives to euthanasia.

SECULAR HUMANISM AND MILITANT HUMANISM (MARXISM)

Just as hot air currents and cold air currents collide and react to form a windstorm that destroys the land, so, too, have the turbulent humanistic movements formed to rip apart the biblical foundation that built the strongest nation in the history of the world.

AMERICA'S CHRISTIAN ORIGINS

Although American history as it is taught in the public schools today has been deliberately robbed of its true Christian fiber, "52 of the 55 Founding Fathers who worked on the Constitution were members of orthodox Christian churches."[40] Their Christian backgrounds no doubt influenced the new government's philosophy and laws. Our Founding Fathers believed that no nation, no government, could survive without God at its head. George Washington said, "Of all the dispositions and habits which lead to political prosperity, religion and morality are indispensable supports. In vain would that man claim the tribute of patriotism, who should labor to subvert these great pillars."[41] According to Patrick Henry, "It cannot be emphasized too strongly or too often that this great nation was founded, not by religionists, but by Christians, on the gospel of Jesus Christ!"[42] Abraham Lincoln is quoted as saying, "[F]or I know that the Lord is always on the side of the right. But it is my constant anxiety and prayer that I and this nation should be on the Lord's side."[43]

The University of Houston did an exhaustive 10-year study on 15,000 key documents in America's foundation. After distilling these 15,000 to the most crucial 3,154 works (the Bill of Rights, the Declaration of Independence, Washington's first inaugural address, etc.), the researchers were amazed to see that the most-quoted source in the documents was the Bible. Thirty-four percent of the quotations were taken directly from the

Scriptures. "Sixty percent of the Founders' quotes are taken from men who had used the Bible to arrive at their own conclusions."[44]

Woodrow Wilson sounded a prophetic warning that today is completely ignored: "A nation which does not remember what it was yesterday, does not know what it is today, nor what it is trying to do. We are trying to do a futile thing if we do not know where we came from or what we have been about."[45]

Take a look at the American history books read by students in elementary school, junior high school, high school, and college, and you'll see that less than 1 percent (in many cases, zero percent) of the texts refer to our country's biblical roots. History should be the accurate documentation of historical events, not a biased indoctrination of slanted intent.

AMERICA'S EDUCATIONAL SYSTEM

Author Herbert Schlossberg wrote, "One of the most useful tools in the quest for power is the educational system."[46] Abraham Lincoln underscored this truth when he said, "The philosophy of the school room in one generation will be the philosophy of government in the next."[47] Proverbs 23:7 (NASB) says, "As a man thinks, so he is." The worldview that controls the schools controls the country. Let's discover the mandate for American education.

John Harvard founded Harvard University in 1636 as the flagship of American universities. Harvard said, "Let every student be plainly instructed, and earnestly pressed to consider well, the main end of his life and studies is to know God and Jesus Christ which is eternal life (John 17:3) and therefore lay Christ at the bottom, as the only foundation of all sound knowledge and learning."[48] Harvard's original motto was *veritas christo et ecclesiae* ("Truth for Christ and the Church"). That has all been drastically altered. Today Christ is openly scorned on Harvard's campus.

What the *Pinta* was to the *Nina*, Yale was to Harvard. Yale described itself as a college "for the liberal and religious education of suitable youth" and required that, since "God is the giver of all wisdom, every scholar, besides private or secret prayer, . . . shall be present morning and evening at public prayer."[49] Today Yale and Harvard freshmen receive sex kits, complete with condoms, rubber gloves, and instructions for decadent homosexual and heterosexual activity.

From America's founding until well into the mid-twentieth century, almost all legitimate public education in America was based on the Bible. For example, for 200 years (1690-1890) the most common textbook of American schools was known in every state as the *New England Primer*.[50] Every young American learned to read with this classic textbook. A large section of the book was dedicated to alphabetical memorization. It read like this (notice the source of each quote):

A "A wise son maketh glad a father" (Prov. 10:1).
B "Better is a little with righteousness" (Prov. 16:8).
C "Come unto me all ye that labour" (Matt. 11:28).
D "Do not this abominable thing that I hate" (Jer. 44:4).
E "Except a man be born again, he cannot see the kingdom of God" (John 3:3).

Another example of the Bible's being the taproot of American public-school teachings is the *Bible Study Course*, which was required reading for graduation from high school.[51] The book dealt with subjects such as the pre-existence of Christ, and it charged students to memorize scriptures like John 1:1-4.

In 1962 prayer was outlawed in public schools.[52] The following rather generic prayer went to the high court for trial and was declared unconstitutional in the historic *Engel v. Vitale* case: "Almighty God, we acknowledge our dependence upon Thee, and we beg Thy blessings upon us, our parents, our teachers, and our country."[53]

In 1963 the Supreme Court ruled that it was unconstitutional to have Bibles in public schools. In 1980 displaying the Ten Commandments in public schools was declared unconstitutional. In 1987 discussing God in the classroom was declared unconstitutional. In 1991 prayer at graduation ceremonies was declared unconstitutional. In 1992 prayer at sporting events was declared unconstitutional.

In 1993 the state courts in Louisiana declared that teaching about traditional, monogamous heterosexual relationships was a "religious" activity and therefore unconstitutional, even if there were no biblical references in the curriculum.

Meanwhile, materials from the most militant antibiblical, antifamily organizations in America are being taught in schools all over the country. For example, Planned Parenthood's recommended reading book for adolescents, *Boys and Sex*, contains the following statements:[54]

More and more people are coming to understand that having sex is a joyful and enriching experience at any age.

Playing with girls sexually before adolescence . . . increases the chances for a satisfactory sex life when a boy grows up.

Premarital intercourse does have its definite value as a training ground for marriage. . . . [B]oys and girls who start having intercourse when they are adolescents . . . will find that it's a big help. . . . [I]t's like taking a car out on a test run before you buy it.

It is estimated that three-quarters of America's schools now use materials from Planned Parenthood.

Since 1962, when our courts began to purposely dismantle God's system in our schools, the following disturbing trends have appeared:

- The pregnancy rate among 15-year-olds has risen 500 percent.[55]
- The rate of sexually transmitted diseases among teens has risen 200 percent.[56]
- The number of teens contracting AIDS doubles every 14 months.[57]
- The rate of violent crime perpetrated by teens has risen 700 percent.[58] "Between 1960 and 1980, the number of serious crimes (murders, rapes, robberies, burglaries) increased 332 percent."[59]
- The rate of sexual abuse of children has risen 2,000 percent.[60]

AMERICA'S LEGAL SYSTEM

Early in America's history, the recognized authority on law was British jurist William Blackstone. His *Commentaries on the Laws of England* was the American lawyer's bible for 160 years.[61] Blackstone summarized American law thusly:

Man, considered as a creature, must necessarily be subject to the laws of his Creator, for he is entirely a dependent being. . . . And consequently, as man depends absolutely upon his Maker for everything, it is necessary that he should, in all points, conform to his Maker's will. This will of his Maker, is called the law of nature. . . . This law of nature . . . dictated by God Himself, is of course superior in obligation to any other. . . . No human laws are of any validity, if contrary to this. . . . The revealed or divine law . . . found only in the Holy Scriptures . . . are found upon comparison to be really part of the original law of nature.[62]

Men such as the great evangelist Charles Finney were often converted to faith in Christ just by reading Blackstone's *Commentaries*.[63]

Because of Christian jurists like Blackstone, early American law (including Supreme Court rulings) was based on the Scriptures. John Jay, the first chief justice of the Supreme Court, said, "Providence has given to our people the choice of their rulers, and it is the duty as well as the privilege and interest of our Christian nation to select and prefer Christians for their rulers."[64] In their rulings, the early justices made statements like these: "Our laws and our institutions must necessarily be based upon and embody the teachings of the Redeemer of mankind. It is impossible that it should be otherwise. In this sense and to this extent, our civilization and our institutions are emphatically Christian," and "Where can the purest principles of morality be learned so clearly or so perfectly as from the New Testament?"[65]

SECULAR HUMANISM

A secular humanist is someone who believes that man is the center of the universe. A humanist believes there are no moral absolutes—if it feels good, do it. A humanist believes no deity will save us—we must save ourselves. A humanist believes there is no God, there is no soul, there is no need for the "props" of traditional religion.[66]

The best-known humanist is Charles Darwin (1809-1882), who claimed in his theory of evolution that the universe had not been created by God but was the result of a cosmic explosion (see Resource E). Another humanist and Darwin's contemporary, Julian Huxley, said, "I disbelieve in a personal God in any sense in which that phrase is ordinarily used. . . . For my own part, the sense of spiritual relief which comes from rejecting the idea of God as a supernatural being is enormous."[67] In this century, we have Carl Sagan, former spokesperson for the American Humanist Association: "We are, in the most profound sense, children of the Cosmos. . . . It makes good sense to revere the Sun and the stars because we are their children. . . . In the beginning Man. . . . It is said that men may not be in the dreams of gods, but gods are the dreams of men."[68]

Secular humanism is rampant in our society today, with strongholds in our government and the media. The popularity of this worldview among Americans bodes ill for conservatives and Christians, because traditional, Judeo-Christian values are increasingly coming under attack.

For example, Congress is debating passage of the Freedom of Choice Act (FOCA), which has President Clinton's complete support. This bill "would eliminate every law regulating abortion anywhere in the United States. It would be legal to kill unborn children throughout the nine months of pregnancy—even five minutes before delivery. In a nation that imposes a $5,000 fine on anyone who destroys an eagle's egg, it will be open season on full-term babies!"[69] Clinton was quoted by the Associated Press as saying, "The new Supreme Court Justices must be abortion rights supporters"—the first time in America's history that a president has openly dictated ethics to the judicial branch of government.[70]

The secular media's attacks have been more personal. The *Washington Post*, in a front-page article, called Christians "poor, uneducated and easy to command."[71] Hugh Downs, on ABC's *20/20,* compared Christians who speak out for family values to Hitler and the Ku Klux Klan.[72] Ted Turner, Humanist of the Year in 1990, said, "Christianity is for losers."[73]

Secular humanism is not the only enemy conservatives and Christians have to face these days. We're fighting a two-front war: secular humanism on one side and militant humanism on the other.

MILITANT HUMANISM (MARXISM)

"Every religious idea, every idea of god, every flirtation with the idea of god, is unutterable vileness"—V.I. Lenin.[74]

"To achieve the real happiness of the people, it is necessary to abolish the illusory religious one. . . . The first step in this direction must be an attack on religion"—Karl Marx.[75]

Militant humanism, like secular humanism, views religion (read: Christianity) as irrelevant and even detrimental to mankind's striving toward a perfect society. Between 1919 and 1980, the Soviet Union, in the name of Marxism-Leninism, crushed 39 countries and murdered 60 million civilians. Another 30-40 million were killed on the battlefield. The number of Russian Orthodox Christian churches was drastically reduced, and thousands of clergy and laypeople were murdered in cold blood.

The Soviet government, through its programs and laws, attempted to "liquidate" religion from every aspect of society.[76] God and religion were banished from Soviet life. Organizations such as the Soviet Institute for Scientific Atheism were founded "to spread the atheistic world view, the atheistic behavior pattern, the atheistic way of understanding ethics, and so on." Beginning in the schools, the Soviet people were to be brought up as atheists.[77]

Though the Soviet Union is no more, militant humanism lives on. Alexander Solzhenitsyn, in his book *The Mortal Danger*, revealed the ultimate goal of Marxism-Leninism: "The authorities make no attempt to hide the fact that they are crushing the Christian faith with the full force of their machinery of terror."[78]

A FINAL WORD

The battle is on, fellow Christians. A good coach always knows the opponent's defense before calling the plays. As you go through high school and college, and when you get married and start a family, be sure you have prepared your mind with God's Word, prepared your intellect against the schemes of the world, and prepared your heart with prayer.

Ephesians 6:10-18 speaks clearly to us when it instructs us to "gird" ourselves for battle. Paul was addressing us as well when he told Timothy, "For God did not give us a spirit of timidity, but a spirit of power, of love and of self-discipline" (2 Tim. 1:7).

Heed the will of God in 2 Chronicles 7:14: "If my people, who are called by my name, will humble themselves and pray and seek my face and turn from their wicked ways, then will I hear from heaven and will forgive their sin and will heal their land."

Pray for our nation. Get a good education. And make it your objective to get into positions of influence that will enable you to help re-create the biblical environment in which America began and which made it the finest nation on earth.

FURTHER READING

For a more detailed study of these topics, I recommend the following resources:

ALCOHOL AND OTHER DRUGS

Arterburn, Stephen, and Jim Burns. *Drug-Proof Your Kids (A Prevention Guide and Intervention Plan)*. Colorado Springs, Colo.: Focus on the Family Publishing, 1989.

——————. *When Love Is Not Enough: Parenting Through the Tough Times*. Colorado Springs, Colo.: Focus on the Family Publishing, 1992.

Dunn, Jerry G. *God Is for the Alcoholic*. Chicago: Moody, 1986.

Leman, Kevin. *Smart Kids, Stupid Choices*. Rev. ed. Ventura, Calif.: Regal, 1987.

Ohlemacher, Janet. *Desperate to Be Needed: Freeing the Family from Chemical Codependency*. Grand Rapids, Mich.: Zondervan, 1990.

Sanford, Doris. *I Can Say No: A Child's Book About Drug Abuse*. Sisters, Ore.: Questar Publishers, 1988.

Spickard, Anderson, and Barbara R. Thompson. *Dying for a Drink: What You Should Know About Alcoholism*. Dallas: Word, 1986.

Tirabassi, Becky. *Life of the Party*. Grand Rapids, Mich.: Zondervan, 1990.

White, John. *Parents in Pain*. Downers Grove, Ill.: InterVarsity, 1979.

PORNOGRAPHY

Kirk, Jerry R. *The Mind Polluters*. Nashville: Thomas Nelson, 1985.

Schlafly, Phyllis. *Pornography's Victims*. Alton, Ill.: Pere Marquette, 1987.

U.S. Attorney General's Commission on Pornography, U.S. Justice Department. *Final Report of the Attorney General's Commission on Pornography*. Nashville: Rutledge Hill Press, 1986.

SAFE SEX/AIDS

Redfield, Robert, and Wanda Kay Franz. *AIDS and Young People*. Washington, D.C.: Regnery Gateway, 1987.

Rozar, G. Edward, Jr., and David B. Biebel. *Laughing in the Face of AIDS: A Surgeon's Personal Battle*. Grand Rapids, Mich.: Baker Book House, 1992.

Smith, Shepherd, and Anita Moreland Smith. *Christians in the Age of AIDS: How We Can Be Good Samaritans Responding to the AIDS Crisis.* Wheaton, Ill.: Victor Books, 1990.

Wood, Glenn G., and John E. Dietrich. *The AIDS Epidemic: Balancing Compassion and Justice.* Sisters, Ore.: Questar Publishers, 1990.

ABORTION/EUTHANASIA

Baker, Don. *Beyond Choice: The Abortion Story No One Is Telling.* Sisters, Ore.: Questar Publishers, 1985.

Dobson, James C., and Gary Bauer. *Children at Risk: The Battle for the Hearts and Minds of Our Children.* Dallas: Word, 1992.

Garton, Jean S. *Who Broke the Baby?* Minneapolis: Bethany House, 1979.

Koop, C. Everett. *The Right to Live; The Right to Die.* Lewiston, N.Y.: Life Cycle Books, 1981.

Koop, C. Everett, and Francis A. Schaeffer. *Whatever Happened to the Human Race?* Wheaton, Ill.: Good News, 1983.

Pierson, Anne. *Fifty-Two Simple Things You Can Do to Be Pro-Life.* Minneapolis: Bethany House, 1991.

Powell, John. *Abortion: The Silent Holocaust.* Valencia, Calif.: Tabor Publishing, 1981.

Tada, Joni Eareckson. *When Is It Right to Die? Suicide, Euthanasia, Suffering, and Mercy.* Grand Rapids, Mich.: Zondervan, 1992.

Willke, J.C., and Mrs. Willke. *Abortion: Questions and Answers.* Rev. ed. Cincinnati: Hayes Publishing, 1988.

WORLDVIEWS

Geisler, Norman L. *Is Man the Measure?* Grand Rapids, Mich.: Baker Book House, 1983.

Geisler, Norman L., and William D. Watkins. *Worlds Apart: A Handbook on Worldviews.* 2d ed. Grand Rapids, Mich.: Baker Book House, 1989.

Hitchcock, James. *What Is Secular Humanism?* Ann Arbor, Mich.: Servant, 1982.

Nash, Ronald H. *Worldviews in Conflict: Choosing Christianity in a World of Ideas.* Grand Rapids, Mich.: Zondervan, 1992.

Noebel, David A. *Understanding the Times: The Story of the Biblical Christian, Marxist/Leninist, and Secular Humanist Worldviews.* Manitou Springs, Colo.: Summit Press, 1991.

Phillips, W. Gary, and William E. Brown. *Making Sense of Your World from a Biblical Viewpoint.* Chicago: Moody, 1991.

Sire, James W. *The Universe Next Door: A Basic Worldview Catalog.* 2d ed. Downers Grove, Ill.: InterVarsity Press, 1988.

Sproul, R.C. *If There's a God, Why Are There Atheists?* Wheaton, Ill.: Tyndale House, 1989.

Whitehead, John W. *The Second American Revolution.* Westchester, Ill.: Crossway, 1982.

Zacharias, Ravi. *A Shattered Visage: The Real Face of Atheism.* Grand Rapids, Mich.: Baker Book House, 1993.

GAME PLAN FOR
A DAILY QUIET TIME

1. Preparation for Each Day

    A.   Equipment: Have a Bible and pen and paper handy to
         record your thoughts.
    B.   Time: Choose a specific time each day to spend with the Lord.
         This may mean getting up in the morning 30 minutes before
         you usually do.
    C.   Place: Find a particular spot where you can limit distractions (e.g.,
         living room, patio, bedroom).
    D.   Pray: "Open my eyes that I may see wonderful things in your
         law" (Ps. 119:18). Ask God to teach you from His Word.

2. Observation

    A.   Read the prescribed chapter in its entirety each day.
    B.   Read the chapter again, writing down your observations. Look
         for the main ideas in the passage, and record them on your Daily
         Quiet Time Work Sheet.
    C.   Ask and answer the following questions of the passage:
         Who are the personalities involved in this passage?
         What is taking place?

Where is this passage happening?
Why did God include this passage in His Word?
When is this passage taking place?

3. Application

A.   Pray for God's direction to plan one unselfish action to help
     another person. This may or may not relate to the specific
     passage for the day.

B.   Here are some ways to reach out to someone:
     1.   Write a letter of encouragement.
     2.   Call someone on the phone.
     3.   Explain the good news of the gospel.
     4.   Visit a friend or someone who lives alone.
     5.   Help a person in need.
     6.   Disciple someone.
     7.   Visit people in hospitals, retirement homes, and so on.
     8.   Help someone with homework, auto repair, chores,
          and so on.
     9.   Encourage a person at work, in school, at home, and
          so on.
     10. Lead a friend away from a bad idea, and lead a friend
          toward Jesus' ways.

C.   Be a servant. Pray for an open mind and a willing heart for God
     to work through you.

4. Prayer

A.   Praise God for who He is. (Adoration)

B.   Ask for forgiveness (be specific). (Confession)

C.   Thank Him specifically for all He has done for and given you.
     Choose what you feel are your most important blessings (they
     could be your health, family, school, work, finances), and thank
     God for them. (Thanksgiving)

D.   Pray for yourself and others. Write down your request each day.
     When God answers it, record the date and circumstances.
     Periodically review all the answered prayers. This will increase
     your thankfulness to God and your faith in Him to answer other
     prayers. (Supplication)

5. Meditation

A.   Choose a key verse from the day's passage, and write it on a note card or memorize it. Think about it as you drive, as you exercise, and during times you are still and quiet.

6. At the End of Each Day (Before Bedtime)

   A.   Reread the passage.
   B.   Look for additional lessons to learn.
   C.   Review the verse you are memorizing.
   D.   Reflect on the application (did you follow through?).
   E.   Pray again for your needs.

7. Team Effort

   A.   Get a friend or parent to be your partner. Phone and encourage each other to be disciplined and faithful in continuing the commitment. Discuss together what you have been learning each week.

IMPORTANT: Keep a master copy of the Daily Quiet Time Work Sheet to use to copy more sheets when you run out.

BIBLE STUDY
DAILY QUIET TIME WORK SHEET

Date:_____

Scripture:_____

Theme:_____

I.   Pray for Godly Insight

II.   Topic (write it here)

III. Key Verse (write it here and memorize it)

IV. RSMM
     R - Read the Chapter
     S - Study the Key Verse
     M - Memorize the Key Verse
     M - Meditate on the Key Verse All Day

V.   Observation   (What does the passage say?)

     Who?   (Who's speaking?)

     What?   (What's going on?)

When?   (Time)

Why?   (Why was it written?)

Wherefore?   (What does it say to me?)

VI.   Application and Commitment (in what practical ways will I apply what I just learned today?)

VII. ACTS   (write prayers in prayer section)

A -   Adoration (praise God for who He is)

C -   Confess (verbally confess your sins)

T -   Thanksgiving (thank God for what He has done for and given you)

S -   Supplication (pray for others and yourself)

READ STUDY MEMORIZE MEDITATE

Day	Topic	Theme	Key Verse	Key Paragraph
Week 1				
Day 1	Godly Wisdom	A Gift and Reward	Eccl. 2:26	Eccl. 2:22-26
Day 2	Godly Wisdom	All Wisdom from God	Dan. 2:20	Dan. 2:19-22
Day 3	Godly Wisdom	God Is So Wise!	Rom. 11:33	Rom. 11:32-36
Day 4	Godly Wisdom	A Greater Than Worldly Wisdom	1 Cor. 1:20	1 Cor. 1:18-21
Day 5	Godly Wisdom	Ask for Wisdom	James 1:5	James 1:5-8
Week 2				
Day 1	Worship	Satan Seeks Worship	Matt. 4:10	Matt. 4:1-11
Day 2	Worship	Worship in Spirit and Truth	John 4:23	John 4:1-26
Day 3	Worship	Worship the Living God	Acts 17:29	Acts 17:16-34
Day 4	Worship	False Worship	Col. 2:18	Col. 2:16-23
Day 5	Worship	Worship in Heaven	Rev. 4:10	Rev. 4:1-11
Week 3				
Day 1	God's Calling	Rejoice in All Circumstances	1 Thess. 5:18	1 Thess. 5:12-24
Day 2	God's Calling	Submit to Authority	1 Peter 2:13	1 Peter 2:13-17
Day 3	God's Calling	Testing and Proving	Rom. 12:2	Rom. 12:1-8
Day 4	God's Calling	Caution to the Disobedient	Matt. 7:21	Matt. 7:21-29
Day 5	God's Calling	Avoid Immorality	1 Thess. 4:3	1 Thess. 4:1-8
Week 4				
Day 1	Holy Spirit	Day of Pentecost	Acts 2:4	Acts 2:1-13
Day 2	Holy Spirit	Lying to the Holy Spirit	Acts 5:3	Acts 5:1-11
Day 3	Holy Spirit	Spirit Empowers Forgiveness	Acts 7:60	Acts 7:51-60
Day 4	Holy Spirit	Spirit Teaches Spiritual Truths	1 Cor. 2:13	1 Cor. 2:6-16
Day 5	Holy Spirit	Body as Temple of the Holy Spirit	1 Cor. 6:19	1 Cor. 6:12-20

Week 5

Day 1	Parents	A Commandment	Exod. 20:12	Exod. 20:1-17
Day 2	Parents	Obedience	Eph. 6:1	Eph. 6:1-3
Day 3	Parents	Christian Home	Col. 3:20	Col. 3:18-25
Day 4	Parents	Wisdom from Parents	Prov. 1:8	Prov. 1:1-19
Day 5	Parents	Society Today	2 Tim. 3:2	2 Tim. 3:1-9

Week 6

Day 1	God the Father	Father of the Fatherless	Ps. 68:5	Ps. 68:1-10
Day 2	God the Father	Father of Jesus	John 3:16	John 3:14-18
Day 3	God the Father	Daddy of Believers	Gal. 4:6	Gal. 3:26-4:9
Day 4	God the Father	Protection of the Father	John 10:29	John 10:27-30
Day 5	God the Father	God Disciplines His Children	Heb. 12:7	Heb. 12:3-11

Week 7

Day 1	Sanctification	God Is Working in You	Phil. 1:6	Phil. 1:3-11
Day 2	Sanctification	The Spirit Gives Life	Rom. 8:9	Rom. 8:5-11
Day 3	Sanctification	It Is the Will of God	1 Thess. 4:3	1 Thess. 4:1-8
Day 4	Sanctification	Make No Provision	Rom. 13:14	Rom. 13:8-14
Day 5	Sanctification	Useful to the Master	2 Tim. 2:21	2 Tim. 2:20-22

Week 8

Day 1	Your Body	You Have Been Wonderfully Woven	Ps. 139:13	Ps. 139:1-16
Day 2	Your Body	God Sees Not as Man Sees	1 Sam. 16:7	1 Sam. 16:1-13
Day 3	Your Body	You Are a Temple of God	1 Cor. 3:16	1 Cor. 3:10-17
Day 4	Your Body	Buffet My Body	1 Cor. 9:27	1 Cor. 9:24-27
Day 5	Your Body	Body of Humiliation	Phil. 3:21	Phil. 3:17-21

Week 9

Day 1	Your Mind	Sin Begins Here	2 Sam. 11:3	2 Sam. 11:1-5
Day 2	Your Mind	Whatever Is Pure	Phil. 4:8	Phil. 4:4-9
Day 3	Your Mind	Renew Your Mind	Rom. 12:2	Rom. 12:1-16
Day 4	Your Mind	Gird Your Mind	1 Pet. 1:13	1 Pet. 1:13-16
Day 5	Your Mind	Set Your Mind	Col. 3:2	Col. 3:1-4

Week 10

| Day 1 | Peace | Given by Jesus, Sustained by the Spirit | John 14:27 | John 14:26-29 |

Day 2	Peace	Christ Is Greater Than the World	John 16:33	John 16:32-33
Day 3	Peace	Peace Through Grace	Rom. 5:1	Rom. 4:22-5:3
Day 4	Peace	Live in Peace	Col. 3:15	Col. 3:12-17
Day 5	Peace	Through Humility	1 Pet. 5:6-7	1 Pet. 5:6-11

Week 11

Day 1	Witnessing to Friends	Salvation Through Jesus	John 3:16	John 3:14-21
Day 2	Witnessing to Friends	Process of Salvation	Rom. 10:9-10	Rom. 10:1-17
Day 3	Witnessing to Friends	Roman Road	Rom. 5:8	Entire Chapter
Day 4	Witnessing to Friends	Saved by Faith, Not by Works	Rom. 4:13	Rom. 4:1-13
Day 5	Witnessing to Friends	The Great Commission	Matt. 28:19-20	Matt. 28:1-20

Week 12

Day 1	Agape Love	The Love Chapter	1 Cor. 13:13	1 Cor. 13:1-13
Day 2	Agape Love	To Family	Ruth 1:16	Ruth 1:1-22
Day 3	Agape Love	To Friends	Phil. 2:15	Phil. 2:1-16
Day 4	Agape Love	To Enemies and/or Authorities	Rom. 12:20	Rom. 12:10-21
Day 5	Agape Love	To God	Phil. 3:8	Phil. 3:7-21

Week 13

Day 1	Discipline	Blessing of Discipline	Ps. 94:12	Ps. 94:10-13
Day 2	Discipline	Why We Need Discipline	Prov. 5:23	Prov. 5:21-23
Day 3	Discipline	Discipline of a Loving Father	Heb. 12:7	Heb. 12:5-9
Day 4	Discipline	Discipline to Make Whole and Protect	Job 5:17-18	Job 5:17-19
Day 5	Discipline	Danger of Denying Discipline	Prov. 13:18	Prov. 13:16-20

Week 14

Day 1	Selflessness	In the Body of Christ	Phil. 2:3	Phil. 2:1-5
Day 2	Selflessness	Living in Christ	Luke 9:24	Luke 9:22-25
Day 3	Selflessness	Why Avoid Self-Ambition?	James 3:16	James 3:13-18
Day 4	Selflessness	To Please God and Live Happily	Ps. 119:36	Ps. 119:34-38
Day 5	Selflessness	The Reward	Mark 10:31	Mark 10:29-31

Week 15

Day 1	Joy	Joy in Heavenly Reward	Luke 6:23	Luke 6:20-23
Day 2	Joy	Joy in the Power of Prayer	John 16:24	John 16:23-27
Day 3	Joy	Joy of Fellowship	Rom. 15:32	Rom. 15:30-33
Day 4	Joy	Joy in the Face of Trials	James 1:2	James 1:2-4
Day 5	Joy	Joy in God's Reward/Power	Heb. 1:9	Heb. 1:8-12

Week 16

Day 1	Jealousy	God's Jealousy	Exod. 20:5	Exod. 20:4-7
Day 2	Jealousy	Evil of Jealousy	Rom. 13:13	Rom. 13:12-14
Day 3	Jealousy	Sign of Worldliness	1 Cor. 3:3	1 Cor. 3:1-3
Day 4	Jealousy	World Is Jealous of Christians	Acts 5:17	Acts 5:15-19
Day 5	Jealousy	Don't Be Jealous of Worldliness	Prov. 23:17	Prov. 23:15-19

Week 17

Day 1	Anger	God's Anger at Disbelief	Heb. 3:11	Heb. 3:8-13
Day 2	Anger	God Is Angered by Bad Motive	Rom. 2:8	Rom. 2:5-11
Day 3	Anger	Controlling Anger	Eph. 4:26	Eph. 4:24-27
Day 4	Anger	Anger Is Part of Old Self	Col. 3:8	Col. 3:5-10
Day 5	Anger	Anger Prevents Righteousness	James 1:20	James 1:19-22

Week 18

Day 1	Giving	Giving Anonymously	Matt. 6:4	Matt. 6:1-6
Day 2	Giving	God's Gift of Testimony	Acts 14:17	Acts 14:15-17
Day 3	Giving	Giving in Sacrifice	Luke 21:4	Luke 21:1-4
Day 4	Giving	Giving of Mercy Never Stops	Rom. 11:29	Rom. 11:26-32
Day 5	Giving	What God's Law Gives Us	Ps. 19:8	Ps. 19:7-11

Week 19

Day 1	Patience	Patience Builds Character	Rom. 5:4	Rom. 5:1-11
Day 2	Patience	Run with Endurance	Heb. 12:1	Heb. 12:1-3
Day 3	Patience	Trials Bring About Patience	James 1:3	James 1:2-4
Day 4	Patience	Be Patient with All Men	1 Thess. 5:14	1 Thess. 5:12-15
Day 5	Patience	Be Patient, Jesus Is Coming	James 5:8	James 5:7-11

Week 20

Day 1	Fellowship	Brotherly Love	Heb. 13:1	Heb. 13:1-3
Day 2	Fellowship	Fellowship of Christ's Sufferings	Phil. 3:10	Phil. 3:8-16
Day 3	Fellowship	Fellowship Involves Serving	Gal. 5:13	Gal. 5:13-15
Day 4	Fellowship	Bearing One Another's Burdens	Gal. 6:2	Gal. 6:1-5
Day 5	Fellowship	Confronting in Love	Eph. 4:15	Eph. 4:14-16

Week 21

Day 1	Creation	The Biblical Dinosaur	Job 40:16	Job 40:15-18
Day 2	Creation	God Spoke Creation into Existence	Heb. 11:3	Heb. 11:1-3
Day 3	Creation	The Flood	Gen. 6:19	Gen. 6:8-22
Day 4	Creation	God's Way	Gen. 1:1	Entire Chapter
Day 5	Creation	God's Word Is God's Word	2 Tim. 3:16-17	2 Tim. 3:14-17

Week 22

Day 1	Sports	Who's Your Audience?	Heb. 12:1	Heb. 12:1-4
Day 2	Sports	Eyes on the Prize	Phil. 3:12, 14	Phil. 3:12-16
Day 3	Sports	Who's Your Coach?	Col. 3:23	Col. 3:23-25
Day 4	Sports	Courage	Deut. 31:6	Deut. 31:1-6
Day 5	Sports	Rules	2 Tim. 2:5	2 Tim. 2:1-13

Week 23

Day 1	Sex and Dating	Flee Immediately	1 Cor. 6:18	1 Cor. 6:15-7:1-3
Day 2	Sex and Dating	Dating/Marrying Non-Christians	2 Cor. 6:14	2 Cor. 6:11-18
Day 3	Sex and Dating	Abstain from Sexual Immorality	1 Thess. 4:3	1 Thess. 4:1-8
Day 4	Sex and Dating	God's Help to Escape Temptation	1 Cor. 10:13	1 Cor. 10:6-13
Day 5	Sex and Dating	Make No Provision for Flesh; Put on Christ	Rom. 13:13-14	Rom. 13:12-14

Week 24

Day 1	Salvation	Plan of Salvation	John 3:16	John 3:16-21
Day 2	Salvation	Jesus Christ—Our Only Means of Salvation	Acts 4:12	Acts 4:10-12
Day 3	Salvation	Spiritual Armor	1 Thess. 5:8	1 Thess. 5:1-8

| Day 4 | Salvation | Sharing the Message of Salvation | 2 Tim. 2:10 | 2 Tim. 2:1-13 |
| Day 5 | Salvation | Grace Brings Salvation | Titus 2:11 | Titus 2:11-15 |

Week 25

Day 1	Grace	Saved by the Bell of Grace	Eph. 2:5	Entire Chapter
Day 2	Grace	Under Rule	Rom. 6:14	Entire Chapter
Day 3	Grace	A Just God	Titus 3:7	Entire Chapter
Day 4	Grace	A True Gift	Ps. 84:11	Entire Chapter
Day 5	Grace	Fallen But Not Sunk	Rom. 3:23-24	Entire Chapter

Week 26

Day 1	Obedience	Love Me	John 14:15	Entire Chapter
Day 2	Obedience	That Small Voice	Ps. 103:20	Entire Chapter
Day 3	Obedience	Just Do It	Eph. 6:1	Entire Chapter
Day 4	Obedience	Don't Be Conformed	1 Pet. 1:14	Entire Chapter
Day 5	Obedience	Under a Rule	Rom. 13:5	Entire Chapter

Week 27

Day 1	Friends	At All Times	Prov. 17:17	Entire Chapter
Day 2	Friends	Count the Cost	John 15:13	Entire Chapter
Day 3	Friends	Wrong Friendships	James 4:4	Entire Chapter
Day 4	Friends	Stick to It	Prov. 18:24	Entire Chapter
Day 5	Friends	Unequally Yoked	2 Cor. 6:14	Entire Chapter

Week 28

Day 1	Trials	Count It Joy	James 1:2	Entire Chapter
Day 2	Trials	"Daddy's Home"	Matt. 24:30	Entire Chapter
Day 3	Trials	Believe Me, It Happens	Mark 4:17	Entire Chapter
Day 4	Trials	He Delivers Us	Job 36:15	Entire Chapter
Day 5	Trials	Trials Bring Hope	Rom. 5:3	Rom. 5:3-5

Week 29

Day 1	Jesus of Nazareth	Jesus Prophesied	Isa. 9:6	Entire Chapter
Day 2	Jesus of Nazareth	His Birthday	Luke 2:7	Luke 2:1-20
Day 3	Jesus of Nazareth	Purpose of Life's Ministry	Matt. 20:28	Matt. 20:25-28
Day 4	Jesus of Nazareth	Death and Resurrection	Luke 24:6-7	Luke 24:1-12
Day 5	Jesus of Nazareth	Second Coming	1 Thess. 5:23	Entire Chapter

Week 30

Day 1	Bible Study	God's Inspired Word	2 Tim. 3:16	2 Tim. 3:14-17
Day 2	Bible Study	Hold Fast to Him	Deut. 11:22	Deut. 11:16-22
Day 3	Bible Study	Hearers and Doers	James 1:22	James 1:18-25
Day 4	Bible Study	Staying Pure	Ps. 119:9	Ps. 119:9-16
Day 5	Bible Study	Armor of God	Eph. 6:17	Eph. 6:10-18

Week 31

Day 1	Godly Counsel	Seek First His Kingdom	Matt. 6:33	Matt. 6:25-34
Day 2	Godly Counsel	Holy Spirit Guides Into Truth	John 16:13	John 16:7-15
Day 3	Godly Counsel	Consult Many Counselors	Prov. 15:22	Prov. 15:20-24
Day 4	Godly Counsel	A Wise Man Will Hear	Prov. 1:5	Prov. 1:2-6
Day 5	Godly Counsel	"A Good Listener"	Prov. 12:15	Prov. 12:15-20

Week 32

Day 1	Work	Commit Your Works to the Lord	Prov. 16:3	Prov. 16:1-9
Day 2	Work	Work to Eat	2 Thess. 3:10	2 Thess. 3:6-13
Day 3	Work	Integrity on the Job	Prov. 10:9	Prov. 10:1-9
Day 4	Work	Work Unto the Lord	Col. 3:23	Col. 3:22-4:1
Day 5	Work	Loyalty to Employers	1 Tim. 6:2	1 Tim. 6:1-2

Week 33

Day 1	Holiness	Be Holy as He Is	Lev. 19:2	Lev. 19:1-4
Day 2	Holiness	His Name Is Holy	Isa. 57:15	Isa. 57:12-16
Day 3	Holiness	Chosen to Be Holy	Eph. 1:4	Eph. 1:3-12
Day 4	Holiness	Present Yourself Alive	Rom. 6:13	Rom. 6:6-14
Day 5	Holiness	Prove Yourself Blameless	Phil. 2:15	Phil. 2:12-16

Week 34

Day 1	Divorce	How Does God Feel?	Mal. 2:16	Mal. 2:14-16
Day 2	Divorce	Hardness of Heart	Matt. 19:8	Matt. 19:3-9
Day 3	Divorce	Mixed Homes	1 Cor. 7:14	1 Cor. 7:10-17
Day 4	Divorce	Betrothed Forever	Hos. 2:19	Hos. 2:19-20
Day 5	Divorce	Love as Christ Loved	Eph. 5:25	Eph. 5:22-28

Week 35

Day 1	Faith	Men and Women of Faith	Heb. 11:1, 6	Entire Chapter
Day 2	Faith	Fix Your Eyes on Jesus	Heb. 12:2	Heb. 12:1-3
Day 3	Faith	Faith Is Action	James 2:17	James 2:14-18
Day 4	Faith	Pursue Faith	2 Tim. 2:22	2 Tim. 2:22-26
Day 5	Faith	Reward of Faith	2 Tim. 2:10	2 Tim. 2:7-10

Week 36

Day 1	Humility	Jesus Humbles Himself	Phil. 2:8	Phil. 2:1-11
Day 2	Humility	The Word Humbles the Proud	Luke 1:52	Luke 1:46-56
Day 3	Humility	Pride in High Position	James 1:9	James 1:9-11
Day 4	Humility	Humility Resists Satan	James 4:10	James 4:7-10
Day 5	Humility	Let God Lift You Up	1 Pet. 5:6	1 Pet. 5:1-11

Week 37

Day 1	Prayer	At All Times	Eph. 6:18	Entire Chapter
Day 2	Prayer	No Stopping Us Now	1 Thess. 5:17	Entire Chapter
Day 3	Prayer	Pray and Believe	Mark 11:24	Entire Chapter
Day 4	Prayer	Pray for Whom?	Matt. 5:44	Entire Chapter
Day 5	Prayer	Devoted to It	Phil. 4:6	Entire Chapter

Week 38

Day 1	Reproving	Don't Fight It	Prov. 15:10, 32	Entire Chapter
Day 2	Reproving	The Word	2 Tim. 3:16	Entire Chapter
Day 3	Reproving	Who?	Prov. 9:8	Entire Chapter
Day 4	Reproving	The Formula	2 Tim. 4:2	Entire Chapter
Day 5	Reproving	The How-Tos	Matt. 18:15	Entire Chapter

Week 39

Day 1	Guilt	Another Example	Rom. 2:15	Rom. 2:12-16
Day 2	Guilt	Scared Into Guilt	1 Tim. 4:2	1 Tim. 4:1-5
Day 3	Guilt	Stained in Guilt	Titus 1:15	Titus 1:10-15
Day 4	Guilt	The Blood of Christ	Heb. 9:14	Heb. 9:11-15
Day 5	Guilt	Don't Bite the Hook	James 1:14	James 1:13-18

Week 40

Day 1	Servanthood	Who's Your Audience?	Col. 3:23	Col. 3:20-25
Day 2	Servanthood	Double Duty	Matt. 6:24	Entire Chapter
Day 3	Servanthood	A Good Soldier	2 Tim. 2:4	Entire Chapter
Day 4	Servanthood	Build It Up	Eph. 4:12	Eph. 4:1-16
Day 5	Servanthood	Real Christianity	Phil. 2:7	Phil. 2:1-11

Week 41

Day 1	Second Coming	He Returns for His Children	John 14:3	John 14:1-6
Day 2	Second Coming	Where Jesus Returns for Us	Acts 1:11	Acts 1:10-11
Day 3	Second Coming	The Rapture	1 Thess. 4:16-17	1 Thess. 4:13-18
Day 4	Second Coming	New Bodies, New Minds	1 Cor. 15:51-53	1 Cor. 15:50-58
Day 5	Second Coming	The Antichrist: Economic Dictator	Rev. 13:16-18	Rev. 13:11-18

Week 42

Day 1	Leadership	A Leader Is a Servant	John 13:5	John 13:1-11
Day 2	Leadership	A Leader Is an Example	1 Cor. 11:1	1 Cor. 10:23-11:1
Day 3	Leadership	A Leader Prays for His/Her People	Exod. 32:32	Exod. 32:30-32
Day 4	Leadership	A Leader Has Vision	Prov. 29:18	Prov. 29:18
Day 5	Leadership	A Leader Is Diligent	Rom. 12:8	Rom. 12:1-8

Week 43

Day 1	Praise	Gentiles	Rom. 15:11	Rom. 15:1-13
Day 2	Praise	Praise for Being Chosen	Eph. 1:3-14	Eph. 1:1-14
Day 3	Praise	Sacrifice of Praise	Heb. 13:15	Heb. 13:1-16
Day 4	Praise	Praise with Instruments	Ps. 33:2	Ps. 33:1-22
Day 5	Praise	All Things Praise the Lord	Ps. 150:6	Entire Chapter

Week 44

Day 1	Temptation	God Does Not Tempt	James 1:13	James 1:12-15
Day 2	Temptation	Jesus Understands Our Temptations	Heb. 4:15	Heb. 4:14-16
Day 3	Temptation	A Way of Escape	1 Cor. 10:13	1 Cor. 10:1-13
Day 4	Temptation	Avoiding Temptation	Matt. 26:41	Matt. 26:36-46
Day 5	Temptation	Temptation of Money	1 Tim. 6:9	1 Tim. 6:1-10

Week 45

Day 1	Death	Last Enemy Destroyed	1 Cor. 15:26	1 Cor. 15:20-34
Day 2	Death	Dead to Sin	Rom. 6:10	Rom. 6:1-14
Day 3	Death	Comfort When Facing Death	Ps. 23:4	Entire Chapter
Day 4	Death	Authority Over Death	John 11:44	John 11:38-44
Day 5	Death	Evidence Against Reincarnation	Heb. 9:27	Heb. 9:23-28

Week 46

Day 1	Forgiveness	Forgive Others as God Has Forgiven You	Matt. 18:35; Eph. 4:32	Matt. 18:21-35
Day 2	Forgiveness	Confession	1 John 1:9	1 John 1:8-10
Day 3	Forgiveness	Debt Was Canceled, Nailed to the Cross	Col. 2:13-14	Col. 2:13-15
Day 4	Forgiveness	Complete Forgiveness and Restoration	Luke 15:22-24	Luke 15:11-24
Day 5	Forgiveness	Removed Our Sins Far from Us	Ps. 103:12	Ps. 103:10-13

Week 47

Day 1	Marriage and Family	Honor and Obey Parents	Eph. 6:1-2	Eph. 6:1-3
Day 2	Marriage and Family	Bring Up Children in God's Ways	Deut. 6:7; Eph. 6:4	Deut. 6:4-9
Day 3	Marriage and Family	Love for Wife	Eph. 5:25	Eph. 5:25-33
Day 4	Marriage and Family	Do Not Be Unequally Yoked	2 Cor. 6:14	2 Cor. 6:14-16
Day 5	Marriage and Family	Submission	Eph. 5:22	Eph. 5:22-24

Week 48

Day 1	Heaven	Heavens Were Created	Gen. 1:1	Gen. 1:1-19
Day 2	Heaven	Christ Is Preparing a Place for Us	John 14:2	John 14:1-3
Day 3	Heaven	Not to Worship the Heavens	Jer. 8:2; Rom. 1:25	Rom. 1:24-26
Day 4	Heaven	Heavens Destroyed by Fire, New Heaven Created	2 Pet. 3:13; Isa. 65:17	2 Pet. 3:3-14
Day 5	Heaven	Kingdom of Heaven	Matt. 13:44	Matt. 13:18-52

NOTES

---

chapter 2

1. Judith Newman, "Sex and the Prom," *Seventeen,* May 1991,
   p. 118.

chapter 7

1. Dick Gilling and Robin Brightwell, *The Human Brain* (London:
   Orbis, 1982), p. 13.
2. Leslie A. Hart, *How the Brain Works* (New York: Basic Books,
   1975), p. 39.
3. Dr. Tom and James Elkin, eds., *The Parent's Guide to Current
   Movies* (Jackson, Miss.: N.p., Jan.-Dec. 1988).
4. The movie in question is *Wayne's World.*

chapter 9

1. Jeff Kleinhuizen, "Campus Drinking Targeted," *USA Today,*
   Mar. 6, 1991, p. A1.
2. Gina Kolata, "Teenagers and AIDS," *Seventeen,* May 1990,
   pp. 149-51.

chapter 10

1. Quoted in David Barton, *The Myth of Separation* (Aledo, Tex.: WallBuilders Press, 1991), pp. 108-9.
2. Ibid., p. 115.
3. Ibid., p. 155. See also Harold K. Lane, *Liberty! Cry Liberty!* (Boston: Lamb and Lamb Tractarian Society, 1939), pp. 32-33.
4. Quoted in Barton, *The Myth of Separation,* p. 249.
5. Ibid.

chapter 11

1. "Reject Prudery, Teen Sex Survey Needed," *USA Today,* July 26, 1991, p. A10.
2. *Statistical Abstract of the United States: 1989* (Washington, D.C.: U.S. Bureau of the Census, 1989), table 125, p. 84.
3. *U.S. News & World Report,* Aug. 14, 1989, p. 70. Report on Gallup poll released July 1989.

chapter 12

1. Gina Kolata, "Teenagers and AIDS," *Seventeen,* May 1990, pp. 149-51.
2. "Unwed Mothers Deliver a Boom," *Trumball Edition,* June 14, 1991, p. A4.
3. *Free to Be Family* (Washington, D.C.: Family Research Council, 1992), pp. 28-29.
4. Catalina Comia, "Teen AIDS Increasing," *The Dallas Morning News,* Aug. 20, 1990, p. A6.
5. Paul Wood, "More Kids at Risk from Alcohol Than Drugs," *USA Today,* Nov. 5, 1991, p. A15.
6. Jeff Kleinhuizen, "Campus Drinking Targeted," *USA Today,* Mar. 6, 1991, p. A1.
7. "Teenage Health," *The Dallas Times Herald,* June 9, 1990, p. A4.
8. Vivian Smith, "You Can Help Get Drugs Out of Schools," *USA Today,* Sept. 29, 1992, p. A13.
9. Colin Patterson quoted in Bert Thompson, *The Scientific Case for Creation* (Montgomery, Ala: Apologetics Press, 1986), pp. 12-13.
10. S. Lovtrup, *Darwinism: The Refutation of a Myth* (London: Croom Helm, 1987), p. 422.

11. Lillian Feder, *Crowell's Handbook of Classical Literature* (New York: Crowell, 1964).
12. Josh McDowell, *Evidence That Demands a Verdict* (San Bernardino, Calif.: Here's Life, 1989), p. 23.
13. Kenneth L. Woodward, "Cultic America: A Tower of Babel," *Newsweek,* Mar. 15, 1993, p. 60.
14. Shirley MacLaine, *Dancing in the Light* (New York: Bantam, 1985), p. 420.
15. Quoted in Anthony A. Hoekema, *The Four Major Cults* (Grand Rapids, Mich.: Eerdmans, 1963), p. 271.
16. H.A.R. Gibb, *Mohammedanism* (London: Oxford University, 1980), p. 37.
17. Josh McDowell and Don Stewart, *Handbook of Today's Religions* (San Bernardino, Calif.: Here's Life, 1991), pp. 311, 320.

resource c

1. Joe White's version of *The Littlest Angel*. Original story by Charles Tazewell, copyright © 1946.

resource d

1. Gary Smith, "Ali and His Entourage," *Sports Illustrated,* Apr. 25, 1988, p. 56.
2. "Seein' My Father in Me," by Paul Overstreet and Taylor Dunn. Copyright © 1987 Scarlet Moon Music (administered by Copyright Management, Inc.). All rights reserved. International copyright secured. Used by permission.
3. Tom Heymann, *On an Average Day* (New York: Fawcett, 1989), pp. 54 (Dunkin' Donuts), 55 (Tootsie Rolls), 56 (M&M's), 98 (comics and sports).
4. C.I. Scofield, ed., *New Scofield Study Bible* (New York: Oxford University Press, 1988), p. 1736.
5. William James, *The Meaning of Truth* (New York: Longmans, Green, 1909), p. 304.
6. Patricia Hersch, "Sexually Transmitted Diseases Are Ravaging Our Children," *American Health* (May 1991): 44; Hersch, "Teen Epidemic," *American Health* (May 1991): 42-45; Jeff Kleinhuizen, "Campus Drinking Targeted," *USA Today,* Mar. 6, 1991, p. 1.

7. Nike annual sales for 1993, in *Moody's Industrial News Report* 65, 50 (Feb. 1, 1994): 3277.

resource e

1. George Wald, *Frontiers of Modern Biology in Theories of Origin of Life* (New York: Houghton Mifflin, 1972), p. 187.
2. Robert Jastrow, *Until the Sun Dies* (New York: W.W. Norton, 1977), pp. 19, 24-25.
3. Robert Jastrow, *God and the Astronomers* (New York: W.W. Norton, 1978), p. 116.
4. Wolfgang Smith, *Cosmos and Transcendance: Breaking Through the Barriers of Scientistic Belief* (Peru, Ill.: Sugden, 1984).
5. Charles B. Thaxton, Walter L. Bradley, and Roger L. Olsen, *The Mysteries of Life's Origin: Reassessing Current Theories* (New York: Dover, 1953).
6. Arthur E. Wilder-Smith in "The Origins of Life," a creationist motion picture written by Willem J.J. Glashouwer and Paul S. Taylor (Mesa, Az.: Eden Films and Standard Media, 1983).
7. See Pierre-Paul Grosse, *Evolution of Living Organisms* (New York: Academic Press, 1977), pp. 88, 130. Emphases added.
8. C.P. Martin, "A Non-Genetics Look at Evolution," *American Scientist* 41, 1 (1953): 100, 103.
9. Charles Darwin, *Origin of Species* (New York: Avenal Books, 1979), p. 217.
10. Charles Darwin, *Origin of Species by Means of Natural Selection* (New York: Avenal Books, 1979).
11. Colin Patterson in a personal letter to L. Sunderland, Apr. 10, 1979, in Luther D. Sunderland, *Darwin's Enigma: Fossils and Other Problems,* 4th ed. (Santee, Calif.: Master Books, 1988), p. 89.
12. Gary E. Parker in "The Fossil Record," a creationist motion picture written by Willem J.J. Glashouwer and Paul S. Taylor (Mesa, Az.: Eden Films and Standard Media, 1983).
13. Niles Eldredge in Sunderland, *Darwin's Enigma,* p. 78.
14. Malcolm Bowden in "The Origin of Mankind," a creationist motion picture written by Willem J.J. Glashouwer and Paul S. Taylor (Mesa, Az.: Eden Films and Standard Media, 1983).
15. Stephen Jay Gould, "Men of the Thirty-third Division: An Essay on Integrity," *Natural History* 99, 4 (Apr. 1990): 12-24.

16. *Time* magazine, Mar. 14, 1994, p. 86.
17. Robert Martin, "Man Is Not an Onion," *New Scientist* 75, 1063 (Aug. 1977): 283-85.
18. William R. Fix, *The Bone Peddlers* (New York: Macmillan, 1984), p. 150.
19. Quoted in Michael H. Brown, *The Search for Eve* (New York: Harper & Row, 1990), p. 241.
20. Edmund Ambrose, *The Nature and Origin of the Biological World* (New York: John Wiley & Sons, 1982), p. 164.
21. Stephen Jay Gould in an October 1983 speech reported in "John Lofton's Journal," *The Washington Times*, Feb. 8, 1984.
22. S. Lovtrup, *Darwinism: The Refutation of a Myth* (London: Croom Helm, 1987), p. 422. Emphases added.

resource f
1. Jeffery L. Sheler, "The Bible's Last Secrets," *U.S. News & World Report,* Oct. 7, 1991, p. 64.
2. Ibid., p. 68.
3. Ibid., p. 70.
4. Henry M. Morris, *The Bible Has the Answer* (Grand Rapids, Mich.: Baker Book House, 1971), p. 4.
5. "World News Shorts," EP News Service, Mar. 8, 1991, p. 10; Josh McDowell, *Evidence That Demands a Verdict* (San Bernardino, Calif.: Here's Life, 1991), p. 18.
6. Lillian Feder, *Crowell's Handbook of Classical Literature* (New York: Crowell, 1964).
7. McDowell, *Evidence,* p. 42.
8. Nelson Glueck, *Rivers in the Desert: History of Negev* (Philadelphia: Jewish Publications Society of America, 1969), p. 31.
9. Sir Walter Scott, *The Monastery* (Boston: Houghton Mifflin, 1913), p. 140.

resource g

1. Philip Schaff, *History of the Christian Church* (Grand Rapids, Mich.: William B. Eerdmans, 1910, reprint 1962), p. 109.
2. Cited in Vernon C. Grounds, *The Reason for Our Hope* (Chicago: Moody, 1945), p. 37.

3. Kenneth Scott Latourette, *A History of Christianity* (New York: Harper & Row, 1953), p. 44.

4. Thomas Schultz, "The Doctrine of the Person of Christ with an Emphasis Upon the Hypostatic Union," unpublished dissertation, Dallas Theological Seminary, May 1962, p. 209.

5. Frank Mead, ed., *The Encyclopedia of Religious Quotations* (Westwood, N.J.: Fleming H. Revell, n.d.), p. 52.

6. *Encyclopaedia Britannica,* 15th ed., 1974, p. 145.

7. Tacitus, *Annals,* xv, 44. Shlomo Pines and David Flusser cited in "Christ Documentation: Israeli Scholars Find Ancient Document They Feel Confirms the Existence of Jesus," *New York Times* press release, Feb. 12, 1972, carried by the *Palm Beach Post-Times,* Feb. 13, 1972.

8. Josephus, *Antiquities,* xviii, 33. Ibid.

9. Jeffery L. Sheler, "The First Christians," *U.S. News & World Report,* Apr. 20, 1992, p. 59.

10. Floyd Hamilton, *The Basis of Christian Faith* (New York: Harper & Row, 1964), p. 160.

11. Peter W. Stoner, *Science Speaks: An Evaluation of Certain Christian Evidences* (Chicago: Moody, 1963), pp. 95-98.

12. Emil Borel, *Possibilities of Life* (New York: Dover, 1962).

resource h

1. Brigham Young, *Journal of Discourses* (Salt Lake City: Church of Jesus Christ of Latter-Day Saints, 1966), 1:50-51.

2. Mary Baker Eddy, *Science and Health with Key to the Scriptures* (Boston: Trustees Under the Will of Mary Baker G. Eddy, 1934), p. 361.

3. Josh McDowell and Don Stewart, *Handbook of Today's Religions* (San Bernardino, Calif.: Here's Life, 1991), p. 59.

4. Joseph Smith, *The Pearl of Great Price* (Salt Lake City: Church of Jesus Christ of Latter-Day Saints, 1952), 2:18, 19.

5. Joseph Fielding Smith, *Doctrines of Salvation* (Salt Lake City: Church of Jesus Christ of Latter-Day Saints, n.d.), pp. 189-90.

6. *Newsweek,* Mar. 15, 1993, p. 60; Dave Bass, "Drawing Down the Moon," *Christianity Today,* Apr. 29, 1991, p. 16.

7. Orson Pratt, "The Bible Alone, an Insufficient Guide," in *Orson Pratt's Works* (Salt Lake City: Church of Jesus Christ of Latter-Day Saints, n.d.), pp. 44-47.

8. *The Watchtower,* July 15, 1960, p. 439.

9. Charles Russell, *Studies in the Scriptures* (Brooklyn: International Bible Students, 1912), 5:54.

10. *Let God Be True* (Brooklyn: Watchtower Bible and Tract Society, 1946), p. 111.

11. James Talmage, *Articles of Faith* (Salt Lake City: Church of Jesus Christ of Latter-Day Saints, 1952), pp. 86, 91.

12. Young, *Journal,* 3:247.

13. McDowell and Stewart, *Handbook,* 378.

14. "Islam," *Encyclopaedia Britannica,* 1967, p. 663.

15. Kenneth Boa, *Cults, World Religions, and You* (Wheaton, Ill.: Victor Books, 1977), p. 55.

16. Smith, *Pearl of Great Price,* 2:18, 19.

17. Bruce R. McConkie, *Mormon Doctrine* (Salt Lake City: Bookcraft, 1979), p. 670.

18. Smith, *Doctrines,* pp. 189-90.

19. Talmage, *Articles,* Article 8.

20. Pratt, *Works,* p. 218.

21. Talmage, *Articles,* Article 8.

22. McConkie, *Mormon Doctrine,* pp. 238-39; Young, *Journal,* 6:3.

23. W. Cleon Skousen, *The First Two Thousand Years* (Salt Lake City: Bookcraft, 1953), pp. 355-56.

24. Joseph Smith, Jr., *History of the Church* (Salt Lake City: Church of Jesus Christ of Latter-Day Saints, n.d.), 6:310-12.

25. Joseph Smith, Jr., *The King Follett Discourse* (Salt Lake City: Church of Jesus Christ of Latter-Day Saints, n.d.), pp. 8-10.

26. Smith, *History,* 4:461.

27. Jerald Tanner and Sandra Tanner, *Changing World of Mormonism* (Chicago: Moody, 1979).

28. Joseph Smith, *Doctrine and Covenants of the Church of Jesus Christ of Latter-Day Saints,* ed. by Orson Pratt (Westport, Conn.: Greenwood, 1880, reprint 1971), 84:5, 31.

29. McConkie, *Mormon Doctrine,* pp. 193, 589-90, 751.

30. Young, *Journal,* 1:50-51.

31. Ibid.
32. Bruce R. McConkie in a speech given at Brigham Young University, Jan. 10, 1984.
33. Bruce R. McConkie in a speech given at Brigham Young University, Mar. 2, 1982.
34. "What Mormons Believe," *Newsweek,* Sept. 1, 1980, p. 68.
35. Mary Baker Eddy, *Christian Science Journal,* Jan. 1901.
36. Baker Eddy, *Science and Health;* Mary Baker Eddy, *Miscellaneous Writings, 1833-1896* (Santa Clarita, Calif.: Bookmark, n.d.), p. 170.
37. Baker Eddy, *Science and Health,* 115:13-14.
38. Ibid., 473:9-16, 361:1, 2, 12.
39. Ibid., 25:6-8.
40. Anonymous, "Qualified to Be Ministers," 1955, p. 310.
41. *Let God Be True,* p. 111.
42. *Make Sure of All Things* (Brooklyn: Watchtower Bible and Tract Society, 1953), p. 207; *Let God Be True,* pp. 33, 88.
43. *Watchtower Reprints* 1 (Mar. 1880): 82.
44. Shirley MacLaine, *Dancing in the Light* (New York: Bantam, 1985), p. 420.
45. Neville Drury and Gregory Tillett, *The Occult Sourcebook* (London: Routledge & Kegan Paul, 1978), p. 78.
46. McDowell and Stewart, *Handbook,* p. 238.
47. Ibid., p. 239.

resource i

1. "Alcohol Warning Label Highlights Hazards," *California Capitol Report,* Nov. 1989, p. 4.
2. "Tolerance for Drunkenness Has Dried Up," *USA Today,* Mar. 9, 1989.
3. "Teenage Drug Use Declines," *USA Today,* Mar. 1, 1989.
4. *AFA Journal,* Jan. 1990, p. 12.
5. Ibid.
6. Ibid.
7. Ibid.
8. Ibid.
9. "Alcohol Is Leading U.S. Drug Worry," *USA Today,* Jan. 24, 1990, p. 1D.

10. Robert H. Stein, "Wine Drinking in New Testament Times," *Christianity Today,* June 20, 1975, p. 10.
11. Homer, *The Odyssey,* 2 vols. (Cambridge, Mass.: Harvard University Press, n.d.), Vol. 1, Book IX, pp. 208f.
12. From Hardin B. Jones, "What the Practicing Physician Should Know About Marijuana," in the Narcotic Educational Foundation of America (NEFA) Medical Student Reference Sheet VF 1994 3-56 (published by NEFA; 5055 Sunset Blvd., Los Angeles, CA 90027).
13. Dan Rather, "Crack Babies," *CBS Nightly News,* Apr. 5, 1990; "How to Beat Drugs," *U.S. News & World Report,* Sept. 11, 1989; *New England Journal of Medicine,* Dec. 7, 1989, and "Cocaine: A Little Can Hurt Heart," *USA Today,* Dec. 7, 1989; William H. Bunn and A. James Giannini, "Cardiovascular Complications of Cocaine Abuse," *American Family Physician* 46, 8 (Sept. 1992): 769; Peter M. Marzuk et al., "Cocaine Use, Risk Taking, and Fatal Russian Roulette," *Journal of the American Medical Association* 267, 19 (May 1992): 2635; "The Pulmonary Effects of Crack Cocaine," *Patient Care* 26, 3 (Feb. 1992): 262; Anne Davies, "How Cocaine Could Really Blow Your Mind," *New Scientist* 136, 1848 (Nov. 1992): 16; and Narcotic Educational Foundation of America (NEFA) Medical Student Reference Sheet VF 1994 3-62 (published by NEFA; 5055 Sunset Blvd., Los Angeles, CA 90027).
14. U.S. Senate Judiciary Committee, "Effect of Pornography on Women and Children," Subcommittee on Juvenile Justice, 98th Cong., 2d sess., 1984, p. 227; U.S. Department of Justice, "Report of the Attorney General's Task Force on Family Violence," Washington, D.C., p. 112; Mark Nichols, "Viewers and Victims: Pornography's Role in Encouraging Violence Against Women," *Maclean's* 106, 41 (Oct. 1993): 60; Andrew Phillips, "Porn from the Skies," *Maclean's* 106, 7 (Feb. 1993): 48; John Schwartz, "Sex Crimes on Your Screen," *Newsweek,* Dec. 23, 1991, p. 66.
15. *CQ Researcher* 1, 31 (Dec. 1991): 973, 974. Published by Congressional Quarterly, Inc., in conjunction with EBSCO Publishing.

16. See Dolf Zillmann and Jennings Bryant, eds., *Pornography: Research Advances and Policy Considerations* (Hillsdale, N.J.: Lawrence Erlbaum Associates, 1989).

17. U.S. Department of Justice, Attorney General's Commission on Pornography, *Final Report* (Washington, D.C.: Government Printing Office, 1986).

18. *Family Planning Perspectives* 18, 5 (Sept./Oct. 1986): 207.

19. Theresa L. Cremshaw, "Ten AIDS Myths Answered," *AIDS Protection* 3 (Sept. 1989): 83.

20. James J. Goedert, "Sounding Board—What Is Safe Sex?" *New England Journal of Medicine* 316, 21 (May 1987): 1340, 1341.

21. M.A. Fischl, "Evaluation of Heterosexual Partners, Children, and Household Contact of Adults with AIDS," *Journal of the American Medical Association* 257 (Feb. 1987): 640-44.

22. "Skin Condoms: Unresolved Questions," *Consumer Reports,* Mar. 1989, p. 137.

23. "Sharp Rise in Rare Sex-Related Diseases," *The New York Times Health,* July 14, 1988, p. 234.

24. "An Introduction to Sexually Transmitted Diseases," prepared by the Office of Communications, National Institute of Allergy and Infectious Diseases, National Institutes of Health, Bethesda, Md., NIH publication No. 92-909A, June 1992.

25. "Syphilis," prepared by the Office of Communications, National Institute of Allergy and Infectious Diseases, National Institutes of Health, Bethesda, Md., NIH publication No. 92-909I, June 1992.

26. *Annual Report for Fiscal Year 1989,* Division of Sexually Transmitted Diseases and HIV Prevention, Centers for Disease Control, Atlanta, 1990, p. 4.

27. "Introduction to Sexually Transmitted Diseases."

28. Ibid.

29. Ibid.

30. Ibid.

31. *The Common Appeal,* Nov. 7, 1988, p. A12.

32. *Historical Statistics of the United States,* 93d Cong., 1st sess., House Doc. 93-78 (Part 2), p. 1140; U.S. Department of Commerce and U.S. Bureau of the Census statistics; John Keegan and Richard Holmes, *Soldiers* (New York: Viking, 1986), p. 154.

33. R. Ernest Dupuy and Trevor N. Dupuy, *Encyclopedia of Military History* (New York: Harper & Row, 1970), p. 1198.

34. According to *U.S. News & World Report* (July 17, 1989), 1.6 million abortions are performed every year in the United States. Multiply that number by 20 years, and you have over 30 million babies killed.

35. Anne Catherine Speckhard, "The Psycho-Social Aspects of Stress Following Abortion," unpublished master's thesis, University of Minnesota, May 1985, p. 69.

36. Taken from Focus on the Family's information sheet FX147, "Euthanasia."

37. From Focus on the Family broadcast BR988A, "The Truth About Euthanasia," with hosts James C. Dobson, Ph.D., and Mike Trout and guest Dr. Dorsett Smith, Dec. 1, 1993.

38. Ibid.

39. FX147, "Euthanasia," excerpted from "Euthanasia Education Packet." Reprinted by permission of the Christian Action Council, 101 W. Broad St., Falls Church, VA 22046.

40. M.E. Bradford, *A Worthy Company: Brief Lives of the Framers of the Constitution* (Marlborough, N.H.: Plymouth Rock Foundation, 1982), table of contents.

41. James D. Richardson, *A Compilation of the Messages and Papers of the Presidents,* 1789-1897, published by the authority of Congress, 1899, 1:220, Sept. 17, 1796.

42. Steve C. Dawson, *God's Providence in America's History* (Rancho Cordova, Calif.: Steve C. Dawson, 1988), 1:5.

43. J.B. McClure, ed., *Abraham Lincoln's Stories and Speeches* (Chicago: Rhodes and McClure, 1896), pp. 135-36.

44. Donald S. Lutz, *The Origins of American Constitutionalism* (Baton Rouge: Louisiana State University Press, 1988), p. 141.

45. Stephen K. McDowell and Mark A. Beilles, *America's Providential History* (Charlottesville, Va.: Providence Press, 1988), p. 156.

46. Robert Flood, *The Rebirth of America* (Philadelphia: The Arthur S. DeMoss Foundation, 1986), p. 12.

47. McDowell and Beilles, *America's Providential History,* p. 79.

48. Gary DeMar, *America's Christian History* (Atlanta: American Vision, 1993), p. 40.

49. McDowell and Beilles, *America's Providential History,* pp. 111, 92.

50. Lawrence A. Cremin, *American Education: The Colonial Experience* (New York: Harper & Row, 1970), pp. 393-94.

51. *Bible Study Course, New Testament, Dallas High Schools,* Bulletin No. 170 (Dallas: Public Schools Print Shop, 1946).

52. *Engel v. Vitale,* 370 U.S. 421 (1962).

53. *Engel v. Vitale,* 370 U.S. 421 at 422 (1962).

54. Wardell B. Pomeroy, *Boys and Sex* (New York: Delacorte, 1981), pp. 2, 38, 117.

55. David Barton, *America: To Pray or Not to Pray* (Aledo, Tex.: Wallbuilders Press, 1991), pp. 44.

56. Ibid.

57. Calculated from *AIDS Weekly Surveillance Report—United States Center for Disease Control,* June 1981-1990, pp. 99, 103.

58. Calculated from *Statistical Abstracts of the United States,* U.S. Department of Commerce, and U.S. Bureau of the Census statistics for 1961/62 through 1989/90. Published by U.S. Bureau of the Census, Washington, D.C.

59. Edwin Meese III, "Thinking About Crime," *Harper's* (Nov. 1985), Letters to the Editor.

60. Based on data from the *National Study on Child Neglect and Abuse Reporting,* annual. Provided by the American Humane Association, Denver, Colo., 1976-1986.

61. Lutz, *Origins of American Constitutionalism,* p. 142.

62. William Blackstone, *Commentaries on the Laws of England* (Philadelphia: J.B. Lippincott, 1879), 1:39, 41-42.

63. David Barton, *America's Godly Heritage* (Aledo, Tex.: Wallbuilders Press, 1993), p. 9.

64. Henry P. Johnson, ed., *The Correspondence and Public Papers of John Jay, 1794-1826* (New York: Burt Franklin, 1970), 4:393, Oct. 12, 1816.

65. *Church of the Holy Trinity v. United States,* 143 U.S. 457 (1892); *Vidal v. Girard's Executors,* 43 U.S. 126, 205-206 (1844).

66. See Josh McDowell and Don Stewart, *Handbook of Today's Religions* (San Bernardino, Calif.: Here's Life, 1991), pp. 459-77.

67. Julian Huxley, *Religion Without Revelation* (New York: Mentor, 1957), pp. 17-18, 32.

68. Carl Sagan, *Cosmos* (New York: Random House, 1980), p. 4.

69. James C. Dobson, Ph.D., president and founder of Focus on the Family, in his April 1993 newsletter.

70. Ibid.

71. Ibid.

72. Ibid.

73. Ibid.

74. Nikolai Lenin, *Selected Works* (London: Lawrence & Wishart, 1939), 60:675-76.

75. Saul K. Padover, *Karl Marx* (New York: Dutton, 1980), p. 80.

76. William Z. Foster, *Toward Soviet America* (Balboa Island, Calif.: Elgin, 1961), p. 113.

77. Victor D. Timofeyev cited in "A Face-to-Face Interview with Soviet Atheist Leaders," edited by Frederick Edwords, *The Humanist* 47, 1 (Jan./Feb. 1987): 9.

78. Alexander Solzhenitsyn, *The Mortal Danger* (New York: Harper & Row, 1980), p. 58.

FOCUS ON THE FAMILY PUBLICATIONS

Focus on the Family

This complimentary magazine provides inspiring stories, thought-provoking articles and helpful information for families interested in traditional, biblical values. Each issue also includes a "Focus on the Family" radio broadcast schedule.

Parental Guidance

Close-ups and commentaries on the latest music, movies, television and advertisements directed toward young people. Parents, as well as youth leaders, teachers and pastors, will benefit from this indispensable newsletter.

Clubhouse Jr.

Youngsters ages 4 to 8 will delight in the great games, creative crafts and super stories that fill the colorful pages of *Clubhouse Jr.* Every article educates and entertains—all with an emphasis on biblical values.

Clubhouse

Here's a fun way to instill Christian principles in your children! With puzzles, easy-to-read stories and exciting activities, *Clubhouse* provides hours of character-building enjoyment for kids ages 8 to 12.

Brio

Designed especially for teen girls, *Brio* is packed with super stories, intriguing interviews and amusing articles on the topics they care about most—relationships, fitness, fashion and more—all from a Christian perspective.

Breakaway

With colorful graphics, hot topics and humor, this magazine for teen guys helps them keep their faith on course and gives the latest info on sports, music, celebrities . . . even girls. Best of all, this publication shows teens how they can put their Christian faith into practice and resist peer pressure.

All magazines are published monthly except where otherwise noted. For more information regarding these and other resources, please call Focus on the Family at (719) 531-5181, or write to us at Focus on the Family, Colorado Springs, CO 80995.